# SIGHTLINES

—— EILEEN KANE ——

# SIGHTLINES

## BEYOND THE BEYOND IN
## —— IRELAND ——

UNIVERSITY OF TORONTO PRESS

Toronto Buffalo London

© University of Toronto Press 2022
Toronto Buffalo London
utorontopress.com
Printed and bound by CPI Group (UK) Ltd, Croydon, CR0 4YY

ISBN 978-1-4875-4715-8 (cloth)       ISBN 978-1-4875-4535-2 (EPUB)
ISBN 978-1-4875-4499-7 (paper)       ISBN 978-1-4875-5256-5 (PDF)

**Library and Archives Canada Cataloguing in Publication**

Title: Sightlines : beyond the beyond in Ireland / Eileen Kane.
Names: Kane, Eileen, author.
Description: Includes bibliographical references.
Identifiers: Canadiana (print) 20220266816 | Canadiana (ebook) 20220266832 |
ISBN 9781487547158 (cloth) | ISBN 9781487544997 (paper) |
ISBN 9781487545352 (EPUB) | ISBN 9781487552565 (PDF)
Subjects: LCSH: Rural development – Ireland – Donegal (County) | LCSH: Donegal (Ireland :
County) – Rural conditions. | LCSH: Donegal (Ireland : County) – Social conditions – 20th
century. | LCSH: Donegal (Ireland : County) – Economic conditions – 20th century.
Classification: LCC HN400.3.D66 K36 2022 | DDC 307.72094169/3 – dc23

We welcome comments and suggestions regarding any aspect of our publications – please feel free
to contact us at news@utorontopress.com or visit us at utorontopress.com.

Every effort has been made to contact copyright holders; in the event of an error or omission,
please notify the publisher.

We wish to acknowledge the land on which the University of Toronto Press operates. This land is
the traditional territory of the Wendat, the Anishnaabeg, the Haudenosaunee, the Métis, and the
Mississaugas of the Credit First Nation.

University of Toronto Press acknowledges the financial support of the Government of Canada and
the Ontario Arts Council, an agency of the Government of Ontario, for its publishing activities.

*For my husband, Paud Murphy,*
*and*
*Professor Ward Goodenough and Ruth Gallagher Goodenough,*
*who performed our wedding,*
*and*
*Professor George Huxley, our dear friend*

Sightline: A line from an observer's eye to a distant point

- *Merriam-Webster Dictionary*

But we're beyond the beyond here. We've fallen out of the space-time continuum.

- James Mary Agnes O'Donnell

Your research isn't only about what you want to know. It's also about what we want you to know, and then what we'd like to tell you.

- Mrs. B.

Have you the study done yet? What about the poor sods who are helping you? Will we ever see something in plain English?

- Conor

Get a big notebook. If you ask a man for road directions, you will have learned how to assemble a clock before he's finished.

- Old Donegal saying

*This has become a story about borders, edges, boundaries, and the places and people who fall outside them, who don't fit in. Also, an old lady's underwear, courthouse toilets, and Pádraig Pearse's fingernail.*

- Eileen Kane

# Contents

# Illustrations

# Preface

*Sightlines* is "backstage anthropology," an invitation to come along for the ride, where you'll get an insider's view of doing anthropological research. You'll meet the great Donegal characters who helped me: "God bless your innocence," they'd say, redirecting me to the right paths. I owe them a great debt, even to this day, over fifty years later.

But first, "Write down some general facts about Ireland," the publishers said, "so when non-Irish people read *Sightlines* they'll understand a little more about the country." I don't see why: sometimes Irish people themselves take pride in *not* understanding it. "It could only happen here" is what people said when a body was found in a restaurant freezer, or an image of the Blessed Virgin Mary appeared on someone's closet door in Dublin.

Still, it's worth a try, because the Irish do have a forensic knowledge of minute points of Irish history. So, first, what do I mean by "Ireland"? Since 1921, the island of Ireland has been divided into two parts: six northeastern counties form Northern Ireland, officially named by the British in 1921; and the remaining twenty-six form the Republic of Ireland.

Referring to the twenty-six counties, the Constitution of Ireland, 1937, Article 4, states "The name of the state is *Éire*, or, in the English language, Ireland." Although many in both countries support unification, at the moment (in 2022) when I write "Ireland," I mean Ireland.

Today, Ireland is one of the richest countries in Europe: second in GDP, and eighth when Ireland's particular economic circumstances are factored in, since over 1,000 major international companies in information and communications technology, social media, pharmaceuticals/medical devices, and finance have Ireland as the hub of their European operations, including Apple, Google, Microsoft, Facebook, Medtronic, HP, IBM, LinkedIn, Twitter, Pfizer, GSK Consumer Healthcare, Genzyme, and Allergan. Most of the world's supply of Viagra (County Cork) and Botox (County Mayo) comes from Ireland. According to the United Nations Human Development Index, which factors economic and educational factors in their assessment, Ireland is second in the world.

Since "Brexit," Britain's exit from the European Union, Ireland is the only remaining English-speaking member of the EU. (All member languages, including Irish, are "official," but the EU uses only English and French for its procedural work.) Ireland also holds a disproportionate number of positions in the EU. An early example was Terry Stewart, who, in his earlier career, was the exasperated manager of the doll factory that appears in *Sightlines*.

But *Sightlines* is set much earlier, in 1966–68, when it still was almost beyond imagination that Ireland could reach such heights. Two of the few who understood the potential, both committed Irish speakers, were T.K. Whitaker, the young secretary of the Department of Finance who appears in *Sightlines*, and the Taoiseach, or prime minister, Seán Lemass. As part of a potential move into the EU, and concerned that it might have a negative effect on remote Irish-speaking areas called the Gaeltacht, the government provided impressive financial support to companies, native and foreign, to set up in these areas. Lemass died in 1971, two years before Ireland joined the European Communities, predecessor of today's EU. Whitaker, described as "The Man Who Made Modern Ireland," lived to be 100; the Wikipedia entry touches on his genius.

When these plans were being made, some Gaeltacht communities already had small, government-subsidized factories, often based on traditional activities, such as tweed production and machine knitting. That's what I wanted to study: would Gaeltacht farm owners sell their poor land to other farmers and go into the factories for a steady wage while the newly expanded farms produced a living for their owners? Could this plan curtail forced emigration and keep native Irish speakers at home? And would the model help to save threatened languages in other countries? My story should interest students of anthropology, but also students of Irish studies and those concerned with minority languages and attempts to maintain them.

A special goal is to honor the memories of those who helped me so long ago: as one reviewer said, "they emerge in their own complexity, curious, and often with acute anthropological insights and questions of their own." Unless they were well-known figures, I've used fictional devices, changing names and sometimes occupations, but I've tried to keep the person's essence as I saw it.

Some, like Mrs. B., are here in full cry, personality unaltered, at the request of her admiring descendants. But all represent real people, in their full humanity and glory. I hope they will "ring true" to Irish readers.

## The Website

*Sightlines* has a website, Sightlines.ie, which contains information that may be useful to readers who would like to know more about Ireland. The first priority, however, will be for students and instructors. The fledgling website contains a list of questions that will help you move from the anthropology of the 1960s to current times. Each question provides links to helpful internet sources. Some may be useful in the preparation of term papers. Both the questions and the sources will be updated periodically.

For other readers, this is a great time to learn about historical changes in Ireland. The year 2012 ushered in the "Decade of Centenaries," remembering significant points in Irish history. For example, the Rising (1916), the War of Independence (1920-21), and the Civil War (1922-23). Also celebrated is the 1918 extension of the vote to women over thirty who had certain property qualifications, the 1922 extension to all women over twenty-one, and now to everyone at age eighteen. Happily, 2021 also marks the first time since the Great Famine that more Irish people have returned to Ireland than have left.

It's also the 1500th birthday of the hotheaded St. Colmcille,[1] patron saint of the communities I studied. And perhaps the patron saint of plagiarism, as you'll see. May his memory be a blessing, or at least an eye-opener.

Michael D. Higgins, poet, sociologist, philosopher, and president of Ireland, recently referred to Irish history and its "hospitality of theories." This phrase gently discourages all-out war among and between historians, and good luck to it. On the *Sightlines* website (Sightlines.ie), I will be discussing some of what I see as "long-tailed" historical events, ones that have repercussions even to this day. Disputing my choices will enrich the discussion. As they are posted periodically, they will include the following:

- The plantation of Ulster
- The famines
- The Wyndham Land Act of 1903, which facilitated tenant ownership of land held by landlords
- The Irish language
- The Rising
- The War of Independence
- The Civil War

---

1 For ancient poems about Colmcille, Niall of the Nine Hostages, Deirdre of the Sorrows, the food-crazed MacConglinne, and other figures you'll encounter in *Sightlines*, see *The Project Gutenberg eBook of Ancient Irish Poetry*, translated by Kuno Meyer (2010).

- 1937 Constitution and its recent amendments on same-sex marriage, abortion, and the position of women
- Accession to the European Union
- The role of the Catholic Church

Each will be accompanied by links to a book or two, and, as appropriate, to film and music.

# Acknowledgments

Most of the older villagers are here - the Mapper, the Woman Who Never Had an Orgasm, the Perpetual Smile, and Madame Blue Mould. Over there, the Flycatcher and Jack Ruby. I hear their voices - their stories about Niall of the Nine Hostages, their tales of rogue trout farms and lost loves. Their perennial debates on how the area might develop into a major center for ... something. In fact, that's the Development Committee, right by the wall. They all demand my attention. This is the noisiest graveyard I've ever been in.

Now, as I search for Mrs. B.'s grave, a slim, grey-haired man comes dancing across the hill, hopping around the headstones. "Eileen Kane, you don't remember me, but I'm giving you a big kiss anyhow!" "Séamus?" I ask. "Pádraig," he says. It's my old neighbor, "Pádraig Twin," eleven when I last saw him and his brother.

This is what the local people are like. (The welcome, not necessarily the kiss.)

Since I began writing this book, many local people have helped me. I don't name them because I don't want anyone living today to be seen as responsible for my story of fifty years ago. There's one exception: I want to thank Diarmuid Bryce and the Bryce family for allowing me to write about their mother, my landlady, Mrs. B., in all her glory.

I am grateful to the people of Carrick and Kilcar, as well as to those in Teelin and Glencolmcille, then and now. I particularly want to thank Kilcar's history and folklore committee, Cumann Staire agus Seanchais, for interrupting their meeting so I could read a chapter of *Sightlines* to them, and for introducing some of the descendants of my characters who were sitting around the table.

I also want to thank Lelia Doolan, my sister Patrice Price, the indispensable Simone Pires De Oliveira, and my dear friend and award-winning builder Declan Kilmartin, who reassures me that Conor's shenanigans are still standard building practice.

At the University of Toronto Press, I thank my commissioning editor, Carli Hansen, for trusting in the book, and for her meticulous reshaping and editing; Janice Evans, for her calm, excellent management of the final production; Leanne Rancourt, for her rigorous copy editing; Stephanie Mazza, for her marketing services; and Sandra Friesen, for the book's jacket design. I couldn't have had more knowledgeable and congenial companions.

# SIGHTLINES

SIGHTLINES

# Prologue

**What Do I Know?**

Our kitchen looks like an abattoir. Red globs splatter the stove, the wall, my father, who's in our way.

"I'd rather see you dead than leave the Catholic Church," my mother says when I tell her I want to be an anthropologist. We're canning tomatoes. My father is laid off.

He eases himself up from the table where he's reading the Deaths in the *Youngstown Vindicator*. "Anthropology's not about religion," he says. He pulls down the ancient encyclopedia from the top of the refrigerator, our library.

"No," I say, swiping at the sticky red sweat pooling between my breasts. "It's about people, ordinary people like us, our families, our food, our clothes ..."

"Ah, here it is," he says. "Anthropology is the study of ..." He licks his finger and turns the page. A happy couple in minimal covering smile out of a photo.

"... of New Guinea?"

Yes, but anthropology was about us too, and everyone else in Youngstown, Ohio. It examined the ideas that many Youngstowners held: that some racial and ethnic groups – Irish, Central European, Italian, Black – were inferior to others. Those groups covered most of us living down by the factories and steel mills that kept Youngstown alive. So, were these ideas true? Some locals said yes. But anthropology, in a long-winded way, said no. And I wouldn't give my mother the satisfaction, but anthropology *was* about religion. It was the cross-cultural study of everything: family, politics, economics, law, art, economy, you name it. I was drawn to its scope, looking at all the world's cultures now and down through history.

So I stayed with it. I got a post-graduate Mellon fellowship, and now I face my second big challenge, the PhD thesis. We Ohioans are not airy-fairy people; if you spend seven years in university, the least you can do is produce something useful at the end. But what?

I'm reading the Irish Census, 1961, and about 700,000, or a quarter of the population, say they can speak Irish, Ireland's First Official Language. Only about 64,000 of these live in the Gaeltacht, the poor, remote western seaboard areas where Irish is the daily language. To save the language from extinction, the Irish government supports factories there. The planners think some small farmers will be enticed into this factory work, and they'll sell their land to other farmers to make more profitable farms. Everyone will have a decent living. Their children won't have to emigrate. The language will survive!

But is it working? I decide to study that. I have a little Irish from my native-speaking grandmother. My earliest memory is learning the names of the days and months. *Mí na Bealtaine*, May, is the month of my birthday. *An séú lá déag*, the sixteenth day.[1]

---

1 Words in the Irish language in this book are written in their modern form, *cló Rómhánach*. The wonderful *Dineen's Irish Dictionary* is written in the old *cló Gaelach*, now used mainly as a decorative font.

"Try Japan. Ireland's not exotic," my professor at the University of Pittsburgh says. Odd, because I've overheard him boasting that I am exotic, a "catch" for the department, a rare female student, and even more far-fetched, from a poor, mill-working background. "Youngstown," he'd said, the way some say "jungle," although anthropologists like jungles.

"What do you know about factories?"

What do I know? The daily mill whistle, soot-choked air, strikes, injuries, men making steel, women making do. Grandmothers, aunts, cousins, sisters all pulling together, filling in the cracks during a layoff, sharing whatever's needed to stave off disaster after a job loss, remaking the world after a breadwinner's death. My great-grandfather and grandfather died in the mills, and my uncle is crippled.

I go back to my professor with a barrage of recipes for blood pudding, pigs' trotters in caul fat, earthy curses in old Irish script, and recordings of uilleann pipe music. Exotic enough? He relents. My mother is delighted. The Irish will see to it that I go to Mass, whereas the Japanese might not.

I tell my father, who's worked in a factory since he was sixteen. We're sitting on the front porch, white petunias glowing in the dusk, fireflies rising and sinking.

"Why? The mills here are closing down."

"They can't ..." Not possible, I think.

He coughs, the same convulsive eye-watering wrack that doubles him every morning.

"They don't admit it. But I was hired as a tool and die maker. Now I just patch things up. Baling wire, welding, soldering jobs on old machines, out of date, dangerous. Closing – I see it."

I'm ashamed I know so little of what he does. And what do we do for him? We used to live only six streets from the mills; now we live in this nice white house on a country road. All of it, the whispering birch leaves, the big lawns, his never-ending garbage wars with raccoons – we owe it all to this man, wiry, five-foot-seven, who works six days a week, overtime if he can get it. Do we ever thank him, I wonder? Of course not.

"We still got open hearths and old steam-driven rolling mills. Ten, twelve years they'll be finished and the town'll collapse. Your brothers, they'll have to leave home to get work." I'm the oldest of six; those boys are ten and eleven. The backs of the younger boy's hands are still dimpled. It hurts to think they'll be like my father's thickened slabs and splayed, scarred fingers.

"Those Irish factories won't save nothing. A factory can close overnight."

I'm stunned, but proud in a way. My father, the covert forensic mechanic.

Three years later, and I'm off to Ireland. I've learned that hundreds of European languages are endangered to some extent, from "critically" to "vulnerable": among them, Scots Gaelic, Basque, Yiddish, Romani, Walloon, Sicilian, all the Scandinavian Sami languages, and, of course, Irish. Anthropologists and linguists know the critical importance of saving them – group reflections of human conditions – but how to save them? Ireland is trying an economic approach: factories. I have a year's grant money from the Wenner-Gren Foundation, some tiny savings, and some books such as Leach's *Political Systems of Highland Burma* and Levi-Strauss's *The Raw and the Cooked* in case anyone in Ireland asks me something. And how would I explain the fascinating cargo cults of Melanesia unless I have Worsley's seminal work? Some great names in anthropology, replacements for the lost saints of my childhood.

We drive along the Ohio River, my parents, the boys, and my sister Patrice, eight. Our trip runs through farm country, half an hour and a planet away from the mills. Rolling fields, a glorious gold in summer, are leached now after the last few night's frosts. We run along the Ohio River, past Freedom, Economy, Harmony Township, and then, as we near the Moon exit, I know we have very little time left. It's a road I haven't taken since my wedding three years ago when my husband and I flew out for our honeymoon. Now our marriage has ended, and the divorce is pending. What we've learned in those three years is marriage offers a unique opportunity for exquisitely designed torture, even for those of us who were high school sweethearts, from families that hadn't seen a divorce in 2,000 years, or so we're being told.

My father knows this route in his sleep, but later he'll go over it on one of his many tattered maps, tracing the places where he took my mother when they were courting, like the picnic ground where a 1930s photo shows him in his new ice cream suit. To him, maps aren't for finding his way around. They let a shy man talk about his life: the Croatian Club where he's a non-Croatian honorary member; the street where his young father was hosed down in freezing weather on a factory picket line; St. Pat's, the church he was buried from a few weeks later. In our house, when a map comes out it's story time. I disappoint him; I can't even follow a map unless north is on top.

How can I leave my family? I didn't have much of a job while I was in college, so each of them, parents, three boys, two girls, has lost something on my account: jeans, a new Easter hat, a kit for mounting butterflies, today's fresh bread. But for decades, the eldest girl in Irish and Irish-American families sacrificed to pave the way for the younger children, working as maids and cleaners. These days, maybe with a PhD and a university job, I'll be able to help mine? Otherwise, it's a job on the "Whoop and Holler," Youngstown's telephone system, because a failed PhD in anthropology isn't in much demand.

The plane is called sooner than we expect. I run, turning at the plane's stairs to wave at the sad little cluster by the gate. My father is bent over, pounding his chest, coughing; my mother, still willowy after six children, pats his back, and the kids wave their little starfish hands at the wrong person.

Airborne. Clean air! Fresh insights! And here's one: I know seven types of canoes used by the Haidas of British Columbia, and I could identify an Ainu of northern Japan at fifty paces. But the anthropologists who wrote the books on them haven't told much about how, day to day, they went about getting their information. It seems as if one just jumps in and "the people," grateful and receptive, reveal all. My only previous experience, a training program among the Paiute Indians of Nevada, succeeded mainly thanks to the Paiutes taking charge of my research, fearing that if I "got a bad grade" on it, they'd be seen as Failed Indians.

Another fresh insight: I've never met a farmer.

# November/Mí na Samhna 1966

## A Face like a Map of Ireland

*Don't mention sex, politics, or religion.* I remember the guidebook's advice as I get off the plane from New York to Dublin and step into a sea of pink faces. The few anthropological studies done here, like Arensberg and Kimball's 1930s classic, *Family and Community in Ireland,* touch on the last two but avoid sex, giving the impression the locals do, too.

My first appointment is at Gael Linn, with Dónall Ó Móráin. I've read he's the new face of the Irish language; inventive, urbane, charismatic, with exquisite Irish. The non-profit organization Ó Móráin founded, Gael Linn, uses a kaleidoscope of activities to support the language: football pools, seaweed processing, scholarships, bingo, music records and filmmaking, furniture, a theater, women knitting sweaters at home, beekeeping, and a boiler-making/lobster factory. I love this: what kind of mind juggles such a collection?

Ó Móráin's office is at the top of a botched art deco building on upmarket Grafton Street. Behind the last door lies a jumbled lair stacked high with anything the occupant might need for disasters, boredom, lawsuits, rain, hunger, formal evening events, or fishing. Ó Móráin, early forties, balding, with a square ginger mustache, is positioned in the center of this maze, presumably so he can enjoy the sight of disoriented visitors wending their way toward the Presence.

"Good afternoon, Doctor," he says, beaming like a child who's just been presented with a circus pony.

"Not yet, I'm just starting my PhD, I ..."

"I have your letter to hand here. Not for the faint-hearted, I'm afraid, a whiff of the academicals about it. Simple English, please, for a simple man. Where are you from?"

"Youngstown, in Ohio ..."

"Famous for anything? Beer? Baseball matches?"

"The Mafia." I'd considered not mentioning this.

"The bombing and shooting Mafia? Cement-boots stuff? Tell me more."

"A few years ago the *Saturday Evening Post* called Youngstown 'Crime Town, USA' and 'Bomb City, the Murder Capital of the U.S.'"

"Ah!" he says, delighted. "And is it?"

"I don't know. My father says it's an understatement."

"Your letter said you want to study factories in a rural place. Why factories?"

It would be hard not to be interested in factories. "Youngstown's a small city, but we have twenty miles of steel mills along the river. When I was little my father told me stories of what came out of his plant – the beams for most of the New York skyscrapers, the gates of the Panama Canal, the world's first Ferris wheel."

It's beyond me to convey all the pictures in my head. In Youngstown, steel and steel-related industry is the grit-spewing, sulfurous core of our existence. It shapes us, defining our neighbors as machinists, puddlers, pig machine operators, batch picklers, stripper crane men, cindermen, all strong, all completely dispensable. Men leave the school bell for the factory whistle and except for strikes and layoffs they won't be released until they're dead, crippled, or old. Youngstown is still recovering from the longest steel strike in U.S. history, and most of us are still struggling to move up a rung or two of the ladder into the lower middle class.

Ó Móráin rattles the letter. "But you want a factory in an Irish-speaking place."

"I've read about the government's plan to put factories in Irish-speaking communities in the west, to keep people at home and the language alive. It seems like quite a leap."

I explain that in Youngstown the factory is the center of a family's life. The man goes in, he gets paid, the family eats. If it closes, we'd have to move. But here it seems the factory will be expected to do a lot more.

"If the plan works, it might help in other places where languages are dying. If it doesn't, then what? Also," I add, "Ireland is one of only two places I know of where a government subsidizes rural industry. The other is Cuba. My Spanish is non-existent." The implication is my Irish is fluent when, in fact, most of my vocabulary focuses on sex, scandal, or tragedy: my elders spoke Irish only when they didn't want me to understand.

"Ah. So you're not just looking for an excuse to find your roots."

"My *roots*?"

"Well, it's clear you're Irish, the red hair, the face like a map of Ireland." I don't like the idea of having a face like the map of Ireland. I'd prefer one of the more symmetrical western American states, Wyoming, say.

He plucks a map from a drawer. "*Ceart go leor*, all right. Irish is the first official language, but most people can't speak it, even though their knuckles are beaten raw in school. So native speakers are important. Eight out of ten live in what's called the Gaeltacht, these scattered communities." He pinpoints places along a line north to south down the west and south coasts.

"And they get a lot of support?"

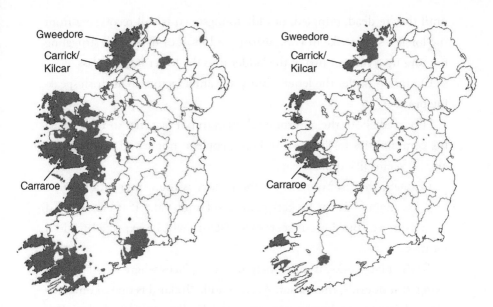

Map 1. Gaeltacht areas of Ireland in 1926 (left) and 1956 (right).

"Some incentives, yes. But you couldn't pay some of their children to take over the farm or live that life. And the idea that farmers will sell land to create bigger farms!" He laughs. "As if an Irish farmer would sell so much as a *scaob* of land."

I gather a *scaob* is very modest, as real estate goes. "Do you have any suggestions for a place I might study?"

"Only a dozen communities in the Gaeltacht have factories. You'll need a place where one has a good chance. You might try Donegal. Some see a difference between northern places like Donegal, hard workers there, as opposed to ones further south, like Galway."

"Why?"

"Some people say laziness. Some say high rates of mental illness in remote rural areas. Or that there's no economic mentality. But others think that's true for both north and south."

"No economic mentality?"

"That they don't try to get ahead, they don't make rational economic decisions, they're suspicious of change. You see grown men just standing around on the village street in the daytime. Some people think they don't know what's good for them."

There's a lot of "some people" here. "Do you agree?"

"This isn't the moment to ask me. When you know me better, say the words 'trout farm.'"

I underline *trout farm* in my notes.

"Also, some Gaeltacht people think the language is a handicap – when their children emigrate to England, they can't get decent jobs. And some outsiders are dead set against special grants for the Gaeltacht." He forages in a drawer. "This is something a Captain Giles, a member of the Dáil, the Irish Parliament, said during a session: *I have travelled around the Gaeltacht areas and I say they are nothing more than national slums and a disgrace to the nation. The inhabitants are almost a primitive people living as State paupers ...*"

He taps a wall map. "I think you might consider communities like Kilcar and Carrick, neighboring villages in southwest Donegal. Kilcar has a large factory, Carrick has none but they're both interested in development. Or you could go to Tourmakeady in County Mayo. They have a knitting factory."

"Tourmakeady? My grandmother comes from near there."

"Does she now? What part?"

I didn't know it had parts. My understanding is its population is about the size of a small orchestra. "Ballyglass, I think."

"Oh, that's outside Tourmakeady." He laughs and points to a blank space on the map. "Ballyglass. Does she know any of the Stantons or Jenningses or Gillins?"

He's named her family tree. "She's a Stanton. Her people were stonemasons to the Moores. She remembers George Moore, the writer; his family were her landlords."

He stands up. "You'll come down with me, so, to the Wicklow Hotel for a quick bite of lunch. We'll celebrate your return home."

## Needs Must When the Devil Drives

It's less than a month to the shortest day, and in the afternoon darkness it seems too late for lunch, but Ó Móráin and I make our way up and down dusty staircases, along an attic, and through mazes of hallways, emerging about four buildings down from his office.

"Never let the bastards know what you're doing," he says, grinning.

In the Wicklow Hotel, an imperious waiter marches us to a table. Ó Móráin orders a bottle of red wine. I cover my glass. "You'll have just a tincture," he says, pouring. When I mention to the waiter that I'm a vegetarian, he sighs and whips my menu away.

"I knew that fellow when he hadn't a trouser to his arse," Ó Móráin says. "Michael Collins, our Civil War hero, gave the order to shoot a porter in this hotel, right out in front." The thought seems to give him some satisfaction.

A short, bald man with a paper bag enters, disappears into the kitchen, and returns wearing a chestnut wig. He begins to play the piano.

"How long will you be here?" Ó Móráin shouts at me.

"A year, more if my grant money lasts."

Throughout lunch he pulls folder after folder from a capacious valise, making precarious towers of papers and maps on a nearby table. He outlines, among other things, the history and pre-history of Ireland, the Civil War, and the work of the semi-state body in charge of setting up the Gaeltacht factories, Gaeltarra Éireann.

I wonder if all the Irish talk so much and so fast. Experienced anthropologists say an hour's conversation or observation takes three hours to type up. I have six hours so far, already wine-spotted and unreadable in places.

"That's Arabic you're writing?" he asks.

"Gregg shorthand. Backwards, for left-handers. Not much use in Irish, though."

"Invented by a fine Irish speaker, Robert Gregg, from County Monaghan. And those yellow cards you're writing on?"

"McBee Keysort cards." They're rectangular cards with small holes punched around all sides.

"You write on them, assign a hole to each topic on the card and snip them open. When you want to retrieve that topic from a set of cards, you run a knitting needle through its hole, and it falls down." I tear a cut through a hole and run a fork tine through it.

"So what topics will you choose for this one?"

God knows. I lie: "Oh, I always wait a day."

"Well, your first order of business will be to see Cathal MacGabhann, Gaeltarra Éireann's general manager. Tell him *I* sent you," he says with a wolfish smile.

I say I'm fascinated by his boiler-making/lobster factory in the Gaeltacht village of Carna. Salvador Dali's telephone has nothing on this. He winces and says it sounds better in the abstract.

He moves on to politics and religion. "The Church here has a stranglehold on sex, and the politicians follow them like sheep. No divorce, of course, but would you believe contraceptives are banned? The priests ask women in Confession why there's a space between their children. And yet the politicians are whoring around in Groome's Hotel."

I'm grateful. How long would it have taken to acquire this kind of insider information, since I can't ask about these subjects?

"People are forced to practice wddwrl," he mutters, "and the Church even frowns on that."

"Practice what?" The pianist finishes a loud dirge, which may or may not have been a slow version of "Oklahoma."

"Wddwrl!"

"Sorry?"

"Withdrawal!" he shouts. The waiter, approaching our table for the dessert order, stops in mid-stride. "Or else, they're forced to resort to aynlss." But the pianist is now pounding through "My Boy Bill."

"Well, of course," I say, mortified that I've placed him in this position. "Anyone would," not having a clue what he's said.

"Anal sex is not to everyone's taste, of course. But as the Brits say, 'Needs must when the devil drives.'"

What? But I avoid the knowing nod in case it might be elaborated upon. We've been here three hours, finishing with small brandies. There's no charge for my lunch: "Sure it was only vegetables," the waiter says.

What some people do in church – ruminate, repent, resolve – I usually do in bed in the middle of the night. Tonight, owl-eyed, I cringe at the discomfort I must have put that poor man through. I'm sure he forced himself to discuss delicate topics just to help a naive visitor ease her entry into Irish society. But I do have some questions to add to my study: factories that lose money don't last long, even government ones. Could the supposed "laziness," or lack of economic mentality, or high rates of mental illness have anything to do with the losses? And if the factories are failing, what am I doing here?

## The 1955 Morris Minor

My first car, and I'm only in Ireland three days! I'm living in some comfort, too, none of this perching-in-a-tree stuff that anthropologists like to boast of. At the Mount Herbert Guest House I get a bed, breakfast, and an evening meal for five pounds a week.[1] The instigator of all this good fortune is Mr. Lenihan, my airport taxi driver, an urban sociologist in mufti.

After a brief investigation into my mission, he'd outlined the history of the country, the different "tribes" of people, and how to catch Weil's disease from rats. A funeral procession halted traffic, and he explained the deceased was a former president of Ireland, "A good man in his own

---

1 In 1966–68, the period of this study, one Irish pound could buy goods and services that would cost almost seventeen times more in 2021.

way, but a 'creeping Jesus.'" I wrote this down. He rejected my choice of hotel as too expensive, took me to the Mount Herbert, and instructed the owner on my care and feeding.

Two days later I'm surprised to see Mr. Lenihan at the front desk again.

"I said to myself I'd see how you're getting on."

I've already learned what to say: "Not a bother." But I do mention I'm cold. "They keep the bedrooms at fifty-five degrees."

"You Yanks are demons for the heat, but it weakens the body. Too much heat and you can't go the course."

I wouldn't like that. He tells me a hot water jar is my only man. I understand every one of those words, but not in that combination.

"You mentioned you'll be needing a car." He folds a newspaper to the automobile ads and we set out, going from seller to seller, checking for mileage fiddling, evidence of crashes, faked logbooks. Finally, Mr. Lenihan chooses a proper dealership, on the grounds the owners are Protestants, Quakers who are "too nice to be let out by themselves, really."

So now I have a car with a split-screen windshield, fender-mounted mirrors, and, magically, two "traficators" or direction indicators, motorized wands that swing out from the pillars between the front and rear doors. Car plus tax and insurance, £150.[2]

At the Mount Herbert I find a package from my mother at the bottom of my suitcase.

I found your old Sacred Heart medal! It's still Advent but here's a wool nightgown and some baklava and kolache for Christmas. Dad's getting some new steel-toed work shoes and I'm knitting Patrice a poncho.

Kolache, lasagne, kielbasa, sauerbraten, "fried mush," borscht, and Amish wilted lettuce are all among my Irish-American mother's

---

2 The pounds in this study are Irish pounds.

specialties, all learned from our neighbors. My medal has become embed-
ded in the baklava.

The letter has a postscript from Patrice. "I was very moanfull when
you left."

## A Few Sound Men

Tonight, five days into my trip, I got my first taste of Dublin nightlife.

"Ó Móráin here," a low Mafia-like voice says over the phone at the
hotel desk. I assume he's not letting the bastards know what he's doing.
"Tonight, half-nine at the Trocadero, with a few of the great and the
good."

The plush, womb-like Troc, one of the few restaurants in Dublin, is
theater-themed with autographed photos of actors and actresses on all
the walls. The gathering includes the broadcaster and journalist Seán
MacRéamoinn, a cherub-faced polyglot/polymath, and one of the last
speakers of various little-known European languages, although later he
confesses his Serbo-Croat is "not what it used to be." I recognize the raspy
voice before I see him; a few nights ago he was introduced on Welsh television, one of the few non-Irish channels viewable in Dublin, as "argu-
ably the most intelligent man in Ireland," so now he's been laughed out
of his local, The Palace Bar. Soon we're joined by professors of Irish,
David Greene of Trinity College, Dublin, and Seán Ó Tuama of University College, Cork.

Ó Móráin has just visited the manager of the trout farm in Donegal,
in Carrick village. "We'd planned it as a model of development," he says.
But pigs seem to have been introduced, mysteriously. He says the manager is hard of hearing, so inquiries are at a standstill.

"I remember meeting that fellow when I was there with you, at the
launch of the trout caper," MacRéamoinn says. "'The Sultan,' he's called,
I can't remember why. Lovely fellow. A great patriot, deafened during

The Troubles. I knew he was always something of a secret pig aficionado, it was only a matter of time."

"He has them living in the ruins of the burnt-out landlord's lodge," Ó Móráin says. "*Former* landlord, Gael Linn is the landlord now, for all the thanks we get."

"At least you got a grand trout dinner?" Ó Tuama asks.

"The trout have vanished. The pools are empty. The Sultan says the local rock we used was porous, that the locals warned us. So far Gael Linn has lost almost thirty-thousand pounds, but when I say it the local Parish Council gets up in arms. They don't seem to understand things like overheads."

Aha, so that's where the "no economic mentality" comes in? Is this why he suggested Carrick as a research site?

"Who should I talk to for advice?" I ask. Various people are dismissed as being "chancers," "sleeveens," "daily communicants"; members of "the socks and sandals brigade" or "not sound."

"Not sound? What does that mean?"

They look perplexed. "Surely ..." "You must ..." "A man is sound if ..." they stutter and it's clear it's one of those cultural concepts that's so obvious as to need no explanation. I become defensive: "Do *you* understand the Mafia concept of a 'made man'?" I demand. They order more St. Emilion and a nice white.

"You have a problem, say you want planning permission for a site that's not zoned for your purpose. A sound man knows how to handle it, exploiting a loophole maybe, nothing illegal as such ..." Professor Greene says.

"As such," Ó Móráin says.

"A good man?"

"Good God no, not necessarily," MacRéamoinn, the national radio's primary religious commentator, protests.

"Honest?"

"Well, yes, with yourself when you consult him, but no, he doesn't have to be honest with just anyone," Ó Móráin says.

"Take your own case," Ó Tuama says to Ó Móráin. "When you wanted to get that outrageous charge, 'Driving Under the Influence,' handled properly, who was it who got it heard in front of a judge down the country and the report restricted to a line or two inside a local newspaper and written in Irish?"

"Exactly!" Ó Móráin beams. "He saw me right. A safe pair of hands."

"So," I say, "a fixer?"

"You might have such a thing in Iowa," MacRéamoinn huffs, "but ..."

"Ohio."

Alice in Wonderland stuff, but I gather a sound man has finesse, balance, judiciousness, a knowledge of limits and boundaries, yet is not overawed by them. Like my companions. They argue about the next course before we face into the freezing sleet: absinthe or sambuca or both? Both.

"Am I sound?" I ask.

"A woman ..." and MacRéamoinn's big cupid's face looks pained at what he's going to have to say. I wave my hand, saving him the trouble. A woman cannot be sound, I gather.

"Have more absinthe," MacRéamoinn says, peering out at the freezing rain. "A great preventative for malaria."

## An Irish Sampler

I'm following some of the leads I got last night, or the most legible ones from notes that deteriorated over the evening.

Cathal MacGabhann, general manager of Gaeltarra Éireann is first. His work seems closest to my interests, putting factories in Irish-speaking places. At his office, a thin blond man in his early thirties rushes through the front door and snatches up some ledgers.

He's Mícheál de hAl, the accountant. It's tempting to ask people with Irish names, especially names such as Iarlaith Ó Muircheartaigh or

Proinsias Mac Aonghusa, what their names are in English. I'm learning this is a colonial insult: Iarlaith Ó Muircheartaigh *is* the person's name, and maybe Proinsias Mac Aonghusa is happy to be known in English as Frank McGuinness, but that's his choice.

I explain my work. He suggests I talk to someone. "I'm not really here."

"I've phoned ..."

"Oh, the girl's new, not up to speed yet, but we had a little accounting rumpus here and we needed a girl with a first-class accounting degree." I wonder what passes for a "rumpus" in the accounting world. Or why a female with a first-class accounting degree isn't a "woman." And is answering the phones.

I say Kilcar might be suitable for my research.

"Oh, I don't think ..."

"It's one of your biggest? And it employs men as well as women?" I'm puzzled by the current gender make up in most Gaeltacht factories. Many workers are girls in their late teens. By law female teachers and civil servants must leave work when they marry, so most other brides do, too.

Since almost all farmers are men, if a factory employs mainly girls why would farmers sell their land?

"Well, I'd say you'd want to check your Kilcar idea with The Boss. He's not here. Give him a shout sometime." And then the question that seems to interest him most: "When are you returning to the States?"

I write down "accounting rumpus?" and "Kilcar???"

⌒

This afternoon I explore the Old Ireland. My companions at the Trocadero suggested I consult Alf Mac Lochlainn at the National Library about the Lawrence Collection, a set of plateglass photograph negatives taken between 1870 and World War I. He has a selection waiting at the counter. "MacRéamoinn," he says.

The plates show craftwork, markets, street scenes, and people whose gaze defies future viewers to claim they're dead. Two photos are the most searing: in the first, an evicted farm family stands in the foreground with a small jumble of kitchen things, watching bailiffs with a wrecking ball knock in the roof of their cottage. In the second, taken in the rain, the same people huddle in a shallow recess cut into a turf bog, their few bits of crockery arranged neatly on a turf ledge behind them. They stare directly, expressionless, at the camera.

I know from my grandmother's stories of her childhood that these people would have cared for the cottage, renewed its thatch, whitewashed it, and put a Bridget's cross above the fire on the first day of each spring. When she came to America, she brought a large holy picture of St. Joseph, eight bone-handled knives, "the good spoon for the priest," and a feather quilt. The people in the photograph probably had a holy picture important enough that it, too, might have been chosen to make a trip to the New World.

And the man in the photograph? Working that land was his domain, as it was his father's, and his father's father's. Maybe, on a hazy summer's morning before the world was up, he might even forget they were just renters, as most small farmers were. He repaired the stone walls; he knew when the soil was warm enough to plant the neat "lazy beds" of potatoes; and where the evening light fell as the few chickens picked their way home across the yard.

Depressed and back out on the street in a slashing rain, I pass Kevin and Howlin's shop on Nassau Street. Inside are lengths of soft, hand-woven Donegal tweed in startlingly vibrant earth colors, the warp and weft enticingly tactile. I think of gorse and lichen and dark peaty waters, none of which I've seen firsthand, but the words themselves carry sensations: yellow, blackberry, grey-green, prickly, spongy, trickling. I'm told tweeds could and did outfit soldiers in the World Wars; I'm shown others, lengths of gossamer tweed, pulled through a wedding ring.

And finally, at Fred Hanna's, I buy the expensive, 1,500-page Dineen's Irish–English Dictionary, *Foclóir Gaedilge Agus Béarla*, with its lovely gold-stamped green binding. I resolve to learn a few new words, a *cúpla focail*, every day. Flipping through it, on page 780 I discover words and phrases for "venomous," "spite," "a demure maid," "betrothed," "a peevish, conceited little creature, esp. a girl," and "the greatest disgrace ever suffered." On that single page, the makings of a novel.

At the guest house, a maid summons me to the desk phone. It's Seán MacRéamoinn: "How are you keeping?"

"Grand," I say – another correct reply to health inquiries. But after that outing to the Troc, it feels like one of my organs, the gizzard perhaps, is dying. MacRéamoinn says he'll bring a cure.

While I wait, fellow guests wave me into the television lounge to watch *The Late Late Show*. The program's host and most of the audience are angry about Irish censorship, and they mock the twenty-year ban on "indecent" literature. Almost all the great writers of our age are banned by the censors, as well as some medical dictionaries and all men's bodybuilding magazines.

Soon the portly MacRéamoinn sticks his head into the lounge and is greeted by all; he's a television personality himself. He has various objects clutched to his sides: a newspaper, a file folder, and two bottles, one Champagne, one something green. "Pernod," he says, tapping it. "The only cure for a hangover." In my room he pours me a half tumbler and opens the Champagne for himself. "I'll just have this. I'm off the drink for Advent."

I raise the censorship issue.

"The censors here define indecent literature as any work that excites sexual passion or suggests sexual immorality," he splutters. "How do they distinguish between married passion and the 'impure' stuff? Or take account of the reader's age? It would take a lot to get me going these days."

He pours himself a little Pernod. "So if you want sex in this country, you have to be able to read Irish. *The Midnight Court, Cúirt An Mheán Oíche*, eighteenth century, is almost gynecological but the censors don't know enough of their native language to read it."

We get into my car. Apparently many of Dublin's famous men can't drive. Their ladies ("wives or mistresses or both") transport them like eastern potentates and deposit them in their regular haunts. MacRéamoinn has assembled a new crowd for me. I'm warned the Dominican priest has a spanking fetish. A faux-Edwardian dandy, introduced as Seán Ó Tuairisc, sniffs at me and says the country has had enough of "colonial oppressors."

"Dear boy," MacRéamoinn protests, pausing to absorb this rudeness. "It could well be argued our own Irish priests and nuns have colonized America."

I remember Sister Margaret clouting little Tony Mastramico because he'd forgotten the words to "Galway Bay."

"I was simply establishing that we don't need yet another American expert."

"I'm not an expert. I'm just ..." What? "Using one more way of seeing, adding it to the pot ..."

"Another eye," MacRéamoinn says. "*Súil eile.* An old Irish concept. A different line of sight."

I need to work out what I can add, besides a PhD, for myself. For now, though, it's Vin Santo, Armagnac for the flush, a flaming sambuca for me, and we're poured out onto the footpath shortly after 1 a.m.


## Just a Set of Hunches?

Where should I do my research? Everyone has an idea. The Department of Agriculture's musical dance expert, a Mr. Breathnach, suggests, among other places, the meat factory in Sallins, County Kildare. ("Before that, all Sallins had was the hero Wolfe Tone's grave, and sure that's hardly an industry at all.") Few people suggest small western communities and even fewer know that factories exist in these places. An exception is the staff of the Agricultural Institute, where a no-nonsense scholar, Rosemary Fennell, repeats that no farmer going into a factory will ever sell his land; it's his home, a fall back, his history and legacy.

The more I hear of Kilcar, where Gaeltarra has its largest factory, and of neighboring Carrick, home of the Sultan and the Irish-speaking trout farm, the more I think this might be the right area. Both are actively looking for more industrial jobs. Other communities fall through my mental sifter because their factories offer only light work suited to girls just out of school. The national Census shows this is the group most likely to emigrate. It's likely that girls don't want to marry small farmers. But maybe boys don't want to inherit small farms, so they go, too. Would they stay for a factory?

I return to Gaeltarra Éireann to consult the general manager, Cathal MacGabhann. Mícheál de hAl greets me: "Are you still at this caper?" and introduces me to MacGabhann as "the American doctor."

My few experiences in the decadent recesses of the Trocadero with my Irish-speaking contacts haven't prepared me for the thirtyish crewcut MacGabhann, who looks like John F. Kennedy in fashionable horn-rimmed glasses. As I enter he's taking a flurry of calls in French, English, Irish, and Italian.

"*Abbiamo bisogno di un progettista ora. Dov'è lui?*" he's saying into the phone. That's when I catch on; people don't grow up in Mafia Youngstown without picking up the music of Italian, if not the words. "*Sì? È il nostro progettista a Lille?* Oh, sorry. *Est notre dessinateur à Lille?*"

"*Gabh mo leithscéal,*" he says, begging my pardon in Irish. "Our designer has gone missing."

He listens carefully to my story while signing the papers de hAl puts before him and shaving bits off a brown block into an ashtray. "What's your hypothesis?"

A hypothesis! What madness! I'm an anthropologist.

I repeat my mantra. "Will the factory workers sell their farms for con-solidation? Will they go into the factory? Will that maintain the language? How? Will that prevent emigration? Is it just a set of hunches?"

"Fair enough. Of course, if you find the policy's not working, I lose my job, and it's my first year as manager."

He seems calm enough about this and gives me a rundown on what they're doing to attract business to the Gaeltacht.

The incentives are astonishing: massive tax reliefs, cash grants for building, machinery, training, moving expenses, help with recruiting workers, and, if necessary, learning Irish. "Everything but wiping their ..." He stops and quickly arranges the few pages on his desk.

"Who wouldn't be attracted by that?" I ask.

"Someone who wants electricity, water, phones, decent roads, and a keenly enthusiastic workforce?" He laughs. "The first four can be scarce enough, and as for the fifth, I'd rather wait and see what you come up with yourself."

"So, people there don't have an 'economic mentality'?"

"I wouldn't say that. Maybe it's just a different way of seeing things."

"I've heard that in a few Gaeltacht places people don't even speak Irish."

"True. We inherited some old factories from the Congested Districts Board. It was set in the poorest areas of the west by the Brits in the 1890s. A lot were Irish speaking in those days, but some aren't now."

"So those old factories weren't an attempt to save the language?"

"Not at all. They were to relieve the terrible poverty on land too poor to support the population - 'congested,' in other words. But actually, that's the reason the language survived in many of the places. The land was so poor and remote that outsiders didn't move in." He picks up his penknife and curls more slivers of the brown block into the ashtray.

De hAl jabs at the map with a stray sliver. "That board gave up in places like west Donegal. Hopeless."

"We've still got the board's buildings, even in places where the only Irish they have is what's been beaten into them in school," MacGabhann says. "The buildings are old, unsuitable, and not always in the places you'd pick for a modern factory."

"But we've just got the go-ahead from the government to develop some big new industrial estates," de hAl says, nodding at the map.

"Where?" I ask, but neither answers. "Of course," MacGabhann says, "some people object to our work. I call them the Quaint Brigade. They say the charm, the *charm*, mind you, of the Gaeltacht will be ruined by small industry. They're Dublin people who send their children there in the summer to learn Irish so they can get into good civil service jobs. They pop down one weekend and demand Manhattan cocktails in Paddy Mickey Joe's pub."

We're both indignant about this, although I'm not certain what a Manhattan cocktail is. "On the other hand, they resent any special government supports for the Gaeltacht. But not doing anything is what got us where we are today."

"Where are we today?"

"Not in a good place. In a little over a hundred years, the population of the Gaeltacht has dropped by ninety-five per cent. The land's still bad, the farms are small, the farmers are old. Where are those Census results, Mick?" He runs his finger down a handwritten table of figures. "Two-thirds of the farmers are over fifty, and a third of them are single," he reads. "You won't meet many people your own age. Less than a third of the people are between fifteen and forty-five."

"And those are your target population?" I ask.

"Yes, but as I say, the young ones want to leave. Look at Ó Móráin of Gael Linn, trying to interest English-speaking middle-class adults in Irish. And isn't he right? Why should keeping the language alive be the job of only the poorest and their kids?"

All three of us are worked up now. I get a rundown on some of the factories. The established ones are tweed and doll making in Donegal, machine knitwear in Mayo, and toy making in Galway. I ask again which areas will get the new industrial estates. They ask what Ohio is like.

"I'm leaning towards studying Kilcar, that area."

"Kilcar," MacGabhann says. His voice has a flat note, and he glances at de hAl.

Kilcar seems obvious to me. "The factory is much larger than the others, it's been there a long time, it employs settled adult men who will feed their money back into the community, it's based on a traditional industry acceptable to the people, it makes something respected around the world, most people have heard of Donegal tweed. If the plan doesn't work there, it won't work anywhere." I'm selling the man on his own factory.

"And that's the place those politician bastards in Dublin called a 'horrifying *dumpail*,'" MacGabhann says to de hAl.

Kilcar is a dump?

"The thing is," he says, "you'd want to look at some of the other factories before deciding. Explore a little. A thing like a PhD study, you wouldn't want to take that decision lightly.

"Take the factory in Tourmakeady, in County Mayo," he says. "Your own home place."

"My ..." we say it at the same time: "Ó Móráin." News travels fast.

"It's based on a traditional industry, too, knitting jumpers and such. The product is popular around the world. It's about a third of the size of Kilcar. It employs men. Are the people delighted?"

"Are they?"

"Not really."

"Why not?"

"Surely that's the point of your study? How the factory fits into the community, and the community into the factory?"

I suspect he just doesn't want to spoil the surprise.

We plan my exploratory trip to a series of factories in Galway and Mayo: toy making, weaving, knitting.

"Break your trip halfway at the hotel in Leenane. There's a good walk there, if you're a mountaineer: *Magairlí an Deamhain*, the Devil's ..."

"Mother. 'The Devil's Mother,'" de hAl interjects.

"At the end of your trip, call in to a guy in Mayo, Fred Driver in Kiltimagh. He's not one of ours: he manages a private factory. Nobody knows how he does it, but he's a legend. See if you can learn his secret."

I thank them for their advice. MacGabhann's attention to the social factors I hope to study is impressive, even more so since he's an accountant. But what about the brown block? The wisps and shards are piling up. What is he doing with them?

"Oh," he says, laughing and tossing the block into a bin. "I get homesick when I travel, so I take some turf shavings with me and burn a bit each night in an ashtray. I'm on my way to your country tomorrow for a meeting."

Outside, de hAl relaxes. "You made a hit with The Boss. I don't think he's ever told anyone but me about the turf. Most visitors look at the block. They ignore the shavings."

# December/Mí na Nollag 1966

## "You Wouldn't Believe the Things That Happen in This Place"

Some of my classmates do exotic fieldwork in yurts or favelas, fending off the Mongolian death worm or the armadillo. One of the few other female students in the department is now in an African hut, the woman my professor described as "so ambitious I'll bet she doesn't even menstruate."

It's time to look at the Gaeltacht factories MacGabhann suggested and settle on my field site.

I leave Dublin at dawn. Four hours later, at the toy factory in Spiddal, County Galway, a man in his early thirties introduces himself in a Northern Irish accent as Terry Stewart. He has thick black hair and one of those faces that settles into cheerful contours even in distress. He's in distress now, huddled at a table behind some packing boxes. In another corner, diagonally, half a dozen teenage girls sit, glaring.

"Thank God you're here!" he says. "Head office told me yesterday you were coming. We need you."

Rarely does an anthropologist hear this, I suspect.

"The place is in chaos. We have no idea what's going on. We're expecting a walkout. Those girls in the corner are doing nothing. You wouldn't believe the things that happen in this place. There's no explaining them, and anyway, no one would believe you. Fred Driver wouldn't put up with this."

I assume this Driver is the "legend" MacGabhann mentioned.

He nods toward the corner, where a dark-haired girl is flattening another's blonde frizz with a barrette. "What do you make of all this? By the way, I'm only here to spell the real manager. He's on what they're calling 'rest leave.'"

I can't make anything of it; all I know is a barrette is no match for that frizz.

"Those girls are supposed to be learning the doll hair-stuffing machine. Dolls' heads used to be made up in the Donegal factory, in a place called Crolly, 'Crolly Dollies,' they're called, and sent here to Galway to be attached to the bodies. But then the hair machine was transferred here. The Crolly girls were furious. That machine was their pride and joy."

"Hair-stuffing?"

"Yes, the dolls' heads have lots of little holes on top and the machine stuffs little bunches of hair into them. It takes three weeks to learn. Then the hair gets styled. Wouldn't you think they'd love that?"

The girl wielding the barrette looks at me defiantly.

"I gather things were okay a while back," Terry says. "The girls got a set wage, but production was very low, about sixty per cent capacity, and customer numbers dropped. So we put the girls on piecework to speed up production – they'd get more money for more work. At the beginning, they got a good rate for each piece, so they didn't see it as a pay cut. And the few lads here, older fellows, were delighted, they worked away. Still do."

"And then?"

"We cut the rate once they got used to the idea that pay was tied to production. The girls saw that as a pay cut."

"It was a pay cut."

"Not if they worked more. The lads did."

"But ..."

"You have to do these things gradually. First get them used to the idea of well-paid piecework, and then move on to the real problem, increasing their work. If you introduced piecework and on payday they got less than their usual money for the amount of work they'd always done, they'd see it as a pay cut. They'd reject the piecework plan."

"So now they get less pay for the original amount of work they'd been doing, or else work harder to get what they used to get?"

"You might go over and see will they talk to a lady."

My Irish isn't good enough for this issue. The girls eye my thick woolly tights contemptuously, but three are comfortable in English and agree to talk. I ask them about piecework.

"They want us to work harder for less," the black-haired girl says. I can't argue with that. She has a very well-developed "economic mentality," whatever people in Dublin might say.

"Yes, but you have a chance to get paid more if you make more toys. You didn't have that before."

"We're satisfied with what we have." She tosses her hair before each reply; she's probably been told her straight, silky hair is her best feature.

"And the men?"

"The young lads are like us," says the frizz-haired girl, whose mop has escaped the barrette and stands around her head like a barbed halo. "Fed up. The old fellas, maybe they work more."

"And then," the black-haired girl says, "they bring this hair-stuffing thing in, and I, I had to learn it. I hate it. I'm not paid anything extra, so the others said they wouldn't learn it, either."

Wouldn't they like to have more spending money? No, they say. Nothing around here to buy.

I try a broader economic argument. "The factory needs enough toys to sell. It might close, otherwise." I regret these last words instantly; in

Youngstown, if someone uttered "factory" and "close" in the same sentence, it would be all over town by nightfall. But it doesn't seem to faze these girls. "We'll go to England, we will soon enough, anyway."

This kind of line may be what fuels the Dublin argument about the Gaeltacht mentality. But most people are like this. They don't make decisions about their resources on purely economic grounds. City people don't charge their elderly mothers for a bedroom, for example, yet a bedroom is a rental commodity.

"Do I want to be like my mother?" Frizz Hair asks. "Killing herself taking in Irish college students every summer? *Na céadta páistí?*"

A hundred children?

Irish colleges are Gaeltacht schools that take in students from English-speaking areas during the summer holidays so they can improve their Irish and have a chance to get into university or the civil service. Local women get a grant of five pounds weekly to keep each student for three weeks. A woman takes ten students, and later, a second round. She can make about £300 annually. Sending children is a *rite de pasage* in many urban families. Parents, the Manhattan cocktail drinkers MacGabhann mentioned, send their children, assuming they'll be studying; the children plan to be drinking and kissing.

"*Na céadta páistí?*" I ask.

"Well, no, maybe twenty at a time. If she's short of money, she crams in more."

"And feeds them on bread and water, not bread and jam," Frizz Hair snickers. I think that's what she's saying in Irish; I confuse the Irish words for "water" and "whiskey."

All this sounds very much like a strong economic mentality to me. Ireland is a small place, and over half the population is rural. Have their urbanite descendants really forgotten how their recent ancestors lived?

Terry followed this conversation from his table-barricade. When I rejoin him, we reminisce about our own jobs as teenagers, me in the

Youngstown public library, he doing odd jobs. What little money we got, we handed over ...

The thought strikes both of us: "The Mother!" he shouts. "Funny, how you can get a business degree and lose the sense God gave you."

We approach the girls.

"Do you have to hand up your money?" Terry asks. "I had to. Miss Kane had to."

One of the English speakers, a mercilessly freckled girl with hair so red it looks like it hurts her head, speaks up. "We do of course, we hand up our pay packet and the mother gives us ten shillings back. If we're lucky."

"But the men," Terry says, "They're older and married."

"They give the lot to the wife," the girl says, "but at least they get a big lump back in their fists for drink and tobacco."

Terry and the young women scheme. One regular pay packet, another for the extra piecework? The first would go, as always, to the mother in the usual amount. Maybe the rest could be lodged in a private savings scheme in the factory? The girls could save to go to England. This seems to appeal. They huddle over details.

As I leave, a breezy youth with a Mod fringe of light brown hair comes in. I recognize him, David Wagstaff, a British student I met in Dublin at a Trinity College debate.

"The anthropologist" he says. "*Dia is Muire dhuit!*" That's "God and Mary with you" instead of the more common "God with you."

A neat trick, and I'm required to outdo him: "*Dia is Muire dhuit agus Pádraig,*" I reply, "God and Mary and Patrick with you." He could raise the ante, adding "Saint Bridget" to my own greeting, to which I would have to add yet another saint, and so on, but instead, graciously, he winks.

"Gaeltarra's just hired me. I don't start for a week, but I thought I'd have a look at some of the factories."

The girls, two shoving one forward, come closer to see this new specimen.

"*Bail ó Dhia ort*," he says to them, "Blessings on the work," and melds into the group, chattering away in Irish. They're all over him, and I'm still young enough to see why.

I resolve to improve my poor Irish and set out for the next factory. I'm delighted that in such a short time in Spiddal I've been allowed to see the effect of a community's culture on the factory. And the factory might affect the community by ... what? Teaching its daughters to be venal sneaks, I suppose, but production might improve.

## Connemara Mayhem

Connemara is a region that corresponds to nothing but itself. It's not a county, a government unit, or a postal district. It's a little like the concept of the American "Old West," part real, part magic. Tiny cottages fight for space among rocks and boulders perched at impossible angles. The contrast between this geological mayhem and the small line of laundry or the cramped ridge of potatoes is almost comical. I move further inland and north across scruffy brown terrain and the soft, low mountains in their lonely spareness.

Connemara has the highest percentage of Irish speakers in the country, but I wonder how MacGabhann and the others, hard-headed accountants and economists, will fare here; they're moving their headquarters soon. Dial telephones don't exist, and they'll have a poor electric supply and some back roads that might defy a mule. It's a love of the language that fires these men, and this landscape must represent its spirit, as the American West draws people who search for a landscape that encapsulates the pioneer spirit. A touch of romance. None, Ó Móráin, MacRéamoinn, MacGabhann, or Stewart, was born in a Gaeltacht. And they could earn more in conventional businesses.

At the second factory, a locksmith says the workers have pulled up the machinery, Hattersley looms, and thrown them out the window. A woman in a housecoat and bedroom slippers sweeps scraps; she says she lives across the road. "I'm saying nothing," she says. I ask about the boiler-making/lobster factory in Carna, about an hour's drive away. "It's only the size of a hen house, and if you go out there, you'll never come back," she mutters. I head off to Leenane and my night's hotel.

No other setting matches Leenane in moonlight. It's at the head of a nine-mile fjord, and the yellowish light over the black water, emerging and receding through clouds, must have inspired many a Victorian painter. The forbidding black mountain range, Mweelrea, is on my left; on my right, the mouth of the fjord opens onto dozens of dimly lit secret bays where spectral yachts sail on silvery plains. The clouds shift and the ships reveal themselves as islands, some pyramid shaped, some sugar loafs, some gumdrops, like a giant's sweets. To be on this planet and miss what I'm seeing now would be a bitter thing.

I've overshot the hotel, but when I arrive there's no response to my ringing and banging. I open a low window, step in over the sill and follow clinking sounds to the bar. The majority of Irish children leave school at fifteen to work, and this one, small and undernourished-looking, wipes glasses. I say I have a reservation, and I'm starving.

"No food, sorry. Or electricity. No one here but me. I could give you a drink, I can make a Martini cocktail. Or a Manhattan cocktail." My first Manhattan.

He says he'll move to New York when he's eighteen, so he's working his way through a cocktail book. "Right now I'm on a Bourbon Presbyterian." I try one. He goes out and brings my suitcase in through the window. I might want to see to my rear chassis rail, he says, it looks dodgy.

I go to bed with Dineen's dictionary and look up MacGabhann's local climb, *Magairlí an Deamhain*, the "Devil's Mother." "*Deamhain*" is the "devil" part, but "*magairlí*"? The word for "mother" is *máthair*. *Magairlí*. Aha, here it is, "testicles." The Devil's Testicles. I'm charmed; how sweet of de hAl and MacGabhann to give me a genteel English version, but also the correct Irish.

## The Legend

An hour along the road, my chassis rail apparently still in place, I find Tourmakeady. Everyone in the knitting factory looks like me or my family except for the managers, who look patrician. People passing through this tiny village may never guess that inside the old school are eighty-seven people, half of them males, working three twenty-four-hour shifts. Manual and power machines produce knitted garments that are then wrapped, packed, and boxed. There's a canteen, a social club, and vans to transport the workers. The managers, all young, none local, say their main problems are emigration and the fact that many local girls look down on factory work. That, and "local interference"; a fellow in the village who goes "straight to the top in Dublin at the first sign of a problem." They're generous with their time, and I roam freely. The manager suggests I also visit Fred Driver, further north. The legend.

Within minutes of leaving the factory I'm lost. My ancestors knew these netted lanes intimately, so "racial memory" must be nonsense. Finally, I come across a pub-shop, which I suspect may be only a few hundred yards from the factory. Inside a greying man emerges from the back, wiping his hands.

"*Fáilte,*" he says. "*Cén chaoi a bhfuil tú?*"

"*Go maith,*" I say, fine. "I was visiting the factory and I've got lost."

He nods. What now?

"My grandmother came from here," I offer. "She was a Stanton."

He squints, studying my face. "Tomás O'Toole," he says, and invites me into a back kitchen, where he gives me tea and Marietta biscuits.

"Most are happy the factory's here. It postpones emigration. And the new manager is good; I don't have to go to Dublin as much." So this is the "interference."

Various elders are summoned, one of whom announces he made his First Holy Communion with my grandmother in 1892. "So she married?" he asks, sounding disappointed. An agricultural instructor and a teacher appear. Fortunately, they need little prompting, since the Marietta biscuits, first cousin to plasterboard, are stuck to the roof of my mouth.

"We don't have much of a knitting tradition here, and men think it's women's work, anyhow. No man wants to go to the pub and say, 'Well, lads, I knitted twenty Aran sweaters today,'" the teacher says. "Of course, they're not men, they're boys, because no married man could live on that wage."

Tomás is figuring on the margin of a newspaper. "A farmer on the dole, the welfare payment, with a wife and six children might get three-hundred-and-seventy-five pounds a year," he says, "and if he's farming on good land he can have another five hundred pounds after expenses. If he's on poor land, it's more like half that. Both farmers will have their vegetables and turf. But twelve pound a week from the factory and no chance of the dole, is what, about six hundred pounds, all told. And you have to buy everything in, and most workers aren't on anything like twelve pound a week." He draws a flow chart. When you pass a lone shop like this in what is not even the middle of nowhere, this nowhere lacking a middle, you don't expect such an analytical audit of local economic and government benefits. And such an "economic mentality."

He says people emigrate, no matter what, but if the wages were high enough for a married man some would return. "The first red-haired lads you talked to up in the factory, Dinny and Joe, they'd come back after a spell away, their old fellas' farms aren't too bad. By the way, that lad ye met on the stairs isn't the full shilling.

"We need a real factory, something like a big nut-and-bolt factory or tubular steel or electrical appliances," he says. "This one's so small, no chance for promotion, and people don't learn a skill. It's not challenging for a young person to stand at a machine all day. So they leave."

The teacher says something they all agree with. "The factory is government subsidized. It doesn't have to be competitive. It's not a real factory. That kind of thing affects the mentality of the place."

I leave Tourmakeady with a little pang and a greeting to pass on to my grandmother.

An hour and a half through tiny fields and I'm in Kiltimagh town, where I find Fred Driver, a neat little Englishman in his fifties. If he knows he's a legend, he doesn't show it. The factory, Irish Spinning Mills, is a private company, not related to language interests. It has eighty workers, he tells me, with day and night shifts. "Once a man comes in here, he's here for life." Almost all the men are part-time farmers, and men on the night shift can earn up to eighteen pounds a week, three more than the day shift, and slightly above the national industrial average.

"But the girls! When I needed an office girl and factory girl, I got twenty applications for the office and two for the factory. It's a class thing: a girl would rather wear a white coat in a chemist's shop for a pound a week than get nine pounds in the factory. We want to show factory work is attractive and respectable for girls."

Two things seem to have helped this factory survive for the last fifteen years. One is community support: the local development group raised money to buy the site and put up capital to attract the factory.

The second becomes clearer as we talk. Driver outfoxes trouble. A factory bus means workers come in on time, and absences without two days' notice are penalized. But he's part of the community. "I bought the old town hall for sports and dancing. Dances start early on Saturdays and end at 11:30 so people are up for Sunday Mass and the priest is happy."

He spreads out some blueprints. "A canteen and showers," he says. "I had them ready to go, but we all went on an outing to Galway, a little tour and a dinner, and I saw a few were missing. I learned some people are embarrassed to eat in front of others. So I have to get that canteen right. The showers, I'm shifting them around, I don't want any possibility of male workers pranking around the females. I'm the only Protestant around and I don't want word going out that I'm lax ..."

"A lot of managers could learn from you," I say, not mentioning the last three I talked to would like to have the privilege.

"Not at all; I'm only running a factory, I'm not expected to save the Irish language. And you wouldn't believe the things that happen around here. There's no industrial history. For example, most workers don't look after the small things, no attention to detail. The fear of closure, I call it: things are made right but not finished off properly. And they worry about getting a raise in case they'd have to pay more taxes.

"On the other hand, a lot of industrial tradition is almost Victorian, so we're building a new one here, bit by bit. They have to learn, I have to learn."

A girl brings tea on a lace-doilied tray and gives him a smile and a tiny theatrical curtsey. "Go away out of that," he laughs, exactly as an Irish person would.


## The Death of One Man

"That's the last place God made," some say in Dublin when I tell them I've chosen "The Field": Kilcar and Carrick in Donegal, the most northerly county in Ireland. They stand at the end of a remote peninsula in southwest Donegal, "nothing between them and America," someone in the Agricultural Institute said. "Harsh weather, extremely poor land, few services, bad roads. But beautiful."

Kilcar is an obvious choice. But Carrick, three miles away, with its zany trout farm? Historically it played an even stronger role in tweed production than Kilcar, with major agents flocking to its monthly market. But later, when Gaeltarra looked for a place to produce tweed, local political influence sent it to Kilcar.

Is Carrick a stepchild, caught between two more blessed siblings? Their other neighbor, Glencolmcille, has the formidable Father McDyer, celebrated across Western Europe for his attempts to bring in local employment, with full-page spreads in British newspapers. I know enough now to suspect that most rural villages put their own people first when anything good, like a factory, comes along. So Carrick, even more than the two others, needs an alternative to agriculture. Will they look for a factory?

This morning I phone Pat Bolger, the new Donegal County development officer.

"For twenty-five years, Carrick's Parish Council tried to attract new business, but private investors won't set up a business in a remote place just for cultural reasons. Carrick has three fellows who are very committed to development, but ... how can I put it? One can't lead, one won't lead, and one has a great future behind him."

I buy expensive ordnance survey maps of the areas, twenty-five inches to the mile. The latest ones for the Carrick/Kilcar area are dated 1906. I'm impressed by the luxuriously heavy paper, crackling as I unroll it. The clerk points out the detail: not just roads and rivers but bogs, churches, forges, ruins, wells, marshes, fields, houses, almost down to the people walking the lanes. The maps were done to valuate properties for tax purposes, he says. I see that altitudes are based on a "Low Water of Spring Tides observed in Dublin Bay on 8th April 1837." Like most people, I'm comforted by precision, even if it might be precisely wrong.

I pore over the mysterious townland names: Crowanrudda Beg, Umuskan, Straleel North and South.

"You've read the letters of John O'Donovan?" the clerk asks. "A great scholar. He was charged with working out the place names for those townlands and thousands of others. He did it on foot. I'm certain it killed him in the end."

The maps haven't been updated in years. I need to interview people to see who's owned each plot since then. Have some of them sold their land to go into the factory, as the government hopes? Has more land been consolidated with existing farms for a better livelihood? Are people staying? Has the language survived?

I go to the library of the Dáil, the Irish parliament. In one report, a Dáil member says the main concern in the Gaeltacht is how to get a ticket out by car, bus, rail, boat, or plane. I come across a fiery exchange in 1961 about the Kilcar factory. The deputy prime minister attacks a

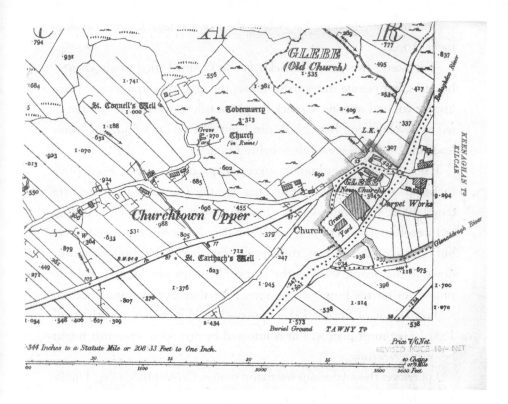

Map 2. Section of an ordnance survey map.

former minister for the Gaeltacht, a member of the opposing party, saying he was "responsible for the death of one man" who took his own life.
He also claims someone was wrongly accused of stealing £100,000 from
Gaeltarra Éireann. But the former minister seems incandescent with
anger, obvious even in this dry report. He defends himself and stands by
his claim that £100,000 was indeed stolen.

Whose death? What stolen money? The bitter exchange ends. I try
to work backwards through the files to see what led up to this, but it's a
maze, and the library is closing. Is this the "accounting rumpus" Mícheál
de hAl mentioned when first I met him? It certainly qualifies.

At the guest house, I have a postcard from my little sister. My father has made "fride eggs and put sinimon on them," she says. My father never cooks. Where is my mother?

## Where I Come From

Tonight I'm meeting the lads for the last time in the Trocadero. Ó Móráin and MacRéamoinn arrive and, over a nice amontillado, Ó Móráin suggests some contacts in Carrick: "Gael Linn got the salmon rights to the bay when we bought the landlord's estate, and we also have part of the river. Michael Boyle is one of the caretakers. Anything to do with the history of the land and farming, he's the best. I suppose I should mention," he says, "the community is still a bit divided over the fact that we bought the estate."

I know now from the way he uses language this could mean anything from a few pursed lips to snipers in trees. "Some people wanted the community to buy it, in partnership with Father McDyer in Glencolmcille. But we were tipped off by a local and got in just in time with a higher bid. James O'Donnell is the man to set you right on any things like that, a great backstage man, James, a bit mad, maybe, but sound, all the same. See him first thing, his pub is on the street. You might stay there until you find a place."

I write down "Michael Boyle," "James O' Donnell," "a bit mad?" and "SOUND?" in my notes. "And you might call in to see old Canon Murphy. Retired as parish priest now, but he's a relic of old decency."

"A relic of old decency?"

"A person ..." Ó Móráin says, "who is ... or does ... or ..."

"A Catholic?"

"Sometimes. More likely it's one of the elderly Anglo-Irish, living off the scrapings of bean tins out in Foxrock."

"It doesn't have to be a person, it could be an action, or a building, or silver tureen ... in the song it was a silk hat ..." MacRéamoinn looks at me pleadingly. "You'd know, yourself."

"I don't," I say. Would they understand what a Youngstowner means when she says dismissively of another woman, "She thinks her ass weighs a ton"?

MacRéamoinn settles like a deflated dirigible, and both of them look weary. I remember I'm the anthropologist, not them. "Can a woman be a relic of old decency?" I ask.

"Yes, of course," MacRéamoinn wheezes. He pulls out a handkerchief so large it might be part of the tablecloth and mops his face. "Indeed, in time you might become one yourself."

Another question. Why, after all our evenings here at the Troc, have I seen so few women diners? "Just those two, with their husbands," I nod toward the neighboring booths.

"But my dear," MacRéamoinn protests, "That's the thing. Those men are *other* women's husbands. Lottie and Orna, the ladies, *their* men are dining in Quo Vadis, with other companions." He beams, happy to have straightened this out.

And your own wives are where? I want to ask, knowing they're at home, supervising homework or candling eggs, certainly not out on the tiles like us.

At the end of the night, it's Slippery Nipples on the house for the small parties still in the restaurant, some sound, some clearly not, one having crawled under the tables and out the kitchen door to avoid paying a long-standing tab. "A bit Irish, that was," someone says, but I'll parse that another day. "To the Field" is the toast. The lads give me a going-away gift: Kuno Meyer's 1906 *The Death Tales of the Ulster Heroes*. "Donegal is in the province of Ulster," MacRéamoinn says. "The site of the greatest tragedies in our mythology. 'Deirdre of the Sorrows' is a good place to begin. Or the hideous death of our great Cú Chulainn." His eyes become misty.

On Christmas day, I join the other guests at the Mount Herbert for a festive lunch. There's sherry in the foyer, fir branches on the mantel tops, and we don strange paper crowns. I think of the huge lit trees at home and the prancing deer on the front lawns, some electrical, others shot and stuffed by the householders. Tomorrow is St. Stephen's Day here, another holiday, and people assure me it's much better in the countryside, where people kill a wren, don disguises, and go from house to house with the body, singing and begging.

I review my time here. I've interviewed officials at heights I couldn't hope to scale in a Youngstown suburb, let alone nationally. I've drunk prosecco in elegant fluted glasses, been seen as sophisticated, and treated as a scholar of some distinction before I have a grasp of what I'm doing.

Now I'm off to Carrick and Kilcar, my "field sites," the kind I've read about in classic anthropological studies. Margaret Mead and Raymond Firth seem to have flourished in theirs. Others, non-mixers, took a "fetch-me-a-pygmy" approach; who, exactly, depends on which anthropologist is telling the story. But few have worked in modern societies where the locals will read what you've written about them. Then I remember *Small Town in Mass Society*, where effigies of the sociologist authors were hanged on a bed of manure.

So am I worried, going from the Mafia "Murder Capital of the U.S." to "The Last Place God Made"?

Yes.

But Christmas reminds me of my father and his perennial Christmas present, the new pair of work boots. I remember his hands on the steering wheel as we drove to the Pittsburgh airport, battered, black-nailed, far from Slippery Nipples. I remember who I am and where I come from.

## A Day at the Races

I'm off! I have my maps, Dineen's Irish dictionary, and Kuno Meyer's *Ulster Death Tales*, all on the passenger seat, handy for quick reference.

After all my grant applications, visas, reading, and consulting, I'm nearing my home for the next year, also home in the fourth century to Niall of the Nine Hostages, he of the delicate black eyelashes and hyacinth eyes; and in the seventeenth century to the great scholars, the Four Masters, the formidably named Míceál Ó Cléirigh, Cú Choigcríche Ó Cléirigh, Fearfeasa Ó Maol Chonaire, and Peregrine Ó Duibhgeannain.

First, though, I have to cross The Border between the Republic and Northern Ireland and back out again, the shortest way to Donegal. I hand my car's logbook and papers to an inspector in a hut, who hands me a card to present to a Northern Irish customs inspector a few yards away. That inspector seals my documents in an envelope, hands it back and sends me to British Customs in the garrison town of Enniskillen, a place that makes Youngstown look like Monaco. I get a year's pass.

As I cross back into the Republic at Pettigo, near Donegal Town, I'm hungry and disoriented by the scenery: honey-brown folds of bare, velveteen mountains, rocks, bracken, heathers, rushes – a bare, scraped landscape like Nevada, but soggy. People who'd told me Donegal was bleak, barren, and windswept were masters of understatement. If the rest of the province is like this, I can see how Deirdre of the Sorrows came to a bad end.

About twelve miles along a particularly austere stretch, I hear a sign of life, a loud motorcycle behind me. I slow down, curious, but there's no sign of a rider. I speed up and the noise increases. Seventy years ago, as a child on a lonely road like this, my grandmother came across her grandfather, a ghost of several hours' standing, riding a horse. I suppose this can't be him now on a motorcycle. I get out, leaving the engine on for a quick getaway.

My exhaust has a hole the size of an orange. I thunder into Donegal Town, where a woman, hands over ears, points me to a garage.

"John Joe Mulhern. It's Stephen's Day, so go to his house if he isn't there. Don't mind him, he washes up well."

The garage is closed. Across the road, someone watches behind grubby curtains but there's no answer to my knock. Eventually, a small grey man in a cap that looks as if it was knitted into his eyebrows opens the door and after a slight hesitation agrees he is John Joe. I doubt he washes up well. Reluctantly, he motions me into the hallway. My explanation is drowned by a medley of ferocious keenings and howlings from the next room. "Quiet, you hoors!" he shouts. The hoors continue. He opens a door just enough to eye the interior, but the wind from the open front door catches it and bangs it open, revealing what must be a sitting-room. The floor is carpeted wall-to-wall in old newspapers. A greyhound exercises on a contraption that's a cross between a small bicycle and a large hamster wheel, while another greyhound coaches it excitedly from the side, barking and trying to bite the shins as they fly past. Sometimes he skids on the newspapers and sends them skittering up behind him.

I assume this must be torture for Greyhound Number One, struggling, panting, and snapped at, but apparently not. "This one," John Joe says, indicating the barker, "wants a go on the machine. Get off, you filthy scut and let your comrade have a go," he shouts at the rider, who hunkers down and keeps going. "Gerroff, I said!" The animal ducks his head into his shoulder, bares his froth-flicked teeth and speeds up.

Suddenly, Greyhound Number Two notices the stranger in the room and lunges. "Run," John Joe shouts, to me I presume, and I do, slamming the door shut as the dog's snout thuds against it. He climbs the door, snapping and growling. I've just outrun a greyhound.

John Joe comes out, swiping at a gob of dog spittle on his forearm. "I train greyhounds."

"I figured it must be something like that."

"What was it you wanted?" He reopens the garage and within half an hour I have a new exhaust. He refuses payment. He's smoothed his hair and rubbed away the tidemark on his neck.

I have a room booked with James O'Donnell, but John Joe warns me not to set out in the dark for Carrick. "Fierce wild people out there." I take John Joe as the benchmark, so I stay in Donegal Town for the night.

## Carrick: "The Rock"

The coast road to Carrick passes through villages like tiny Bruckless, where women in an old schoolhouse make world-famous lace for royalty, Manhattanites, and the trousseaus of commoners. It loops around Killybegs harbor's jam of huge fishing vessels. Vistas appear and disappear at the bends and turns: on my right are cottages set in a moon-mountain landscape, and on my left the sea looks south across to County Sligo. From the hilltops, water and, eventually, Newfoundland.

Finally, 170 miles from Dublin, a sign announces *An Charraig*, "The Rock" in Irish, and underneath, "Carrick." The road sweeps down across a stone bridge and rises again into Carrick Upper, past a chemist/post office, pubs, a shop/petrol pump, a school, a church. Most are brightly painted, spare and neat. The 1966 Census says the village population is 172, a jump of six since 1841, but I just see three elderly men in four visible layers of wools and tweeds, caps angled against the wind, standing in front of the Central Bar.

Across the road a few younger men lean against a corner wall. These must be the sort of fellows whom some Dubliners think are lazy. But they look like farmers. Surely farmers need to exchange news about markets, diseases, new treatments, and fertilizers? I think of my father waiting early at the factory gate to hear about possible layoffs, who has been hurt, what's happening down in Shop 2. Carrick is a rural area with few phones. How are people to know what's going on, except on the street and in the pub?

I park and walk, scanning the buildings for James O'Donnell's pub. I see a few possibilities, one of which is also an undertaker, and none named "O'Donnell." It's sleeting daggers. I stop a small woman. "James O'Donnell?" she asks. "Which one?"

"He has a pub," I say. Her eyes are an extraordinary mosaic of blue and violet flecks, like stained glass.

"Oh, that would be James Mary Agnes." She escorts me to a door, smiles shyly, and hurries away, shoulders huddled in her thin worn coat. The pub seems to be a shop as well, with a stand of withered vegetables at the doorstep. The sign, in faded black paint, says "Ó Floinn."

Inside, everything is the same brownish color – floor, bar, walls, air – like an underexposed sepia print. As my eyes adjust, two customers surface, hunched over the bar, capped and overcoated. They turn minimally and lift their heads enough to examine me.

"Mr. O'Donnell?"

"He said you're to wait," the older man says. "S'out on a run in the taxi." I was supposed to arrive in Carrick yesterday; how long have they been sitting here?

The door bangs open and we're caught in a spray of hail.

"Doctor Kane, the anthropologist, I presume? Ó Móráin sent a note about your study." A tall slim man touches his wide-brimmed fedora and thrusts his hand out. "James."

"Not 'doctor' yet. This is my PhD study."

"Och, aye, isn't that always the way?" He waves at a pile of furry mittens behind a table. "It's the same with me and the taxidermy. I keep my hand in, but it isn't the same as having the certificate." Now the mittens look more like emptied rabbits. James himself comes into better focus, too: a generous smile in a tanned, fine-featured face.

The elder of the men at the bar turns again and ducks his head to view me through a lush thatch of eyebrows.

"Eugene McGinley, down from the hills beyond Owenteskiny," James says. "And my neighbor, Shane Cannon." The younger man, ruddy-skinned, lifts his cap, showing strands of dark hair plastered to his skull.

A new entrant, craggy, eyes watering from the wind, lets in a gust that balloons Shane's newspaper. He nods to the others, and to me, roars, "*Cad é mar atá tú?*" I tell him I'm fine, thanks: "*Tá mé go maith, go raibh maith agat.*" I don't have to draw any further on my store of Irish, because he leaves a flyer about piggery grants and goes.

"That's the Sultan," James says. "He runs the Gael Linn piggery and trout farm above. The hearing's not so great. You could have replied in Latvian."

"I'm glad you didn't think I did. I only have children's Irish, whatever I learned from my grandmother." I seem to talk about her so much, I don't know why I didn't bring her with me.

"And she's from?"

"Mayo, she comes from Ballyglass. Near Tourmakeady. On Lough Carra." I add these extra features because it's about 150 miles away. The men at the bar scrape their stools around a little to get a better look.

"Eugene's wife, God rest her, came from Ballyglass," James says.

"She was a Gillin," Eugene says. "And Shane here," James says, nodding at the younger man, "had an assistant from there."

"A Hughes, he was," Shane says.

"My grandmother's mother was a Hughes. She married a Stanton," I say.

"Ah," James says. "Your grandmother is a Stanton, so." He looks at the men and the bar falls silent. I wait for more, but not a peep. Perhaps they've heard of some of the Stantons? As they study me, I suspect I'm being placed in some kind of historical, social, and maybe even psychiatric niche. Maybe the Stantons acquired a name for something: hot-headedness, being a little slow, or the kind who wouldn't put their hands in their pockets too readily when it was time to order rounds of drinks?

"Well," James says, slapping the counter. "No worries. Sure don't we all have a chance to make our own way in life? Where do you come from yourself?"

"Youngstown, Ohio," and when that goes down all right, I add, "But I've been studying in Pittsburgh, Pennsylvania."

"Pittsburgh! The Duquesne Incline! Almost eight hundred feet long! Thirty-degree incline! Five-foot gauge! You know it will be ninety years old in a few months?" James turns back to Shane and Eugene. "Its terminus is at the exact confluence of the Allegheny, Monongahela, and Ohio Rivers. From thence on, of course, it's called the Ohio River." Shane sighs.

"Were you ever on it?" James asks me.

"A few times." It's a cable railway running up and down Mount Washington in downtown Pittsburgh. I say I always feel that I might end up in the confluence.

"That's part of the attraction. Look at the Katoomba Scenic Railway in Australia, steeper, with a fifty-two-degree incline, people sick on it all the time!"

Soon a table is covered with diagrams of two, three, and four rail systems, plus some blueprints he pulls from under the bar.

"What way did ye come on the journey?" Eugene asks.

"Kells, Cavan, Clones ... I went to Clones by mistake." They nod, as if no one goes to Clones deliberately. They wait. I'm nearly down to Mercator projections when Shane says, "You missed Lisnaskea?"

"No, she couldn't miss Lisnaskea unless she went wrong out of Clones and went to Drumguff or one of them. But then she would have missed Enniskillen."

I sketch the next roads and their arteries in the air. "Lisnaskea, Enniskillen, Pettigo ...," I say, ending in Carrick. I supply my times for each leg.

"Sure you were only touching the road in spots," Eugene says. He nods, imperceptibly perhaps to anyone else, but I'm so pleased to be conversing with a weathered elder that it's as good as a semaphored flag to me.

I remember I need to see Kilcar.

"Ah, Kilcar," James says. "Don't bother your head, take your ease. That's a mighty journey you've made from Dublin. You'll have something to eat." He pulls up a loaf of sliced bread and a package of ham from under the bar and, with lightning slashes, makes a swan-shaped sandwich with a bit of twisted crust for a beak, on a nest of onion shavings. The men say nothing; obviously they expect this of James.

"Catering school," he says.

He gets my bags, boxes, and typewriter from the car and gives an approving pat to Dineen's Irish dictionary and my *Ulster Death Tales*. He leads me upstairs to a small room lined floor to ceiling with books.

"My boyhood bedroom." My eye falls on several I've been searching everywhere for, including Samuel Lewis's A *Topographical Dictionary of Ireland*, 1837.

When I go down James is gone, but Shane is doing the newspaper crossword and Eugene sits more companionably at a sixty-degree angle from the bar, with a full pint behind him, a correct elbow-length away. Here's where scientific observation isn't everything: I know from my short time in Dublin that despite appearances, he's "watching" his freshly poured pint. "Watching" is a complex process: it requires an air of indifference, plus a knowledge of the precise moment when the pint's foam will settle to save the embarrassment of drinking it too early, and good lateral vision because once in a century someone, like the new customer, a burly man who's now engrossed in a road map, might accidentally take the pint. What happens then is unknown; we're all too young.

James returns, sloughing rain from his hairy tweed jacket. "Now," he says to me, tugging at something heavy behind the bar. He lurches out with a scarred Gladstone bag. The frame has disengaged itself from the leather on one side and its mouth gapes even more as he pulls out books, papers, notes, and some old Mass cards.

"Before you step out the door you should have these read," he says. I look through the pile: among them are *The Report of the Gaeltacht Commission 1925–26*; Sir William Petty's *Political Survey of Ireland*, *1672*; *The History of Landlordism in Donegal*; some copied pages from the *Minutes of the Devon Commission 1836–40*, also from the *Griffith Valuation 1850–60*; a recent study of the area by geographer David Symes of the University of Hull, and something from the tourist board titled "Three Heads Are Better Than None."

He sits at the table, the first time I've seen him at rest, and opens Canon McGuire's *History of the Diocese of Raphoe*. Soon he's lost to the bar trade. We're all quiet, as if we're watching a baby sleep, until Shane rises and taps him gently on the shoulder. James puts his finger on the sentence he's reading. "The tongue is hanging out of that lad," Shane says, nodding toward the newcomer. James sighs, rises, pulls a pint, and returns to the books.

"Ahh," the man relaxes as he watches his pint. "And I'm that hungry I could eat a child's arse through a railing. I should have been in Glencolmcille hours ago."

"What delayed you?" Shane asks without lifting his head from the newspaper.

"The mother," the man says. "She took a turn."

The others look up sharply. James sighs, rises, and goes behind the bar. He pulls the last two slices of bread from the tail end of a wrapper, stuffs the remains of the ham between the bread, and with a few lightning slashes of a knife, produces star-shaped canapés topped with curls of tomato.

"Good man," Shane says, back behind the paper again.

The winter light fades, and if I'm to see Kilcar today, I should go. I've written to Mr. Redington, the Kilcar factory manager.

"You're off to pay your respects to the Four Horsemen?" James asks. "The Sergeant ..."

Of course. I forgot the advice of my various mentors in Dublin. Before doing anything in a rural community, it's courteous to explain one's purpose to the informally recognized leaders: the parish priest, the sergeant of the Gardaí (Ireland's police), the doctor, and the headmaster.[1]

"You can start with the priest, up above."

"Kilcar ..." I say. "As a courtesy to the factory manager ..."

"Redington's away, putting out a fire in Galway." Maybe the "fire" is the factory whose machines have been thrown out?

"And Kilcar has been there since the time of Saint Carthaigh in 540 AD. I'd say it will be there tomorrow."

I didn't see it, but was it possible to hear a nose-wrinkle of contempt when he said "Kilcar"?

I set out to find the priest.

## The Four Horsemen

At the church, three little boys and a yellow dog dance around the priest's knees as he hands out broken pieces of Peggy's Leg, a rock-hard candy. "Away you go now, here's a lady," shooing them and smiling at me. "Father Devlin," he says.

"Good afternoon, Father. I'm Eileen Kane. I'm staying with James O'Donnell."

"James O'Don ... oh, yes, James Mary Agnes. A lovely, dreamy sort of man."

---

1 The official name of the national police system is "Garda Siochana," Guardians of the Peace. The collective noun is Gardaí. An individual member is called a "Garda" in Irish, and a "guard" in English, but in Carrick and Kilcar, when speaking in English, the English and Irish terms were used interchangeably.

"I'm an anthropologist. I'm here looking at the impact of factories on communities, like the factory in Kilcar."

"Well, you couldn't be a geographer, anyway. Kilcar is the next parish over. Tell me this and tell me no more, dear, what is anthropology when it's at home?"

Of course that's the point. It never *is* at home. "Anthropology is the study of other cultures," I say, which is a standard, dated explanation, one whose banality is now obvious: "other" to whom?

He views his surroundings, as if seeing them anew. "I suppose it *is* another culture," he says. "Perhaps we'd be happier if we thought of it that way." He looks at my leatherette carry-all, jammed with maps and local histories. "Do you always carry so much?"

"Only when I'm in the field."

"The field," he says softly. He looks around again at the shop fronts, the church, the mountains beyond. "I like that. Oh, I like that." He offers me a "penny mouse" sweet and moves off, smiling.

At the National School, I'm told by the boys I saw a few minutes ago the master is not there, it's a school holiday. He'll be back at half-three. "Why are you here, then?" I ask one of them, a freckled black-haired boy, who says, cheerfully, "We're here for slaps."

"Slaps?"

"We didn't give our copies to the master last week and he's coming at half-three to slap us," says another.

The smallest boy giggles. "But he never does." The yellow dog barks and they dance with it, waving a sweet over its head.

"I heard he slapped a big boy once," the first protests.

"Yes, but yer man, he needed a slap. We don't," the small boy says, trumping the discussion.

The Garda barracks has a plaque above the door: "*Garda Síochána,*" Guardians of the Peace. Inside, Garda Hamilton says his boss, Sergeant Rooney, has taken "a poor bastard to The Mental. Hospital," he adds.

I introduce myself and say I'll call back tomorrow. I go next door to the surgery.

James mentioned two doctors in the practice: "The Doctor" and "Mrs. Doctor." The only person in the waiting room is a petite, elegant lady in her early seventies, dressed in pastels, a rose cardigan over a pale green and rose tweed skirt. Her silvery hair is pulled back in a soft French twist with a tortoiseshell comb in its fold.

"I'm Nellie Brennan, ex-national teacher," she says. "You're welcome to Carrick. The tourist board says we're to be nice to visitors, but Donegal people don't have to be told that."

We're interrupted by a little boy who creeps up behind us and whacks me across the shoulder with a stick, hooting. He races into the doctor's office. Mrs. Brennan rises, posture perfect. "They say the doctor himself was wild as a child, and he's fine now. But you'd want to be fierce sick to come here on a school holiday. Better to try your chances tomorrow." So one out of three appointments so far.

It's almost four now, and when I get back to the school, it's locked. The dancing boys, slapped or unslapped, are gone.

On the way back down the hill I see Shane looking at my car. In this better light, I see his natural expression is that of a man who expects disaster and is resigned that he'll be the one who has to fix it.

"You've a flat. I'll get the spare out and change it." It starts to sleet shards.

"Thanks, I can change it."

"I'm sure you can. You Americans can do everything, but if you changed this tire you'd inconvenience every able-bodied man on the street."

"How?"

"They'd have to hide. A woman changing a tire? A *visitor*?"

We discover that my spare, 40 per cent patches, is also flat. He rolls it down to the petrol pump, returns, and changes the tire. I stand around looking like a damsel.

"I haven't had much success today seeing the people I needed to see," I say brightly, as he grunts to release the rusty jack.

"Who did you need to see?"

The rusty screw breaks, and the jack collapses. The car crashes down, grazing Shane's shoulder.

"The priest, the doctor, the sergeant, the headmaster. I only saw one," I say, looking at him from between my fingers.

"I'm the headmaster," says Shane, rising and dusting his knees. "What was it you wanted?"

"To introduce myself." He turns away slightly, brushes his hand casually across his shoulder and looks at it. No blood.

"Did you slap those boys?" I ask, to distract him.

"Indeed I did not, the bold wains! Did they say that? I've never raised a hand to a child, although God knows I've been provoked enough."

We agree I can come to the school tomorrow. "And listen, take care on the roads. The children have never seen a woman driver."

Inside, James says I must be perished with the hunger and produces rashers, steaming scrambled eggs, and homemade soda bread.

"My wife, Liz, is wild mad for panto,"[2] he says. I can't begin to think what this means. "The niece, too, so they've gone to Dublin. So I'm the chef. Sorry we've nothing else tonight, but a grand girl like you, I'd say you eat anything."

I fancy the idea of this, me as someone who eats anything – bugs, larvae, rat brains – everything a proper anthropologist would eat, but instead here I am, almost a vegan, balking at eggs and a rasher.

"The priest was here. He's a bit annoyed. I'd warned him you'd be visiting, and he waited in all afternoon."

"I talked to the priest." It was my one clear-cut accomplishment. I eat one slice of bread, and drawing on years of dietary deceit, I crumble the other one, artfully blanketing the rashers and egg.

---

2 Pantomine is a slapstick comedy performance, popular around Christmas.

"You talked to the curate, Father Devlin. It's the parish priest you need to talk to."

Apparently, the curate is a priest, but not *the* priest. He's *the* priest's assistant.

"Also the rest of the headmasters. We have half a dozen around the area, plus the headmaster of the vocational school."

I push back from the table and indicate with a satisfied rub of my stomach that I can't possibly eat another morsel.

"That's what I like to see! Never trust a picky eater." He picks up my copy of Dineen. "This is meant only for reference. You'd never get through this. The same Irish word might mean a gate, a turnip, a small hole for storing objects, a point halfway along a cow. But we could take your notebook at night and write a few words for things you might want to say. '*Antraipeolaíocht*,' for example. 'Anthropologist.'" He opens the notebook I carry for names, directions, Irish words, and on the last few pages he writes "*Taighde*, study; *monarcha*, factory; *Meiriceá*, America." He taps the pencil, thinking. "*Spaire*," he writes.

"What's *spaire*?"

"Spy." He laughs. "Don't worry. Whatever you do, people will talk. They are, already."


## You Could Go Weeks without Hearing a Word of Irish

In bed last night I lay swathed in fine, soft old linen and wool blankets, but my joints ached with cold. I'd got up a few times to stamp my feet into circulation before remembering James is in the room below. Why hadn't I chosen a warm place like Hawaii as a field site? Or Oaxaca, in Mexico, as a colleague had? For hours "Oaxaca" hammered in my skull, like a woodpecker.

Around six, I fell asleep. At breakfast, James presents me with more eggs, accompanied by baked beans and rashers. I deny I'm a restless sleeper.

He picks up three lengths of metal, each about eighteen inches long, and arranges them on the bar counter. Beside them are a big ring, a blowtorch, and a soldering iron.

"What's that?"

"Oh, this, it's just in the development phase. An anchor. I'm hoping to sell it to the Irish Navy for their small craft." I'm impressed. I see now the long metal bits are flukes. When I was a child, my father *invented* a collapsible anchor in our garage. I tell him.

This is the first time I've seen James in a good light without the big fedora. His eyebrows are even more luxuriant than old Eugene's, exuberant frames to his pale blue eyes. His hair is flyaway raven, greying, but when it falls over his right eye he looks about eighteen. But it's his light graceful movements that define him, complementing what seems like an untethered brain: cable cars, anchors, stuffed rabbits. It's hard to tell, but he must be about fifty.

"You've just missed the curate," James says. "He came in after the funeral. He couldn't talk about anything except Miss Kane."

"What did he say?" Ever since "*spaire*," I'm nervous people might see me as a spy. Dublin people warned me about the fate of Brinsley Mac-Namara, author of *The Valley of the Squinting Windows*, set in his family's village, Delvin in County Westmeath. Delighted locals gathered for its first public reading but after a few pages were outraged at the portrayal of them as sneaking, treacherous gossips. Copies were publicly burned, high court cases taken, and the author's father, the local headmaster, had to emigrate. Everyone speaks of the book as though it has just been published. In fact, it appeared in 1918 and hasn't been reprinted since.

"He's calling Carrick 'The Field' now," James says.

I set out in a downpour to introduce myself to the rest of the Four Horsemen. James says I won't understand the parish priest's Irish ("few do") because he comes from Gweedore, a more northerly Gaeltacht. The housekeeper says he's occupied with mourners. "James sang like an

Archangel at the funeral this morning," she says. Next is the sergeant. I pass the same three old men sheltering in the doorway of the Central Bar. I haven't seen anyone my own age, in their twenties or thirties. Not surprising: the Census shows the fifteen to thirty-four age group dropped by 70 per cent in the last twenty-five years.

Sergeant Rooney is hearty and affable, a non-local as all guards must be. I explain my work, which brings him to the subject of the Irish language. He speaks a different dialect of Irish and points out that the Sultan speaks yet another. Things would be a lot better if everyone just spoke "the King's English." Garda Hamilton, his assistant, calms him: "Thanks be to God," he says, "you could go weeks here without hearing a word of Irish." In fact, I haven't heard much of it since I got here, although James says everyone is well able to speak it. I sense a hairline crack in my thesis.

The sergeant says there's little crime: a bit of poaching, sometimes, motor tax violations, one or two bicycles without lights. "All in all, though, I have damn-all to do here. It's on me to measure the rainfall at 10 a.m. each morning, but you can be sure it's not done on the dot." For a man who doesn't come from this area, he shows a certain pride in the figures: the yearly rainfall reached ninety-eight inches at one point. This is the wettest area in Ireland. He quotes a study by the Agricultural Institute: the local conditions are said to be much less favorable than elsewhere in the country. He's heard an industrial estate might be coming, cross fingers. Have I anything to do with that?

A scholarly looking man interrupts us, looking for a dog license. "This is Leo McLoughlin," the Sergeant says. "An important man here, chairs the Parish Council."

"We're disbanding the Parish Council," the chairman says when I tell him about my development interests. His shoulders sag as if the topic is too wearisome to discuss.

"Maybe James can fill me in?"

"Oh, indeed? I'd like to be a fly on the wall when he does. Has he mentioned the funicular railway yet?"

But he, too, asks me if I know about the two new industrial estates Gaeltarra is planning. "It's critical the area gets one of them. If we form a *serious* group this time, we could join forces with Kilcar." I say I'm not connected to Gaeltarra. He looks at the sergeant, surprised, and leaves. The sergeant winks. "Say nothing," he says. "Your secret's safe with me."

Back at the pub, the blowtorch is still on the counter and the wood is badly scorched. No sign of James. Eugene and another elderly man sit in the dark. "I've brought this fellow with me, Charles, he heard you're studying history." "Charles" is pronounced "Charliss" here.

"I'm not ..."

"Here, you, Charlie, give out 'Deirdre of the Sorrows.'"

Charles raises his head, shuts his eyes, and bays the tragic story of the beautiful Deirdre.

"No, in English for her," Eugene says, tears already forming in his eyes.

"It can't be told in English," Charles says, annoyed.

But they piece it together in English: Deirdre, doomed by a seer from birth to cause the death of Ulster's greatest warriors. Rejecting her intended husband, Conchubar, King of Ulster, our province, she flees with her fated love, Naoise, one of three brave brothers. Conchubar lures them to his court and has the brothers killed. Deirdre dies of grief for the handsome, noble Naoise.

"I told you it's better in Irish," Charles says to Eugene, but Eugene is still red-eyed and sniffling.

"There *is* a fellow here who could make a better fist of the English," Eugene admits. "I'll see can I get him to talk to you some night."

Poor fist or not, I can only imagine how sad it must be to lose your fated love, and I say goodnight, a little morbid.

# January/Mí Eanáir 1967

## Many's the Man Who Lived by the Spade

"May I ask you something?" I look up at James from my hard-boiled eggs and kipper. He's delighted because Liz is due back from Dublin this evening.

"*Bien sûr*," says James. His hand is bandaged.

"The Stantons. Is there something ..."

"No, no. I wouldn't bother my head about that."

He tends the fire. I sneak the kipper to a dog at the door and slip the eggs into my handbag. Today is New Year's Day, not a public holiday but a Holy Day of Obligation, the Feast of the Circumcision, and people are making their way to Mass.

"It all depends on what interpretation you want to take with these things," he says, sweeping the ashes.

I know the big taboos in Irish life, the things a family can't overcome. A baby out of wedlock, tuberculosis, mental illness, or having a "spoiled priest" – a man who leaves the seminary before ordination. Which of these marked the Stantons? I remember a mug on my grandmother's sideboard: "Life's Just One Damn Thing after Another."

James lets me spread my local ordnance survey map in the bar's snug, a secluded little room where he says I'll be safe from male attention except for "the rare fellow who might try his hand." People, usually women, can nip in and have a drink unobserved. One might imagine the type of woman – cigarette dangling from a lipsticked mouth – but no, I'm joined by a grandmotherly lady in long black wool skirts, shawled and booted.

"A wee gin, please, a Shéamuis," she calls out to James. "When a body's old it helps them make their water," she tells me.

Ireland was the first country in the world to be completely mapped in detail: houses, sheds, plot dimensions, everything but owners' names. My father's maps tell stories; ones about his teenage pranks, like rigging the Pentecostal Church bell to ring at 2 a.m.; or the spot down on the east side, where my uncle Chicken Shit John ferments hootch in chicken manure. My maps tell stories, too, but what? Did farms' owners change when the factory came? More ex-farmers in the factory? Land sales, suggesting farming may no longer be a desirable way of life?

The curate puts his head in. James presents him with a steaming hot whiskey, salutes, and leaves.

"You have some interesting-looking books," the curate says, indicating the little shelf James set up so "your reference materials can be instantly to hand." My favorite, Raymond Firth's We, the Tikopia, nestles between Evans-Pritchard's The Nuer and Malinowski's fascinating Argonauts of the Western Pacific, about the "Kula rings" of the Trobriand Islands. Worsley's Trumpet Shall Sound, on Micronesian cargo cults, is missing; James reads it and takes notes between filling pints.

"Not one book by Margaret Mead?" the curate asks.

There isn't, I realize. "A popularizer, Baggy Maggie," my professor had said. Nor have I any by Ruth Benedict, whose work shaped the Allies' post-war treatment of Japan. "A gorgeous gal" is all another professor said of her. The first female president of the American Anthropological Association is brushed off as "loose." But I don't need Mead or Benedict: I know them by heart. They're applied anthropologists. They've used anthropology for practical purposes, as I hope to do.

I do have Goodenough's *Cooperation in Change*, Arensberg and Nie-hof's *Introducing Social Change*, Spicer's *Human Problems in Technological Change*, and Foster's recent "Traditional Cultures and the Impact of Technological Change," plus a slew (Irish *slua*, crowd) of articles from the applied anthropology journal *Human Organization* – founded by Mead, Arensberg, and Chapple. One of the reasons I admire these authors is not only do they deal with real problems, they write in clear English. "Oversimplified," one of my professors said in a review of Arensberg, which I suspect means no lunges into the passive voice and professional backside-saving obfuscations.

What I'm short on is theory. In the nineteenth and first half of the twentieth centuries, the focus was on anthropology as a science, provid-ing explanations of the workings and changes within culture, such as evolutionism (stages of cultural development), which reappears more modestly in the 1950s and 1960s in the work of Julian Steward, Leslie White, and Marshall Sahlins; diffusionism (the movement of cultural products from one culture to another); and structural functionalism (the internal integration of cultural ideas and customs within a culture). But by the 1950s and early 1960s, overall grand theory is dormant.

Also, during World War II, our older professors, such as George Mur-dock and Melville Herskovits, along with hundreds more, had drawn on anthropology for the war effort and are anxious now to return to more abstruse scholarly activities, hence the slight dismay at my interest in applied anthropology.[1]

---

1 For more on anthropology during the war, see David Price's *Lessons from Second World War Anthropology*.

What I like about anthropology is the "four fields" approach, learning about archeology, physical anthropology, cultural anthropology, and linguistics, and we can read the literature in each, even though we will specialize in one. Another strength is our enthusiasm for learning about and borrowing from other disciplines, among them medicine, psychology, psychiatry, history, economics, politics, kinesics and proxemics, the arts, and literature. Discovering anthropology, an anonymous practitioner of one of these has said "Anthropology is too good for the anthropologists."

But perhaps as a sign of things to come, the traditional belief that anthropology (and other social sciences, including economics) is "scientific" is weakening: the best we are doing is "triangulating" our information by using multiple and diverse methods to strengthen our information - observation, interviews, multiple sources, records. All the things you use when your child comes home and says your neighbor tried to sell him some heroin.

But do you use a questionnaire? We don't either.

⌒

When I explain my questions about the land to the curate, he tells me to call up to Michael Boyle. "What he doesn't know, his father, old Máirtín Boyle will."

Michael's house in Carrick Upper sits on a hill overlooking the road. Most Irish farmers here have impressively good "housekeeping": whitewashed farmhouses and land carefully fenced with stone. Everything clean, neat, and spare.

A slim teenaged blonde, Una, says Michael is "abroad" on the mountain (there's a fox after his sheep), but her grandfather, Máirtín Boyle, is here. Máirtín, thin and white-haired, sits by the kitchen stove, a blanket covering his legs. Una's sister Fiona, pale and freckled, spoons leaves into the teapot from a canister over the fire. Máirtín has a tiny guest, introduced as Wee Robert, who seems almost as old as Máirtín.

"I'm ninety-one years old," Máirtín shouts. "I'm a *cliamhan isteach* – I married into this farm – so I had to give up my own work to see to it. I was a shoemaker. I apprenticed to a master for three years with no pay. I had to pay *him*. Forty years ago I made women's shoes for seven shillings sixpence, eleven and six for men. I could only make four pairs a week, so there wasn't much money in it." Wee Robert nods.

I think Máirtín is so accustomed to people asking him about the past that now he just reels it out, unbidden. I show him his entry on the 1901 Census, a son in a big household a few miles from Owenteskiny.

| Boyle | Máirtín | Son | RC | RW | 22 | Boot maker | Single | Donegal | IE |
|-------|---------|-----|-----|-----|-----|-----------|--------|---------|-----|

"It says you're a boot maker, single, you can read and write, and speak Irish and English." The "RC" is Roman Catholic.

"Here, let me see that." His face lights up as he spreads the document. "They have my age wrong, you'd better correct that. I remember that day. I answered the questions for the house. I always said the constable who took it down was a bit slack in the head." Wee Robert nods. I ask if there were more "mental problems" in the past, and he said there were plenty, but no more than now. We move on.

"When I was a child, I worked building the priest's house, Canon Murphy's, for a penny a day. My brother went to a hiring fair, all the boys and men standing on the street, hoping to be hired. He got on one of the hardest farms in the Lagan for twelve pound a year. Girls went off as servants for six pound a year." I don't know "the Lagan" and he explains: "In east Donegal, strong farmers squeezing every penny out of you."

"And I remember a fellow working on a gang in Kilcar. His father died that day, but still he went to work. The ganger asked why, and the fellow said, 'The shilling is wanted at home.' But the ganger sent him home and told him he would get his shilling." Máirtín slaps his knee. "Many's the man who lived by the spade and the shilling a day."

"Grandda, have your tea," Una coaxes. Wee Robert is asleep.

"In my day, young boys wore skirts," Máirtín says. "Not a stitch under ..." This must be a story he trots out for the girls, because they cover their mouths and blush. "And some girls were matched by a match-maker. He and the groom would go house to house with a bottle of whiskey until he got a wife and then they all drank. Sometimes the girl came with a dowry. The matchmaker was always a man, but not a priest, that was bad luck."

He was excited now and speaking in Irish. "English!" the girls shouted, waving at me.

Two cheerful giants enter. "It's time you were home, Dada," they shout to Wee Robert, who wakes, startled. One of them sits him into the crook of his arm. Wee Robert smiles at all of us. "It's a good job I married a big woman," he says, "otherwise these boys would be able to thrash grain under a bed."

In the village, James's wife, Liz, a short, strapping woman with an easy air about her, is back from Dublin. She's propped at the bar drinking hot milk and whiskey. James flits around her like a hen with a chick. She apologizes for the state of the place while she's been away.

"God love her, she's put her back out getting off the bus. She can't sit," James cries. "Here, have another drop of that. It'll do you nothing but good. You're off to bed, then."

He carries her down the hall, aiming her head-first like a pole as she laughs.

"It's all the heavy bar work that has her as she is. She's very delicate." He ushers me to the table.

"I can't eat a thing," I say. "The Boyles gave me tea."

"I have just the thing for a poor appetite," he says, producing a ragged booklet. "MacConglinne's *Vision*. MacConglinne was a scholar, like yourself. He had a vision, a land made entirely of wonderful food: oozy lard, custard, hung beef, cheese curds, bacon, tripe, corned beef; good,

stomach-rumbling stuff." I take the booklet and see MacConglinne, like
me, was staying in a cold guesthouse at the time.

"Did you know this fellow?" I ask.

"Not personally. The tale is from the eleventh or twelfth century."

He hands me a letter from home. No one has written to explain why
my father was frying eggs. Could my mother be sick? Patrice encloses a
happy photo of herself in front of the Christmas tree wearing her main
gift, the orange and mustard poncho. I recognize the yarns, unraveled
from our childhood sweaters.

While I fill a hot water bottle for bed, James turns away from *The Trumpet Shall Sound* to add some words to my notebook: *mapa*, obvious; *eastát
tionsclaíochta*, industrial estate; and, with a tapping finger, *bean phósta*,
married woman. "People are asking," he says. But about which?


## A Floundering Trout Farm as a Model for Development

"Aren't you the grand girl, a doctor at your age?" people say in shops.
"What's this your study is about again, the Kilcar factory? Well isn't that
a nice compliment to us, you staying here instead of Kilcar? And why
wouldn't you?"

I consult James about going to Kilcar. "I suppose you might as well
put in an appearance," he says, with a dismissive flick toward something,
Kilcar, perhaps. "Of course, Kilcar has been there since ..."

"I know, 540 AD and will probably be for another five hundred years
but I won't." I wonder if he's insecure about Carrick village being here
only since the 1840s. It was built as residences and shops for the well-off
middlemen handling the output from the once-flourishing fish business
in neighboring Teelin village.

"Of course there's a lot to be doing *here*."

"I'm doing it," I say. Even if people weren't selling land to make bigger
farms, they could stay if there were enough local businesses. "I've made

appointments to visit the vegetable co-op, the furniture-making place, the co-op, Manus McLoughlin's construction business, the knitting center here, Father McDyer's enterprises out in Glencolmcille ..."

James thinks little of Kilcar but less of Glencolmcille, known as "Glen." He'd broached the subject obliquely when I first arrived, under the guise of giving me local proverbs. "Put a hat on a stick and you'll get a wife in Glen," he'd said. And "If you marry a woman from Glen, you marry all of Glen." But tiny Glencolmcille, with a population of only ninety-one, is actually part of the same parish as Carrick, and the parish priest here is Father McDyer's boss.

"Surely I need to know what the people of Glencolmcille think about the developments out there?" I ask as Shane comes in with a pile of tests he's correcting.

"The malign say they've lost the ability to think," Shane says. "They just do what McDyer thinks. He's not as popular here in this part of the world," "here" meaning Carrick. "In fact, we and Glen used to play football against Kilcar, but now we've joined Kilcar against Glen, the feeling is that strong."

I can see myself becoming a prisoner in Carrick. "I'm going to Kilcar," I say.

Shane laughs and offers a parting shot: "If you think everyone is looking at you, it's because they will be. When St. Colmcille passed through Kilcar, the locals stared so much he put a curse on them. It hasn't stopped them."

I drive over the bridge and south out The Line, the road along the sea bay. Through gaps in the thorny winter bushes I see the river, a deep clear amber, dancing over rocks. A postcard view opens across the bay to Teelin harbor and village. Its cliffs blaze in a fan of sun rays and its boats roll in a Mediterranean-blue sea. This kind of sight is what makes prospective visitors imagine Ireland as a warm, verdant place. I don't hold the same hope for Kilcar: in one of James's books, Lewis's *Topographical Dictionary*, 1837, it says, "There is not a single tree in the parish."

I focus now, because the first impression an anthropologist makes in a new field site is critical: no longer is it acceptable, for example, to be borne in on a howdah by natives. I'll drive to the top of the town and walk back down to the river and the factory.

I enter the T-junction in Kilcar's main street. On the right-hand corner a few men take note of my Dublin registration plate and then resume their huddled conversation. As I'm turning, though, the Morris's traficator sticks: the lighted wand won't come out of its pocket in the door and I can't indicate my turn. I roll down the window and bang on the door. No traficator. I bang harder, then furiously. The traficator pops out. The men, one of them very old, hasten over to the car and ask if I'm calling them.

Do I look like a person who'd thump on a car door to summon people? I thank them and say no, it's just that my traficator is broken. They look at it. It goes down again. They stand silent. I pretend I'm trying to make it go up again. "See, it won't go up," I say, smiling, hands up. "I'm going to Killybegs," I lie. One man nods, leans on the open window, settles in and points left. This would be a great opportunity for casual talk, but I don't seem to have any. The man withdraws, stepping backwards, as one does with a queen.

About ten miles out the road, I remember I'm a grown woman and far too self-conscious; my mother has me ruined. I drive back, scanning the landscape. If a tree has grown since Lewis was here in 1837, I don't see it. But the larger view is magnificent: the village sits snug in a valley of stone-walled fields, ending in the glittering bay. The recent Census shows 229 people in Kilcar. I figure about 8 per cent of them were there in the "traficator" group. As I re-enter the village, the men look up from their corner and at that moment my thumb knocks the horn on. Usually you have to pound it twice, hard, to make it work. I give the men a little military salute and bang it off. Haltingly, they salute back.

~

A small shop offers the *Irish Times*, the *Irish Press*, or the *Irish Independent*. I've been told in Dublin if a man dies, the headline in the rather religious *Independent* will say "Priest's Brother Dies"; in the politically focused *Press*, it will refer to his party, "Fianna Fáil Supporter Dies," and in the once British-oriented *Times*, "Rugby Fan Dies." I don't want to reveal my leanings, so I settle for last week's *Donegal Democrat*. The shop assistant fusses with her burnt nimbus of dyed, permed hair. "You're Nancy's granddaughter! The girl from New Jersey!" she cries.

Suddenly I'm exhausted. For weeks I've radiated cultural sensitivity toward everyone around me, and now this indignity. I, too, have a culture. We Youngstowners are not a vainglorious people, the label "Bomb City" hindering any serious pretensions we might have, but experts agree we are part of a narrow linguistic corridor in which American English can be heard in its most "neutral" accent. All across the country, regardless of local speech, broadcasters are trained to use this accent. So my speech is as far from a New Jersey accent as the English language and common politeness permits. This is not to say everything about our local language is exquisite: we say, "That dog needs washed," for example, and sometimes "yu'ns" for "you" plural. The shopkeeper can't be expected to know all this, but I can't be expected not to be irritated. But I just say "No, I'm not. I'm doing research."

"Oh," she says, "folklore. The Teelin people, they're the ones for folklore. But tongues like razors. They can skin a flea in Irish."

"And Kilcar?" I ask.

"Kilcar? Och, what would we have here to study? Nothing at all. Nothing."

It occurs to me I don't have a good local explanation of my study, one that's true, brief, and travels well. All my versions, for my professors, the foundation grants people, the Dublin nabobs, were tailored to each audience. But in Carrick, I haven't had to explain anything; James seems to have accepted whatever Ó Móráin told him and slipped it into his local conversations.

As I get in the car, I realize I haven't seen the factory. I'll drive past and return another day. It's a large white 1950s modern building with welcome signs saying "*Céad Mile Fáilte*," a Hundred Thousand Welcomes. I hope so.

## The Haystack Report

James produces bacon and eggs and "tea the way you like it, you could trot a mouse on that."

"What am I studying?" I ask. To me, it's clear; if some people get work in the factory or other business and neighbors can farm on bigger pieces of land, emigration will decline and the language may have a chance of surviving. That's my informal research statement, the map that suggests what I look at and what I might spend less time on, but it's not something you could shout out the car window or tell a shopkeeper who's got three impatient customers.

"You're studying the social factors associated with development in the Gaeltacht," he says. "Mind you, by 'social' I mean cultural, economic, and historical. Do I pass?"

That's it, of course. I can say I'm studying local development.

"Don't worry, every living creature in the region already knows," he says. "But don't mention the plan for a new industrial estate or you'll be pestered to death."

"I won't. So I hear the Parish Council is being abolished. What now?"

"Aye, what now, indeed," he says.

I try another tack. "What about the funicular railway?" I recall Chairman Leo McLoughlin mentioning it.

He brightens. "Now you're talking. Your average tourist is aging. How will he haul himself up to the top of one of the steepest sea cliffs in Europe?"

"Which is where?"

"Here! Slieve League, just down the road! A funicular railway is your answer. Look at the Katoomba, with its fifty-two-degree incline, steepest in the world. Our grade is too steep but we certainly could run it part way up."

"Have you discussed this with the Parish Council?"

"Amn't I blue in the face discussing it? They can't get beyond the subject of factories. But it would benefit the community. People are so relieved to get off a funicular railway that men make for the nearest pub and women the pew."

He dismisses the council and pulls a notebook from his jacket.

"This is the Haystack Report." Head high, chin out, a stance suited to a Roman plinth, he begins. "The report ..."

"A wee word, A *Shéamuis*, if you please," an authoritative voice says to James from the door. Nellie Brennan, the lady I met in the surgery, sweeps in with the light step of a dancer. Her braided silver hair is up in a coronet, and the long train flowing from her shoulders is obvious from her bearing, if not quite visible.

"*Dia daoibh*," she greets both of us. "You'll excuse us," she says, shepherding James toward the snug. "I have some business with this gentleman." I scrape most of my breakfast under the toast. I hear a muffled but firm exchange and they return.

"You'll have a mineral,"[2] he says, coming out. He pours her a Club Orange, and she turns to show me a pin on her lapel, a shield bearing a symbol of the Sacred Heart. She, like James, is a pioneer, a teetotaler. Also like James, she wears a second, ring-shaped pin, a gold *fáinne*, indicating she's a fluent Irish speaker.

"I'm surprised a lady like Mrs. Brennan would come into a pub," I say later.

---

2 Commonly used in Ireland for a soft drink.

"Mrs. Brennan, ex-national teacher, is impervious to iniquity. She has an impermeable membrane. She doesn't go into other people's worlds, she brings her own with her."

"I sometimes wonder, do you like eggs at all?" he asks, poking a finger at the cold lumps under my toast. What *do* you eat?"

"Potatoes, carrots, cauliflower, spaghetti ..." I say.

"And for *food?*" Then he slaps his head. "Could it be you have a *geas*, a taboo? Our ancient warrior hero Cú Chulainn had a *geas* against eating dog meat. When a hag offered him some, he, of course, had to eat it and lost his strength for battle."

I certainly draw the line at dog meat.

"Mrs. B. is right," he says. "I'm in and out all the time, and poor Liz ... a sandwich or a fry is all we can manage. Mrs. B. says you're welcome to stay with her." He puts his hands up, as if expecting a mutiny. "And she's a devil for the vegetables."

"I'll miss our talks."

"Don't worry your head. I'm reading *The Trumpet Shall Sound*, the cargo cults, and I'll be down to discuss them. And Mrs. B.'s will love the company. Most people are terrified of her."

I pick up the notebook. "The Haystack Report?"

He opens it, but its luster seems a little diminished. "Last autumn I attended the making of two haystacks," he says. "I've jotted the figures down."

"The figures for what?"

"You asked me yesterday about the *meitheal*, neighbors and friends helping each other cut turf or giving a hand with farm work. It's not so common now. However," he says, voice pitched for a classroom, "the haystack is an exception. Haystack Number One is owned by Tommy. Five men helped him: three neighbors who always help each other, a brother-in-law, and a neighbor who bales his own hay now, but Tommy used to help him. When he's finished, Tommy will have to help at four other stacks."

A head peeks around the door.

"Máirtín Boyle," James calls, bowing to the old man. "And son, Michael." Michael is a tall, gaunt man, his pale, wind-honed face as smooth as marble. Spare, like his farm, he hasn't an extra inch of flesh or needless sprout of hair. It gives him a surprising beauty. Máirtín shuffles toward me, and Michael lurches behind him, his arms forming an invisible cage, the kind his father probably made for Michael when he took his first steps. Michael suggests a table, but Máirtín makes straight for a bar stool and, with a surprising strength, hauls himself up. Michael moves three other stools to form a barricade against falls.

"I was saying some people still give a hand with haystacks," James shouts at Máirtín.

"Oh, the women finished that off. In my day, they made a big breakfast for the helpers. Now, in *his* day," he waves at Michael, "they don't."

"Because they had to spend until dinner time making the breakfast," Michael says.

"I always tell him, if you don't have your neighbor, you have no one." Máirtín lifts a shaking glass. "I mind the early days, a man would be driving his sheep to the market and a buyer would approach him before he was halfway. The buyers, they'd work in twos and threes along the road. The first one offered a price, then the second offered less, and the third, closest to town, offered least. The first would pass by then and ask the farmer, 'Did you better my price?' But if you went straight into the village, a neighbor might advise you that you were asking too little."

"Haystack Number Two," James shouts. "Let's say 'John's.' Six people helped: two fellows John always helps, the two sons of a couple of other men he helps, a neighbor who gets a free patch from John to grow potatoes, and a fellow who's a wee bit simple who helps everyone, and everyone does him small favors back."

"Of course the artistry of the haystack is gone," Máirtín says. "Each part of the stack has a name, and some people still know them, but in the old days, men sat around smoking pipes and criticizing the work for hours, days even. Only an expert, always an older man, was allowed to finish the top."

"Sat around for hours and days," Michael repeats. "And the women still cooking." I like Michael.

"The oldest man opened the hay season," Máirtín says. "He would go out after Patrick's Day and touch his bare backside to the ground to test was it warm enough for planting. "

"Of course that doesn't happen today," Michael says quickly.

"Indeed it doesn't," Máirtín says, "and it won't as long as I'm the old-est man."

He finishes his drink, and I put my question to Michael: are farms still going to the eldest son, and if not, who do they go to? He says he's the youngest son himself, the only one prepared to stay on the farm. And if a farmer married young and is still active when his eldest is grown, it could go to a younger son. I show him my ordnance survey map with its wonderfully detailed plots and explain what I need to know. He stretches it out on the bar and traces the lines, nodding as he comes to the end of each. "I'll come down one of the days and we'll go over it."

They leave, Michael repeating the protective dance as Máirtín lunges uncertainly toward the door. Máirtín winks at me as he goes out, as if we were comrades well accustomed to humoring the overworried but well-meaning people of this world.

As I help him clean up, James says, "I wish you'd let me explain my ideas on funicular railways to you in Irish," he says. "It's so much more ..." He closes his eyes. "It's richer? Prismatic? See, the problem with English is it doesn't have adequate words to describe the wonders of the Irish language."

"I can't ..."

"There's an old saying, *Is fearr Gaeilge briste, ná Béarla cliste*. Better bro-ken Irish than clever English."

He rips the pages from his notebook and puts the Haystack Report into mine. "Keep that. You never know how it will contribute to the Big

Picture." He adds a few new words to my notebook. *An staidéar na forbartha*, the study of development. *Uibheacha*, eggs. *Mála láimhe*, handbag.

I go to bed, wondering how terrifying Mrs. B. is.

## People Don't Ask the Women a Thing

I moved to Mrs. B.'s yesterday. My visa says I'm supposed to report any change of address to the guards.

"Sure the world knows that, didn't we all see you go? Anyway, it's only a few yards you moved, the immigration system won't implode," Garda Hamilton says. "The Big Day will come when you move to Kilcar. I wonder have the authorities the staff for that."

Still, I'll miss James. He has a kaleidoscopic intellect, and he gives good advice.

"That James, he'd have your ears blistered with his old blather," the Garda says. "Ah, here we are. Just the thing," he says, rummaging in a cupboard and bringing out a black record book. "The sergeant says you can have a gawk at it and bring it back when you're finished." It's a handwritten copy of the 1966 Census returns, quite detailed. As I scan the pages it's clear the majority of household heads are listed as farmers, as I expected.

The Garda was cheerfully dismissive when I worried about the legality of this. "Why wouldn't we make a copy of the Census, it's ourselves who collected it, and don't we know all these people, anyway? As for farming details, people here think the Census is a means test, so they'll say anything. If we want real agricultural information, we just go out and ask a few local people in the know. So don't ask anyone about farming, they'll think you're with the Census, and your study will say no one here owns a blade of grass or ever clapped eye on a cow, except maybe in another parish."

There goes a central part of my study.

At Mrs. B.'s I'm welcome to use the oilcloth-covered kitchen table for my writing. Behind the kitchen a small pantry holds the gas cooker and electric kettle, but the heart of the house is a cast-iron, yellow-enameled Stanley stove that heats the kitchen and water and is used for most cooking. Mrs. B. appeases it constantly, feeding in turf, adjusting drafts, emptying ashes, banking up the embers at night. Under no circumstances must we let it go out, she warns.

She's a widow, retired after teaching many of the area's now middle-aged adults, a few of whom do seem terrified of her. Others say she's prudish and "difficult." My mother holds the world's record, I suspect, so I'm not too worried. Mrs. B.'s five children, whose careers she proudly outlines for me, are grown and living in distant places.

"I told James you were getting very peaky on his cooking." I say I hope to make some of the dishes I miss, like my mother's pierogies or lasagne. Or baklava. Youngstown is a culinary melting pot, although her own Irish cuisine has made almost no impact.

Mrs. B. sits at the big table now and peeks at the Garda's Census, which she calls "The Tillage."

"There's no word of truth put on these forms," she says. "The same with the tax. I said to a young priest once I shouldn't have to pay twenty-five pounds a year out of my four-hundred-and-thirteen-pound pension. I spend six pounds a year just on stamps, five on the television license, over six on the ground rent for electricity, a pound for the water rate, a land tax ... He said 'Well, be sure you don't report every penny coming into the house.'"

"Then how will I meet my Lord when I die?" she'd asked. "He explained it to me: 'The authorities ask too much of us, and we must do them any way we can.' So I do."

"Who was this priest?"

"I don't remember his name. It was last year. He called to the house collecting money for the missions."

I begin copying bits of the Census into my notebook. Only six people replied in Irish, five teachers and James. The teachers are paid £50 a year for teaching through Irish. Far from being the abbreviated facts I've seen published in the national Census every five years, this book is a copy of the original raw data collected on the lives of everyone in the area. Copying it, and even more, lending it out, especially to a stranger who's been in the village less than three weeks? Is that why I've been allowed to borrow it? I'm seen as a bird of passage?

A boy appears at the pantry door. "The lady is wanted up in McGinley's pub."

"McGinley's! Who wants Dr. Kane?" Mrs. B. demands.

"A farmer. Says he has some information."

I get out my ordnance survey maps of Carrick and go up.

"Duck," the man says. He's sitting in the snug. "It's The Perpetual Smile. Lord, spare me this cross! Get down, he doesn't need to know our business." From our crouched position, he sticks out his hand. "Frank Doherty," he says. "Frank by name and Frank by nature." I've greeted him once or twice on the street, a short, hunched man whose face is framed in reddish-grey whiskers with bits of tobacco and food stuck in them. He wears a greasy tweed jacket and crusty-looking trousers. James has explained the word in Irish for "hair" is *gruaige*, but when people refer to their own hair, they say *mo chuid gruaige*, literally "my portion/share of hair." The same is true of teeth: *mo chuid fiacla*, "my share of teeth." Frank's portions are a little unfair: sprigs of faded red on top and a few teeth short of a set.

"I hear you want to know about farming," he says. I explain it's a little more specific than that. I show him the maps.

He offers to sell me fifteen acres of good land, "since you're in the market."

"I'm not ..." I study the plots he's offering. They're commonage – common land.

I thank him, and remove his hand from my knee.

"Ah, now," he says, giving me a pinch, "What harm? A great girl like yourself. I have a shop in the village, you know," he says, waving across the street toward a nicely decorated place. "Tell me this, if I threw my hat in the ring, would you throw it out?"

I smile, as if he's paid me a witty courtesy, which he may have, and pack up my maps.

Soon he drifts out toward the men in the front bar. I hear him mutter a word in Irish.

Back at Mrs. B.'s, I have a note of names I want to ask about: "James Mary Agnes," and "The Perpetual Smile," but her mind is fixed on my trip to McGinley's. I tell her, phonetically, the word the man said as he left.

"Well! The scoundrel! Pay no attention."

"But what does it mean?"

"'*Scubaide*.' 'Hussy,' she says. Who's this that fellow was you met?" she demands. She's speaking Irish, but in English.

"Frank Doherty from Teelin. Unmarried, I think."

"There are forty-five bachelors in Teelin this minute," she says. "Frank Doherty; there's five or six. Och, aye, I have it now, he's called 'Better.'" He has a whiskers?"

"A whiskers?"

"That dirty herbaceous border round his face."

"Yes. Why 'Better'?"

She pauses, her lips a tight seam, then, "One day some lads going the road heard a fellow in the hedge, saying to a girl, 'Can you do a little better, Miss?' So that was the end of the good name his mother gave him. He's a terrible man for giving a girl what he calls a 'fondie,' a pinch here or there."

I wonder if she's had a fondie. "And what can James Mary Agnes have done to earn a long name like that?" I ask her.

"We have only eight or ten family names in this place, and a child often gets its Christian name from a grandparent, so if you have a group of brothers and they all follow this custom for their children, you get a lot of people, some very old, some very young, with the same first and last name. If you go looking for James O'Donnell, there are three or four of them."

"So you give him a nickname," I say.

"Aye, if he earns one, like 'Better' did. Otherwise he'll probably just have a string of family names, so we know which O'Donnell he is. We might take his first name, and add his father's first name, and sometimes a grandparent's. In English it would be 'James Mickey Pat O'Donnell,' for example, the son of Mickey O'Donnell and the grandson of Pat.

"Or he might get the place where he lives as part of his name: James Dún, because he lives by the fort, *dún*. Or his hair color: *ruadh*, red-haired. Or his occupation, *táilliur*, tailor.

"But James Mary Agnes's father, an O'Donnell, he came from outside and died young before he was known to many, so it was his mother's name, Mary Agnes, that was added to his."

"And the name above his shop, Ó Floinn?"

"Flynn, his mother's father's name. It came down through her."

"And you are?" I ask.

"I was born 'Nora,'" she says, "but I was always called 'Nellie.' So up in my home place, I was 'Nellie Paddy Seán' after my father and grandfather. But here, I'm Mrs. Brennan, or in Irish, Nora Bean Uí Bhraonáin ... Nora, the wife of Brennan. Although I'm a widow now, so 'Bean' becomes 'Baintreach.' That's falling out of use, though."

"What about outsiders?"

"Most of the married women here are from another place, so if they have a surname different from the common ones here, we're only too delighted to use it."

None of this explains The Perpetual Smile. "Well, some say he's naturally cheerful. Others say he's too proud of the teeth he paid for."

After evening tea of ham, cheese, lettuce, and tomatoes, we watch the news on television. The Northern Ireland Civil Rights Association has been formed to address sectarian bombings and shootings, some of them by "an illegal organization."

"You can't say 'IRA' on the national network," Mrs. B. says. "I've half a mind to join it, the law is so ridiculous."

After she says her nightly Rosary we sit by the dying fire in the Stanley, I in a kitchen chair and she nested in a low armchair layered with faded cushions, like the princess and the pea.

"Well, I'm glad they sent a woman for this study," she says. "People come here and don't ask the women a thing. I'll tell you this now, there's a lot wrong with that rhythm method of birth control!"

"It's a sin?"

"Indeed it isn't. But you have to have sex when you don't feel like it, and you can't have it when you do." She sits back, obviously pleased to have put me right on the subject. "You can put that in your notebook." She banks the fire, and we say good night.


## Showing the Black Breast

Not everyone here is a farmer. We're nestled in mountains and hills that are blanketed in fields, some grassy, some stony, some seamed in thin chocolate bogs, but Carrick also has shopkeepers, teachers, publicans, guards, nurses, a mechanic, a pharmacist, a social welfare officer, women knitting at home for agents, carpenters, casual laborers, electricians, and builders. Sometimes there's one of each, or one holds two or three posts, but most also have some connection to land: a bit of turf bog, some sheep in a field, a patch of potatoes.

I visit some of the businesses, starting in Carrick's twin in the parish, Glencolmcille, named for St. Colmcille. A Glen teacher, Art Sweeney, is my guide. Driving through the bogs, we meet three women in their sixties battling toward us along the windy road. Their faces are stolid when they see me, but when Art leans across to greet them, angelic smiles transform them.

"I worry people won't want to talk to me," I say as we continue.

"Not at all," he says. "You'll be the strange girl here. This place used to rock with céilís and dances. A big dance was called a ball. It began about eight and ended at six or eight in the morning. Young girls came from all over, fourteen or fifteen miles away, 'strange girls,' and stayed with relatives in local houses for about a week. Word would go out for miles that a strange girl was in, and the men flocked here to dance mazurkas, barn dances, highland."

We pick up an old lady in a florid headscarf. "We had no slow dancing," she says, continuing the story. "The lads just caught a girl and swung hell out of her. It wouldn't be right until a fight broke out over the strange girl. The man who walked out with the girl was the champion."

"Were any of the ladies we saw on the road strange girls?"

"Indeed they were. But the dance could be sad, too," she says. "Two or three boys might set off right after the dance and walk to Derry to get to Scotland for work. People would say 'He's missing,' and nothing more would be made of it. They'd write when they got there, sometimes not. My sweetheart never did."

"Oh!"

"Never mind, what would I do with an old man now?"

We stop to pick up a Mrs. Campbell, a teacher in Art's school. She mentions some other old-time amusements. "First the lantern slides, later on the flicks, with melodramas and tear-jerkers where the girl lays down and dies when the boy leaves her. We saw a lot of English propaganda films."

The jilted old lady points out a haystack. "It's many a jag I got in the old days, courting in haystacks," she giggles. We drop her and Mrs. Campbell at a shop and promise to continue this line of discussion.

In Glen, an old school houses the new machine-knitting factory brought in by Father McDyer. Four teenage boys run the machines and six girls do the assembly, 200 items a week. The manager says they'll all emigrate.

Next is the small Gaeltarra Éireann weaving factory. Father McDyer's idea was to hire young unmarried women to keep them here at home, but now only four of the thirty workers are women. Pat, the manager, says "It used to be *mile* murder to get workers in on time, but now they're here 8:30 to 5:30 and work on their farms in the long evenings." It's hard to picture it in this serene landscape, but *mile* murder means trouble, chaos.

Pat is a great fan of Father McDyer because he "presses" to get things done, going to the president of Ireland, if necessary. McDyer, he says, thinks the area's only hope is the locals, using their own labor to create what's needed. Far from being delighted at this vote of confidence, many locals have to be prodded into participating. Father McDyer is the man to do it, Pat says, by a combination of reasoning, nagging, and ordering. The result is a football pitch, the village hall, the electricity, tourist accommodation in private houses, and even piped water, which is quite a feat because the last Census shows only a quarter of rural Irish houses have it.

Celery is next; it's one of the few crops that flourishes in this harsh weather. Art and I turn off at Father McDyer's seasonal Errigal vegetable co-op, which cans vegetables for export. A grower can make about £150 a year, but many are wary after losing crops to bad weather, and the factory is in the red. Some local people eat the celery, the manager says, but "only out of patriotism."

Back in Carrick, Art makes a list of local associations, clubs, and organizations: Glen, with the tiniest population, has the most, fifteen, about six people per group; Kilcar, the largest village, has ten, and Carrick has seven. The Carrick Parish Council, founded in 1940, is defunct, Art says, because of a disagreement. He falls silent. Maybe funicular railways played a role.

In Carrick, the Gael Linn furniture workshop has closed. James explains the problem: "They were young lads. The idea was each lad would rent a machine and eventually pay it off. They worked at home a lot. That's all right for married men, but the young lads, they like to work together, smell the other fellow's socks. You know yourself how it is." He forgets I'm American.

The vocational school teacher who trained them has another take: "The real problem, aside of no tradition of woodworking, was the project was too small to get good wood, and the houses and workshop were too damp: you need six to ten per cent moisture in wood, and we had twenty-five. Everything warped when it arrived in a dry place. So all the boys became carpenters in England."

Mrs. B. says one of her sons worked there but earned only four pounds a week, a fifth of what he'd been making earlier in England. They got a little more "when James got them out on strike." Since James is one of the people who encouraged Gael Linn to come to Carrick, this seems a bit perverse, but James is a man of many hats. Mrs. B. made three novenas to St. Joseph the Carpenter, with an "odd shout" to the Blessed Virgin, saying, "please ask your carpenter to help mine."

What Carrick *does* have is the trout farm/piggery, acquired when Gael Linn bought part of the former landlord's estate. The Sultan, the newest manager, the fourth in a few years, is a gentle man, surprising since local lore suggests he lost his hearing in a blast that occurred while carrying out a patriotic bombing in the Wicklow mountains. Since that area also has a huge military firing range, it's possible he was damaged passing through on a Sunday hike. I don't ask how he got his name; it's reminiscent of Youngstown's Mafioso, people like "Ronnie the Crab," "Cadillac Charlie," and Ciasullo the Animal." But there's a bigger mystery: where are the trout?

Two official agricultural advisors, one in Kilcar, one here, explain. Gael Linn tried to make a model farm, they say, with sheep, cattle, New Zealand white rabbits, grass, chickens, and a rainbow trout farm. But the land is too poor. The rabbits were "dying wholesale." The trout farm never got off the ground because the ground leaked. ("We told them it would," people say.) I recall the assistant postmistress's sour comment: "Hasn't Gael Linn a lot of money that they can be posting dead rabbits off for post-mortems?" The Sultan has been left to his own devices and private passion, pigs.

"That's all we've had," James says. "Here's a title for your thesis: 'A Floundering Trout Farm as a Model for Development.'" He confirms the love affair between Gael Linn and Carrick is probably over. They wanted to buy his pub to develop as a hotel and "I refused, of course," he says. "It came down from my mother - my patrimony! Or 'matrimony'? Whichever, now they've shown us the black breast."

I can't picture this.

"It's from the old custom of weaning a child. A mother smears black soot on her nipple."

This evening Manus McLoughlin, a stoutish man in his late sixties, stands on the corner outside his house. He owns one of the few locally developed companies, a construction business.

"Well," he says, "let me give you my side of the story."

"What story?" I ask.

"Whatever one others have told you."

Nothing at all, except that the older McLoughlins are clannish, Manus has fallen out with the priest over a roof repair, he and his brother fought on opposite sides in the Civil War, he was the first chair of the Parish Council, and he has held one office or another ever since. That when a McLoughlin is born, people are reminded, roughly, of the words of The Charge of the Light Brigade: "McLoughlins in front of me, McLoughlins in back of me, etcetera."

"They haven't told me anything," I assure him. He pats my shoulder.

"I'll tell you something interesting about the church roof," he says. Ah, I think, I'll get his side of the story.

"The timber was salvaged from the wreck of the merchant ship *Sydney*, near here, in 1870. All but two of the sailors died."

Manus leases the local quarry and needs three-phase electricity to make tiles but can't get it. "The powers that be will put up sixteen poles to supply one light bulb but nothing to help the businessman. We wouldn't need government-subsidized factories if we had the utilities the rest of the country has."

He says he trained many of the local handymen who now do him out of work, tax free. "So I work all over the country except here, building, making doors and windows. And I have a very good market in chairs for the hotel trade."

"At least you've trained some fellows well enough that they can stay at home. Or get a better job when they emigrate," I say.

"I hadn't thought of it that way before," he says.

I look at fishing too, down on the bay in Teelin. Once Teelin was the hub of the area's economy, catching and salting fish for the entire west and beyond. Now there's one full-time and six part-time fishermen. Before World War I, fleets of British steam-drifters, sometimes as many as 200, damaged the local herring fishing. In the 1950s, seiners from the town of Killybegs ruined the long lines used by local fishermen and denuded the inshore waters of fish. At best, today's boats can make about £600 a year, roughly a hundred more than a farmer would make.

I watch hundreds of barrels of fish being loaded onto a large vessel, the Irene, to be taken to Dublin. Today, toward the end of the four- or five-month herring season, the Gallagher brothers, who have a house on the pier, salted and barreled 700 crann of herring, which is over 26,000 gallons of fish. According to them, though, it's hard to get daily or weekly help: "The dole has this country ruined." The dole is Unemployment Assistance, which unemployed males can get from the age of eighteen.

I meet a visiting official from the Department of the Gaeltacht who's talking to James. He also says Carrick and Kilcar are not priorities with the department because neither speaks Irish. "They all can, beautifully, but don't." But from what I see so far, it's fairer to say "not consistently": they slip in and out depending on who they're talking to, the subject, and the environment.

"And because we're in the Gaeltacht," James says, "the other depart-ments say they can't help us." The official shrugs.

Back in the bar, James signals me to open my notebook. He explains that since the twelfth century, "The Pale" was a privileged, bounded area around Dublin. "It doesn't have a physical boundary these days, but it's still privileged." I wonder where we're going.

"Write this down. Most of Ireland is Beyond the Pale," he says. "And we here are Beyond the Beyond."

So "Now what?" is on a lot of people's minds. The headmaster of the vocational school is away giving lectures in Irish at the university in Galway, but I introduce myself to an assistant headmaster, Brian McBride, known as "Brian Vocational," a slight man, smoking and gasping as he runs to his car. He's late for a meeting with Gaeltarra Éireann; he wants to ask if they'll subsidize a new small woodworking industry making chairs for the hotel trade. What about damp? What about Manus's hotel chairs?

Tonight, Mrs. B. knits a baby's tiny cap. When she has enough she sends them to an agent, a local middleman who sells them to retailers. "Women are the invisible factories here. Many a bill wouldn't be paid except for this," she says, lifting the needles. We make a rough tabulation of houses in Carrick and Glencolmcille where women knit, crochet, and make crafts, counting over a hundred. A knitter can earn about three pounds a week working every free hour, and getting nothing if the agent finds a fault.

We finish with a book: she's reading to me to improve my Irish. I'd been told in Dublin that the Irish in this area is incomprehensible, but that the Irish up north in Gweedore is *completely* incomprehensible "*altogether*," so I settle for incomprehensible. The book is *Nuair a Bhí Mé Og, When I Was Young*, by the beloved Donegal novelist Séamus Ó Grianna, pen name "Máire." Mrs. B's about the same age, and dabs her eyes as she reads.

In bed, two hot-water bottles cradling my feet and a handknit jumper over my flannel night clothes, I add up the numbers. All the "industrial" activities in the two halves of the parish give employment, some part time, to about 150 people. Then I look at the total number of workers in the kind of full-time jobs the government wants to see. It's fewer than thirty. Most workers are under twenty-five and their employers believe they'll all emigrate.

So yes, I think the black breast is for real.


## The Wolfhound of Glencolmcille

Father McDyer is chairing a women's meeting in the house next to Mrs. B.'s and wants to meet me. I go with some trepidation: he's a dynamo, corralling people into his projects, willing or not; an international figure revered everywhere but here for his accomplishments.

The meeting ends as I arrive. I settle in, notebook in hand, ready to hear a résumé of his works and pomps. But "Where am I going wrong?" he asks. He's a tall, bushy-haired man with the bearing of an Irish wolfhound. "I know I'm not liked. There's my counterpart, the curate here in Carrick; I'm a curate, too, you know, the parish priest here is my boss, and people love the other fellow. He'd be the first to tell you he's not perfect. I can see why he takes a drink, living in this place, but ..."

I know about Father Devlin's conviviality. Indeed, James has shown me the newspaper coverage of a recent escapade: he and a solicitor from Killybegs were involved in after-hours drinking ("etcetera," James says) in a local pub.

"But they *love* him for it," Father McDyer says, "and here's me, working to get what people want, the water, the electricity, and not easily, I can tell you that for nothing, and am I loved? Or even liked? Of course, 'the other lad' says Mass in record time, so that's an attraction."

I've been reading the life of St. Colmcille, a Donegal man. It's one of the books James leaves on Mrs. B.'s kitchen table when he has his nightly constitutional. I've memorized an ancient poem in which Colm-cille laments:

> Should sudden death overtake me,
> It is for my great love of the Gael.

Father McDyer seems like a man who can take the comparison, and he does. "What's new?" he sighs. We discuss what's being done in other western rural areas, new ideas he'd like to try, and the complex logistics of getting anything done in such a remote place. He's just opened a Folk Museum. Next year it's a Holiday Village, thatched cottages that visitors can rent. But he's had a major setback: he planned a farming commune covering 50,000 square acres. Farmers would hand over their lands and titles for seven years. Vast areas would be fenced. Three foremen would handle the hill sheep, cattle, vegetables, and game. Members would get free potatoes, fuel, milk, and seven pounds a week.

Smugly, I picture the outcome: no farmer would hand over his deeds and pool his lands.

Wrong. "I had about one-hundred-and-twenty farmers signed up. The problem was we needed one-hundred-thousand pounds to get started, and the Agricultural Credit Organization wouldn't give it."

"Why?"

"It was the idea of a commune in Catholic Ireland. I was blackened as a communist."

"So now?"

"Now I have seventy-five farmers signed up in a co-op, each on his own land, but working cooperatively. We'll fence, drain, and fertilize the lowlands, and seed to build up our sheep numbers. The vegetable co-op will buy and market our produce."

Father McDyer is an elemental force, fueled by a belief that people deserve a decent standard of living, and I suspect he'd do it all, dig ditches, wire poles, single-handedly if necessary. His barely chained

ambition makes it unlikely he'll have to. But being loved might be more
elusive.

The parish priest, Father Bonner, has been away until now. Outside the
rectory a woman soothes a child who's crying; he can't find his mother.
The woman might be anything from thirty to fifty, but her startling blue
eyes, clear as stained glass, could be those of a teenager. It's the same
woman who directed me to James's pub the day I arrived in Carrick. The
child's mother emerges from the rectory, snaps at the woman, snatches
the child away angrily, and marches off.

The parish is declining, Father Bonner says: fifteen marriages in 1885,
one last year. The population declined by 20 per cent in the last twenty
years. Kilcar's declined, too, but not as much. And he has another complaint: "When people ask me where I come from, I say I'm the parish
priest here and they'll say, 'Oh yes, Father McDyer's parish.' You hear
so much about development in Glen and when you get out there you
realize nothing's going on." No mention of his other "staff" problem, the
curate's scandal.

I ask about the Parish Council. He sighs and lifts his hands to
heaven.

What next? A few men from Carrick work in the Kilcar factory, and
Mrs. B. invites two of them, her former students, to come for tea. "They
made me promise you're not here to close the factory," she says.

I say I'll make my mother's lasagne for them. She's never heard of it
but she's game. But my noodles, thick grey strips, look like linoleum.

"Arrah!" she mutters, edging me aside and dumping my dough into
the slop pail. She starts over with new flour, eggs, salt, and cooking oil.
The result is beautiful translucent noodles layered with my sauce and
awful processed cheese, the only kind available here even though I can
see cows from the window.

When I was studying with the Paiute Indians in Nevada, I taught the
young boys a game popular among Youngstown's Mafia gangs: barbut, an
old Turkish dice game. Afterward, I worried that the next anthropologist

to arrive might try to make a connection between the Paiutes and the Turks. I hope Mrs. B. doesn't introduce lasagne here.

"We're making an Italian dish," Mrs. B. announces when the factory men arrive, and they smile nervously. She introduces them: Peter, a driver, and Gerry, from the office.

Gerry could "talk Donegal tweed for Ireland," Mrs. B. told me, and he does. "An bréidín," he says. "The tweed" is worn around the world, he tells us; an English country gentleman in his shooting coat, a lady in New York throwing a gossamer tweed wrap over her cocktail dress, a Berliner in a herringbone Ulster, he conjures them all with a few gestures. "Now, of course, we make most tweed on power looms, and it's the best in the world, but the handloom, there's nothing to touch it."

"A hundred years ago we had twenty-four-hundred weavers in this area," Peter says. "The tweed was sold at the old market here on the village street."

"So why isn't the factory in Carrick?"

"Politics. Forty years ago, Kilcar had a politician elected to the Dáil. Carrick never had one. He represented the whole area, but naturally he'd want the factory in his home place. And the building was already there, an old carpet factory."

Peter says they have a hundred-odd men, most of them settled and married, long-time employees, a couple from the 1920s. Many are returned emigrants. They come from old weaving families; rarely does a "new fellow" try it. I wonder if the government might try to welcome other Irish speakers back.

"And the women?" I ask.

"They're younger, single. We do have one older girl, forty, forty-five."

The driver, Peter, makes ten pounds a week. "I was offered a good job in the warehouse, but I ..." he looks at Mrs. B. No one speaks. I've learned in my short career that something unsaid is often more important than hours of talk.

"The lasagne! Where's my head!" Mrs. B. cries.

"Are women happy to do factory work?" I ask. Fred Driver, in Kilti-magh, Mayo, said the girls in his factory felt they were looked down upon.

"Aye," Peter says. "They're our daughters or nieces or neighbors. We bring them in when we hear about a job. And they're not doing men's work. Women never weave."

I mention that Navaho Indian women do the weaving.

"Well, they must be strapping big lassies. A lot heartier than our girls."

I apologize for not speaking much Irish. They must be using it in the factory.

"Not at all, maybe a manager or two, but it would be the quare day there'd be any Irish spoken on the factory floor," Peter says. "Nor in the office, unless they're talking to headquarters."

"But everyone *can* speak Irish?"

"Why couldn't they?" he asks. "Even my cows understand Irish."

Mrs. B. returns. "You'll have some lasagne," she orders.

They draw back a little in their chairs and say nothing, two big men trying to be invisible. They make a show of eating but take microscopic bites. Mrs. B. tucks in with gusto.

"We eat the canned celery," Gerry offers, as if they're already doing their bit for the world of bizarre foods. All three think it's a step too far when I say Americans eat their celery raw.

So I mention Father McDyer. "Could his ideas work here in Carrick?"

"Ah, no," Peter says, and Gerry agrees. "This is a different part of the world, a different race of people. You'll see, yourself."

"Well," Mrs. B. says later, "Those lads didn't say much. I suppose they were embarrassed in front of a visitor."

But "wary" would be more like it. I write down "warehouse" and a question mark.

As we watch the flames in the Stanley, she tells me an ancient tale of the handsome seventeen-year-old Cú Chulainn, who was destined to defend Ulster single-handedly against Queen Méabh of Connacht.

Mrs. B.'s voice, her gestures, her eyes, now fiery, now gentle, re-create Cú Chulainn's monstrous rage as he fought from his chariot, slashing, goug-ing, slaughtering; his many trysts; his gallant refusal to kill Méabh when she interrupted the battle to have her period; and his epic three-day fight to the death with his foster-brother, Ferdiad. "We'll get to the tragedy another night," she says.

# February/Mí Feabhra 1967

## Your Man and Your Other Lad

Today, February 1, is the first day of spring according to traditional Irish reckoning. *Lá Fhéile Bhríde*, St. Brigid's Day, was originally the pagan festival of *Imbolg*. Brigid was a powerful fifth-century Catholic bishop whose power exceeded that of any Catholic woman who came before or after her. Each year, her reed-woven cross is hung over mantels and doorways to protect the house from fire and evil. "The evenings are drawing out," people say. Farmers roam their commonage with sheepdogs looking for last year's lambs and give them names. "The White-faced One with Black Horns," Michael says to old Máirtín.

Oddly, Carrick ends at the bottom of its main street, so the vocational school, a few steps further on, is in Kilcar. I catch Brian Vocational shouldering his way out the door, arms full of files. I'm particularly interested in his development-related insights. I've heard he was a moving force on the old Carrick Parish Council. He assures me that indeed he wasn't; he was only one of many foot soldiers. "Around here, you only stand up to be shot down."

Delicately, and with frequent references to "your man" and "your other lad," he indicates there was an "unsettled atmosphere" within the council. I guess on one side of the atmosphere were those involved in encouraging Gael Linn (James and "that crowd") to buy the land-lord's estate, with its bay and river rights; on the other side, those like the currently elected chair, Leo ("your man here"), who wanted to join with Father McDyer ("the lad out in Glencolmcille") to get the estate and water rights for the parish. "But it's not as simple as that," he says.

James has a different account. He'd been the secretary, although that isn't why it collapsed. The Parish Council found themselves issuing a note of censure to the parish priest. Like his predecessors, the priest is *officially* the chair, although now he prefers not to attend. "Of course," James assures me, "not a *damnandas et proscribendas esse*, which only the Church can issue, but a wee scribble asking what happened to some money we'd collected for a special purpose. When we went to the bank to draw on it, it wasn't there. Not a sausage." I imagine the priest has his own account of this event, probably quite different.

But I must look overly interested because James says, "It's all over bar the shouting, now."

"So, what next?"

"We're planning a new council, without the priest." Who's "we," I wonder. "We're asking him to announce the date of the meeting at a Sunday Mass."

I suspect this announcement will require the delicacy of a seventeenth-century Venetian diplomat. I want to be there.

～

My Morris Minor is having gear trouble. Also, I can see the road through a hole beside the clutch, and the brakes ... "Nonsense," James says, "Come, I'll show you something." We drive down the Teelin road, gingerly, to Slieve League, almost 2,000 feet high.

"We'll take our dead ease walking up. You'll be grand, you're always dressed for the Arctic." He dances up the stony path, shouting back that the mountain is largely quartzite, with some tropical limestone far underneath. "Awhile back Ireland was on the Equator," he says. At a cliff, the Eagle's Nest, I balk. James says we're only at 800 feet. The wind flays my cheeks.

"Mrs. B. did this walk to the top recently in a much fresher breeze," James says.

We come to a geological atrocity, a knife-edge rib of rock with, in good places, a two-foot-wide path along its length, running for about 1,000 feet. To the left is a sickening drop of about 500 feet into the sea. I make this inch-by-inch, not looking down, sometimes thinking I should go on all fours, once slipping and being saved by a skin-splitting crag.

Almost three hours into the walk, we reach the summit. My eyes stream, and I've stopped bothering about my nose. James points across Donegal Bay to the area where the poet Yeats is buried, near Ben Bulben, the anvil-shaped mountain in county Sligo. I can also see the curvature of the earth, not a welcome sight.

"Here we are," he says, pointing to a wedge-shaped, broken-topped cement column. "A triangulation pillar! Erected by the ordnance survey mappers!"

"As a sort of celebration?"

He takes a grubby envelope from his breast pocket and draws a line. "Look. That line is my base. I've measured its length. The two ends of the line are what are called my known points. Then I can work out the angles between each of the points and a third place."

"What place?"

"Any place. Walk over there by that bit of grass. You're the third place, and I want to know how far away you are from my base. I go to one end of my base and I point my measuring tool, a theodolite, at you. That's my sightline. I measure the angle between the sightline and my base. I do the same from the other end of my base. I know the distance between you and me. What they did is called triangulation. The British did this, all over Ireland, to make the maps."

"And the pillar?"

"They mounted the theodolite on the pillar to start measuring a new triangle."

I don't ask how they hauled all that stuff up here and whether they brought the pillar with them, or made it on site, in which case they hauled bags of sand and cement. They were tough men. "If I remember right, they did it over a Christmas," James says.

As I did in Carrick, I start making my courtesy visits to the Four Horsemen in Kilcar. I call on the young curate, Father Stevens. He feels BBC television should come in and do an exposé on Father McDyer. The vegetable co-op was down £40,000 last year and £80,000 this year. Nothing is happening out there, he says. We conclude on a somber note: "Even if I say so myself," he says, "the whole place is clergy-ridden."

"I'm delighted to learn new recipes," Mrs. B. says later this evening, watching me make a pizza, her hands clearly itching to roll the dough properly. Her usual diet, like most people's, has as its foundation tea, bread, and butter at every meal. "Shop bread" is what most village people eat these days; Shane Cannon's wife, Margaret, across the road, is one of the few who still bakes all her bread. For breakfast, around nine, people may add porridge, and those going out to work might have an egg. For other meals, Mrs. B. says the difference between "village people" and "country people" is the presence of meat and sweets. Country people might have meat only twice a week; on other days, their midday dinner might be potatoes, chopped cabbage with butter, and a bit of bacon or minced beef for flavor, and to drink, a cup of milk. Mrs. B might have that, or a chop, but she'll also have a sweet at the end. This is a weekday luxury for most people, as are the biscuits at other meals, too. For tea, the meal at five, she might add a slice of ham, a tomato, and a boiled egg, and if other people are coming, whatever cake is in the house. The last meal is supper around eleven, which is porridge with milk, rarely sugar, but not everyone has this.

The pizza she's re-rolling now is just for us. Just as it is ready to come out of the oven, Mrs. B. rushes to the front door.

"Mr. Fitzgerald," she reports back, "from the factory."

"You'll have a cup of tea," Mrs. B. says, giving him the best chair in the parlor. He's a junior manager in the factory, about my age; black hair, baby-faced, with an attempt at a serious mustache.

He gives her a slight, dismissive nod and making a temple of his fingers, quizzes me on my factory study. I explain, but he says nothing. He picks up a book from the side table and flips through it.

Mrs. B. brings in the tea, sits to pour it, and there's a moment when I wonder if he's waiting for her to retire to the kitchen. She stays, though, and asks about his four young children. Most of their care is left to what he calls "my lady wife." Mrs. B. says she must be lonely, knowing few people here. "I'll bet she's the happy woman when you get home from work."

"I'm tired after a day at the factory and all I want is my pipe handed to me and my slippers and the paper," he says. She surrenders and leaves. He passes me the book he's been looking at.

I hesitate, and he laughs. "Whenever I pick something up, I hand it to my wife to put away." He gets up and says he'll be on the lookout for me in the factory, although "I doubt you'll get anything on us."

"Arrah, his old pipe and slippers," Mrs. B. says. "He can put them where the monkey put the nut." She imitates him, making a temple of her fingers.

James appears at eleven, not unusual here and certainly not for James. He waves a scroll.

"I wonder if you know about the space-time continuum? It's all the go in the papers these days."

"Well, not ..."

"We have a variation on that here," he says. He unrolls the scroll. "Here's a rough map I made." It shows all of Ireland, long red roads crisscrossing it, and in the sea, short blue lines extending out to historic figures. "The fellow on the blue line out there in the water is Niall of the Nine Hostages," he says.

"What is this?"

"It shows the mind of Irish country people - us." He moves a finger eastward along the road to Dublin. "We tend to compress time and expand distance. Dublin seems light years away from us, in every sense. Maybe because millions of years ago we were on two different continents. We were on Laurentia, part of North America, and they were on Gondwana."

"James ..."

"So distance is long but history is short. To us, Niall was only yesterday."

He produces a second map of Ireland, netted with ordnance triangulation lines.

"What's this?"

"I explained triangulation, but I want to show you where ordnance survey's sightlines for Ireland begin."

He points to six places on the British coastline. Dagger-like tentacles reach across the Irish Sea to Ireland.

Seeing, in an instant, such a dramatic representation of conquest is unnerving. Ireland looks like a snared sea creature, laced with ropes and hogtied. Britain had this power to draw, to segment, to name. The only comparable shock I've had was when I was called "Mrs. Murphy" only minutes after my wedding.

Mrs. B. comes out of the pantry. "It's late, James, so you can join us for the Rosary." Sheepishly, we both kneel. With a little prodding, I find I can announce the Sorrowful Mysteries like a Mother Superior. If only my mother could see me now.

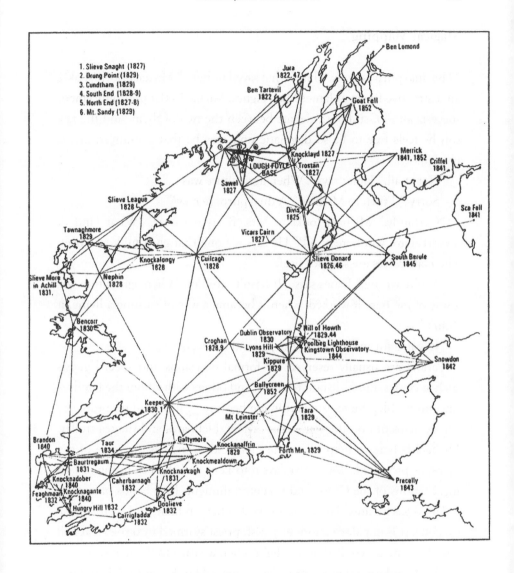

Map 3. Principal triangulation of Ireland, c. 1846.

Source: Trigpointing Ireland, "The History of Ordnance Survey in Ireland,"
http://www.trigpointing-ireland .org.uk/about.php?a=history.

## Magical Mapping

"The dual-purpose cow. That's what saved us here." Michael Boyle shakes an instructive finger at James Mary Agnes. Michael's flat pronouncement suggests an old, stubborn debate between the two of them, and the reason he feels free to be so dogmatic now may be that a stranger, me, is present.

"Not at all," James says. "When agriculture was …"

"Sorry?" I turn to Michael. "A dual-purpose cow?"

"Certainly." Michael looks at Mrs. B. as if to say, "What kind of 'expert' have you here at all?" He says it's one that gives milk and beef. The male calves are sold for beef.

"You're wrong," James says. "It hasn't saved us. When agriculture was a way of life here it worked; when it became a way of earning a living, it didn't."

"It works for me. Between the jigs and the reels."

Parlors are usually reserved for formal occasions and special guests such as clerics, nuns, distant relatives, and others with whom the family is uncomfortable. We're using it tonight because I can spread my ordnance survey maps out on the settee, the ornate sideboard, and the tea trolley. Michael is here to help fill in the plot holders' names on some of the maps, as promised. We're two days into Lent and the beginning of fasting, Stations of the Cross, and no entertainment. Irish bands have gone to Las Vegas because dances are forbidden here in Lent, and even a classical concert is out since a former parish priest stormed into the local hall and shut one down. Perhaps, as light relief, we turn to the maps.

"I'm wondering if more farms have been sold in Kilcar than here since some of the Kilcar men have gone to work in the factory – it's almost thirty years, now," I say. "And has any land been consolidated?" If nothing at all has happened, the government's plan is off kilter.

"I'll start with Carrick's map, so I can compare them. Then I'll check Kilcar's map before and after the factory came in," I say.

"Well, if you just look across to the fields to Kilcar, you'll see they're not doing much farming, sale or not. So you won't need to bother with any maps there." James spreads the map of Carrick Upper, where Michael lives and James has a small garden.

The two men present quite a contrast: Michael, strong-boned, calm; James with his lithe dancer's body and air of trapped lightning. Michael is reserved; James has a hand in everything but still I was surprised to learn from Mrs. B. the other day he's a qualified, respected engineer. Perhaps that explains the anchor and the funicular railway.

"What kind of engineer?" I'd asked.

"Civil," she'd said. "People say he wanted to be a mechanical engineer but the mother thought 'civil' sounded nicer."

"Does he practice?"

"Occasionally. He's in demand, but it's like everything else, he only does it to satisfy his curiosity."

Under the bare overhead bulb, Michael traces the eastern boundary of his lands with his finger – "lands" because his eighteen acres are in three parts. "Here, my land marches alongside Mattie's, and on the west, it's ..." His finger runs along the line as if he can feel it, never lifting it, as if lifting it would lose something. He cranes his neck, moving his finger north toward the commonage. "Here's that wee scrap of land forn-enst the mountain, and below it Wee Hughdie's land marches alongside Owen Bán's."

Soon Michael is lost in his tracings. "I've never seen one of these yokes before." It's likely this map has never been studied by someone who knows the territory so well, field by field, ditch by ditch, stony patch by grassy bowl. He looks like a schoolmaster, alert for mistakes, pleased to find that despite misgivings almost everything is right. "Well, that's okay, so," he announces, pulling back with a little smile. "Them ones, they know it all."

The odd-shaped pieces, parallelograms, rhomboids, blobby bits, are fields, grass, rock and bog to him, places he's worked or knows who worked them. This is almost a private moment, more important to this man than it will ever be to me in my research. I've seen my father looking at things like this: old maps of Youngstown, 1920s photos of the local amusement park or the city trolley, and he comes into his own then, alert, pointing out old haunts, what's gone now, angling the paper, hoping to get at the long-forgotten bits just beyond the edges. Then he gets up from his chair a little stiffly and comes back to this world, as Michael does now. Something has become more complete for him. He seems gratified the fields he's worked all his life are worth the official care that's so obvious on the map.

James is absorbed in the map of the village's main street and the position of his pub. "This is not to any scale I ever heard of," he says. He takes a pencil stub from behind his ear and scratches a drawing in my notebook. Soon we have a rough map of today's village center.

"This ordnance survey map was last revised sixty years ago," I say.

"Yes, but the village can't have changed that much. Those owners are dead, but many of the buildings are the same. I think they've got the dimensions wrong."

Michael looks at James's drawing. It certainly wouldn't fit as an overlay of the earlier map.

The Perpetual Smile, a retired teacher, now a shopkeeper, knocks.

"You've drawn your own place a wee bit too big, James," he says. "Sure I know you have notions of grandeur, but your shop isn't that big."

James hands him the notebook. "Don't let me stand in your way."

A new map emerges, this one with a more modest representation of James Mary Agnes's establishment, and The Perpetual Smile's shop looming over its neighbors. Michael flips the map over and, in a few lines, sketches the river at the lower end, the church at the upper, and neatly fits in all the buildings, Heekin's, Doogan's, Brown's, some names still used even though the people are long dead. James and The Perpetual Smile disagree with his dimensions, too, each for different reasons. I wonder how men who have lived here all their lives can't produce an agreed-upon map of the short central street. But today's street where both my father and I grew up – would our drawings look the same?

"Enough work for the day that's in it," Michael says. "Mind you," he warns, "we've said nothing about *anything* that happens *inside* the houses. You make that clear if anyone asks."

I help Mrs. B. with the supper, but I know not to touch anything to do with the tea brewing until I'm fully trained in its mysteries. The same with the fire in the Stanley; a mistake and we'd have no hot water or heat this bitter evening.

In the kitchen, there's none of the usual fuss, the hostess opening with, "You'll have a cup of tea," the guests responding, "No, no, don't bother." Everyone is starved.

"The Church exempts the elderly and men working at hard labor," Mrs. B. says, and since I'm no longer Catholic we all tuck in.

"The maps you men drew are wrong," she says.

"They need a woman's touch, so," Michael says. "Round up a few and set them to it." He promises that next time we'll go back to my questions about land use and ownership. "I might bring different lads with me," he says. "Country fellows, not city gents."

Michael puts on his cap and James his fedora. They hadn't taken off their coats because Mrs. B.'s parlor would have had to be heated at least a day in advance. Now they go out into the cold night, calling back "Good night" to both of us, "*Oíche mhaith agaibh.*"

"What happens in the houses! I'd like to hear what happens in the pubs!" Mrs. B. says as we wash the cups. "We'll invite some women to draw the village. They always love to get an invitation from me."

In bed, I think about the poor ordnance survey mappers, freezing at the top of Slieve League. And a word I looked up after James's lesson on triangulation: "*sightline: a line from an observer's eye to a distant point.*"

## Playing Jazz, in Wool

"It's a wonder you ever managed to get married at all," Mrs. B. laughs. It's bone-snapping cold and I've upholstered myself in woolens.

But she knows, if only obliquely, that a legal parting is in the works. The high school romance, the boy next door, the marriage that occurred mainly because it seemed to both of us to be the expected, grown-up thing to do, all fading now as if it happened to other people.

Mr. Redington, the manager of the Kilcar factory, is back, and rang to say head office told him to invite me in for a chat. I add furry gloves to my ensemble: where once I thought the Morris's heater was broken, I've since learned it doesn't have one. "Oh," James laughed when he heard this, "that's quite common. Some people take them out because they think a heater is very dear on petrol."

The drive out The Line to Kilcar today must be one of the most beautiful sights in the world. It's a sparkling, azure-sky morning, Technicolor blues and greens, the air so clear everything seems closer, and to the east, dramatic fans of sunlight, the sort I associate with the booming, godly voice of Charlton Heston in a nightgown.

The factory is a two-storey white stucco art-deco-style building, flat-roofed, curved at one end. That sign again, "A Hundred Thousand Welcomes," in Irish. Do the workers see this each day as they enter? I picture the dead-black canyon beneath the Market Street bridge in Youngstown, a reeking cavity of mills and factories, including the one my father works in.

Mr. Redington greets me at the door. "They've sent me a full report on your visit to head office." He shows me a letter from MacGabhann, who seems to have a clearer understanding of what I'm doing than I do.

The weavers! Each sits on his own bench, dwarfed by a high wooden loom. Looms are strung with lengths of yarn to make the warp and the shuttle flies across to make the cross-wise strings of the woof, yet each weaver produces a different piece of magic.

What strikes me most is the men's grace, and music.

They face forward in their rows, straight-backed, heads erect, their arms moving rhythmically, fluidly, like harpists weaving music. The colors and textures sift down and the pattern emerges, line by line. Occasionally a man adjusts his loom, sits back again, and off he goes like a jazz pianist working in wool, his feet pedaling away.

Mr. Redington says Gaeltarra has about 1750 employees, with 170 locals in Kilcar. I'm still transfixed; the weavers continue to shuttle jewel-like colors across the vibrant warp. Some seem to be making a Donegal meadow on a sunny day, others a turf bank along a dark amber river, a few weaving a muted blanket bog in soft rain. Elsewhere, Mr. Redington says, some of the men are machine weaving or spinning, but I don't see them.

"Sixty per cent of the workers are men. Most are married, over forty, here for the long haul, ten years, sometimes twenty or more." I pull out my notebook, reluctant to take my eyes off the patterns accumulating on the looms. "The girls are single, in their twenties. We have one married woman. Most girls emigrate, or leave when they marry."

"Do you encourage them to stay?" I ask.

"No. If they're marrying in the area, that's grand, and we'd hope new girls would come in, stay a while, and maybe do the same."

The men are more individual now; I see a big man with an equestrian bearing and a rider's tight, economical movements; another, a small, wiry man, leans into the loom with his whole body, wrestling a pattern into the wool. All the men work silently, with only an odd comment called out to another. Anyone in Dublin who told me Gaeltacht people are lazy should see these weavers. Maybe they wouldn't be seen as Gaeltacht people, though, because I hear very little Irish.

"Weaving is in the blood here," he says. "Twenty-five years ago, as many as fifteen hundred men were still weaving at home. That's not counting the ones who were working in the factory. The ones you see here are from old weaving families. We don't teach weaving. They learn from their fathers."

"Those other workers are using Hattersley looms. And the rest are fin-ishers, dyers, carpenters, drivers, office people. Whatever they do, they're big on the factory's performance. They see the connection to their wage packets. One fellow here even keeps his own production records."

"It's as if it's in your blood, too," I say.

"My father was the manager here, too, actually the designer, but they needed a production manager, so ..."

"I'm afraid I don't know much about the history of the factory, yet," I say.

"No need, no need," he says. "Too much is made of history, raking things up." He turns back to see the hand weavers, whose fluid motions suggest they must be wonderful dancers, too. "I'll tell you one thing, though," he says, turning back, "If Donegal workers are with you and want to do the job, anything is possible. If they're not, they'll tell you straight out, and you'll get nothing out of them. Not every part of the country is like that."

"Where else have you worked?"

"Everywhere. Some places, you'd be demented. A business degree won't explain some of the things I see in factories further south. Up here, it's not so bad. But still, there are differences between this and an urban factory. A worker here might leave without giving notice. He doesn't want his brothers to know: if he's the last to emigrate, he might get stuck with the farm and the old people. He won't find a girl willing to marry into that." We move away from the weavers.

"Another difference might be that the rates of depression are higher in rural areas than cities," he says. "I was talking to the medical officer in Killybegs. He said the highest rates of mental illness in Donegal are right here on this southwest peninsula."

"So do you have problems in the factory?"

"No, not really. A lot of mental illness comes from loneliness and poverty. These fellows in the factory have comrades and a pay packet. Of course, I don't know everyone, or why some people leave, or why some never apply. Sometimes in the village you do hear of a fellow being taken away, or going off to the mental hospital on his own. But it's not a topic a family wants to talk about."

If a high rate could affect investment from outside, how will I find out more about mental illness here?

⁓

A middle-aged giant of a man wearing a tan clerk's coat over rough denim trousers and thick boots makes his way toward us. He hands Mr. Redington a docket, touching his hand to head, as one might to a cap. To me, he nods and leaves.

"Now there's a case for your study. Tommo was a laborer in the warehouse, and he got to know more about the warehouse than anyone else. When the job came up, I promoted him to warehouse stock keeper. He came to me about six months later, annoyed. He said, 'I have to spend so much time fooling with these figures I hardly have any time for work.'"

Later a young man in overalls appears with some papers for Mr. Redington. "Where's Tommo?" Mr. Redington demands.

The young man rolls his eyes. "Loadin'," he sighs.

"Why aren't you loading? That's *your* job." He taps the papers. "These are *his*."

"Won't let me. I was good enough to load, the last place I was in, but not here, seems like."

I ask about Irish. Mr. Redington says it's the policy to speak it, but people speak what they like. "The managers, we speak Irish."

I recall James telling me the newer Gaeltarra managers' Irish is generally so bad one tries to translate it into English and then back into Irish to figure out what they're saying.

I say I've interviewed a couple of the workers living in Carrick and I'd like to talk to some here. "In different jobs, men, women, younger, older, so I can start to get a picture."

"But surely you'll want to do a proper scientific survey?" he asks. "Here in the factory? I can extend the lunch hour and they can fill in a questionnaire."

How often does a researcher get the chance to stop an entire factory while the workers fill in her questionnaire? But anthropologists prefer to get information by participating, observing, interviewing. We don't get much training in questionnaire design, which often produces more context-free "facts" than "meanings."

But I've been thinking of the ordnance survey mappers. They used a network of triangles across the landscape to establish distances, followed by surveyors, teams to plot the measurements, engravers, printers, and so on to the final map. But another team also "triangulated," to work out the place names to go on the maps: they sought out local people, history, legends, folklore, and possible Irish, Greek, Roman, or Norse root words. When anthropologists triangulate – drawing on many people, perspectives, methods – we hope to weave some sort of "safety net" for our information. Not perfect, but what is? Anyway, I'll try the questionnaires. One more way of seeing, one more sightline.

"Thanks. When I know what to ask, I'll do a survey," I say.

In the canteen, I meet two trainee managers. I mention the Tourmakeady staff say they eat with the workers. "We tend to keep apart from the workers here," he says. "We never know anything about local politics or factions until we see grown men breaking down over local persecution."

Local persecution? Mr. Redington stands and shoves the table back. "What else can we do for you?" he asks, motioning his assistants back to work. He walks me to the front door. "It's better to do things very cautiously in a small place." He looks weary now. "If you have any more questions, just send me a note or drop in."

## A New Parish Council and the "Dinner/Tea Puzzle"

At the end of Sunday Mass today, the priest announced elections for a new Parish Council tonight at the vocational school. No ripple of excitement through the congregation: the women struggled off the kneelers and, as always, most of the men huddled uneasily at the back of the church, despite the priest's past threats to haul them up into the pews personally.

The first Carrick Parish Council was set up in 1940 to protect the community during what was known in Ireland as "The Emergency," and everywhere else as World War II. Some members were Civil War veterans of both sides who could mobilize, and indeed could probably unite now to start a new war if required. Clergymen and medical officers were ex-officio members, and the parish priest could disband the council at will.

I see Brian Vocational buying the *Sunday Independent*, so he must support the Fine Gael political party. I ask who is running.

"Running?" Brian asks.

"*Ag seasamh* ...," I start. "Sorry, I don't know how to say 'Running, as in the election,'" and I hear he's pretty strict about Irish.

"I *know* what you meant," he says.

"Well how is the vote organized? Do people campaign?"

"Do people campaign to catch their hand in a door?"

"Is the priest invited?"

"He just likes to drop in and out, so no." He says nothing about a possible disagreement over the priest's use of money, and he won't. In a community webbed with gossip, Brian is so discreet he barely speaks.

"Whoever turns up for the meeting can vote. Someone will be proposed, and if no one challenges it, he'll be elected."

"He? No women?"

"I think ... I recall ... yes, young Cáit Gallagher! She was the secretary a while back."

Cáit is one of the few young people here. We've moaned about it, about money, men, loneliness. "I've found some figures that will cheer you up," I told her once. "In our age group there are only five hundred single women for every one thousand single men in Donegal."

"I don't want a man in Donegal. I want to go back to my nursing job in London. That council! I went to a meeting once, just to say I planned to organize a young adults' club with my friend Bríd from Kilcar. They told me not to bother, I had enough to do looking after my mother. But I was the only woman, so they elected me secretary on the spot, handed me a notebook, and told me what time they'd like tea."

"We need this committee," Brian says now. "Rural villages don't have local mayors or councils. The county is our lowest level of local government. Unless you get a local person elected to the county, or better, to Dáil Éireann in Dublin, your community gets nothing. The one elected from Kilcar brought in that factory. Our candidates never got elected. We need to organize at the local level if we're to get anything done, and even then, we'll have to go hat in hand to someone who might have 'pull.' Glencolmcille has McDyer, and he's wangled official Glencolmcille signs from Killybegs on out. Soon you'll see signs for Glen right outside the Chicago airport."

He picks up his *Sunday Independent* and wags a finger at me. "Every second week I buy the *Sunday Press*, so don't assume." A careful man, as everyone says.

$\sim$

I've mentioned in a letter home that a British newspaper had a two-page spread on the Youngstown Mafia. On Monday, a note from my mother, on her usual stationery, a paper napkin:

> Ash Wednesday. Both the fire department and the police are out on strike.
> The Youngstown Vindicator says it's the first time in the country's history.
> But it's nice to have a little recognition for something besides Mafia murders. Everything's fine here.

But I know it isn't: Last week I got a note from my father saying he'd love to see a map of the area. On the back, my little sister wrote that she's painted his nails purple. So he's still laid off work.

For how long? And my mother? She hasn't worked outside our home since she married. Is she now? I've asked, but I get no answers.

Wiring money from here isn't easy: the bank comes to Carrick only once a month on Fair Day, so I send a draft from the main branch in Killybegs. I also send a ten-shilling postal order to the Ordnance Survey Office so my father can see the places I write home about.

Mrs. B. says, "I want you to visit a great Carrick weaver, I call him Nijinsky, a great dancer in my day."

This Nijinsky, old Owen, lives with his grandson, himself a weaver, in a modern house. He has a bone-shuddering cough and I fear for him as he prods us toward a weaver's shed in the back where he works occasionally on a single-shuttle loom.

"My people have been weavers since monsters walked the earth. Like Cú Chulainn himself. He was a monster when he went into battle, he twisted himself into an awful deformity. This loom here produces twenty-eight-inch cloth, a power loom produces fifty-six inch," he says. "The fifty-six is popular in factories now for making clothes, but the hand-woven is better." I write "Cú Chulainn, monster."

"Once, a very good man might produce thirty yards in a day. He'd use wool his wife and daughters carded and spun, wool from our black-faced Scottish Mountain and Cheviot sheep. The damp weather here was great for the spinning. It kept the wool from tearing."

His lungs must be in ribbons now, hacking the words out, but he's unstoppable.

"Then the weaver carried his web, sometimes bowed down under sixty yards, to the depot in the market here. An inspector from the Congested Districts Board examined your work and next day, Fair Day, he gave his verdict. Good tweed got stamped and you could sell it to agents from all over, but the poor weaver had his failings pointed out and took it home. But we all knew who was good and who wasn't, we didn't need an inspector."

"That did him a world of good," Mrs. B. says later. I jokingly ask if our Nijinsky was an old flame of hers. She blushes. "Go away out of that."

James arrives at eleven, just in time for a late supper.

"I'm told you Yanks call your dinner 'supper,'" he says. "I'm confused."

Just as I was when I first arrived at my guest house in Dublin. My problem was "dinner" versus "tea." If we'd had lunch at midday, we'd get dinner in the evening; if we'd had dinner at midday, we'd get "tea" in the evening. I couldn't recognize the difference between a lunch and a midday dinner. Cold versus hot? Size? Potatoes or none? Everyone knew, but no one could explain. "That's something anthropology is good at – figuring how people know what they know when they don't know how they know themselves."

James won't give me the satisfaction of asking for the answer, so I tell Mrs. B. It's when the cup of tea is served. Lunch has a pot of tea and is drunk throughout. At dinner, the cup of tea appears at the end. James scribbles under the table.

I ask Mrs. B. if she's attending the election tonight. She's surprised: "I leave politics to the men."


## The Perils of Surveys

No word on the meeting last night, and I've been too busy to ask. I'm minding the house while Mrs. B's away attending a two-day course given by the Irish Countrywomen's Association, four or five hours away by bus. I'm flattered she trusts me now with the never-ending vigilance required to clean, feed, and fire the Stanley.

It's the fourteenth of the month, Fair Day. James says it's more modest these days, there's little home weaving, and vans come to the house to buy sheep and cattle. But in winters past, especially between the two World Wars, men came in at dawn, some with animals, some with tweed. Women were even more involved; some supported their families by knitting, and their socks, jumpers, hats, and scarves would be on display for agents from Magee's in Donegal Town and Molloy's in Ardara.

Today I've arranged to meet Ellen Curran there, one of the few women left who is still crocheting lace, or "sprigging," for an international market. On the street, the burst of humanity and animality surprises me. Stalls of novelty hawkers, used clothes dealers, farmers selling sheep, some of which are roughly penned in, some grouped with their faces to the wall like scolded children, crying, bleating, moaning; men and a few women with eggs, butter, vegetables, fish. Tradesmen sell farming and fishing goods such as ropes and mysterious hooks, nets, and long-handled implements. There's a table with bolts of tweed, whether hand-woven or not, I can't tell. Apart from the others, the little woman with the blue mosaic eyes, the one who comforted the lost child at the rectory, is hunched over her wares, three knitted baby caps.

Big companies sell goods from the backs of their vans: Quinns of Killybegs, Cassidy of Dunkineely, McDevitt of Fintown. The once-a-month bank from Killybegs takes a room in one of the houses, so I save myself the two-hour round trip to wire a little more money home.

No school today, and children dance around a man demonstrating a Pinocchio puppet. Heaps of violently colored comic books and strings of plastic toys bring me back to my childhood. Maybe these children imagine themselves dazzling their friends, impressing their parents, becoming known throughout the glens for their skill, all with a piece of orange plastic or a few lead cars.

James's front bar is thronged with men: farmers, fishermen, traders, agents, fellows in for a bit of excitement. Some call for a round of drinks or sit minding a pint, able to calculate its exact location on the packed bar without seeming to look. More have a glass in hand, knowing with certainty whose round is next. The refreshments are their reward for a morning's haggling or selling the wife's brown eggs at the price she's demanded. The rest are writing on badly mimeographed drink-splattered papers with carpenter's pencils or chewed stubs. A few rub out what they've written; those without pencil erasers are spitting and rubbing holes in the paper. Curses are heard.

The Census? The Tillage? Tax forms?

In the snug. Ellen and five other women whom I recognize are writing, too, pencils and pens jabbing at papers on tables sticky with drink slops from their glasses of orange or blackberry. All look cross.

"Here, you that has an education," a large woman calls to me. "It says on this form 'How many friends, relatives or neighbors have called to your house in the past week?' I can't answer that."

"Why not?" I suspect this is a survey being carried out by the British university geography department whose students come here every summer.

"Because some of my friends are my neighbors and some of my neighbors aren't my friends, but some of both are my relatives."

"This isn't *your* survey, is it?" another asks, digging deep pocks in the table with her pencil.

"I don't trust these things," a lady in a hairnet says, "Last year people from an English university came to the door to ask where I shopped, even for things like linens and cutlery. But I got plenty of those when I married, I don't need to buy them. So I said I didn't. I suppose they went back and told all the other English people we don't use cutlery here." One more reason why I'm reluctant to use questionnaires.

The ladies argue about whether each of them is a friend, a neighbor, or a relative to each other, and faulting each for not calling on the other more often. Soon the discussion becomes one of how they're tied to the cooker all day and haven't a moment to think, let alone ...

I ask Ellen Curran about "sprigging," crochet work with a leaf design, and about local embroidery. "Once, most girls embroidered hankies, so they had parties in the evenings. They'd take a bundle to the local agents, shopkeepers, for credit. Eventually they exchanged it for a dress or tea or whatever the shop sold. They were always 'done.' Cheated. If you were owed one shilling thruppence for your work, the shopkeeper credited you with a penny less in the exchange. Women bringing in eggs, the same thing happened to them."

As I leave, they're irritably counting their relatives/friends/neighbors. Back on the street, I see the little woman hasn't sold her caps. They're beautiful featherweight pieces and I buy one for my grown sister's baby.

At Mrs. B.'s, the Stanley is fine, but the pantry is flooded. One of the Cannon twins, Pádraig Twin, runs to find Mattie Jennings, the plumber.

"Pretend I'm not here," Mattie says when he arrives, and bangs away. Around eleven, he appears at the kitchen door looking rather forlorn. Finally, he finishes up. Mrs. B. will be proud of my efficiency.

But no. Two days later, fresh off the Killybegs bus, Mrs. B. shakes her sodden coat with a whip-cracking snap. "The poor devil, he must have been famished."

"Who?"

"Mattie. No one ever set foot in this house without being offered a cup of tea, even if it's only in their hand. I'm good that way."

"But ..."

"It was mentioned on the bus from Killybegs. *Éirigh as!*" She grabs the umbrella and chases a wet dog that slipped in behind her. I want to go with him.

I retreat to James's. He's composing a letter to the *Irish Times* about Carrick's version of the space-time continuum.

He says he's disheartened about the Parish Council: only two people showed up for the election. Later though, Brian calls in to Mrs. B.'s and says the place was empty when he arrived five minutes late. It doesn't surprise him, though; people had avoided it because all James ever talks about these days is "anthropology, anthropology, anthropology" and how much we could learn from the cargo cults of Micronesia.

"Anthropology? That just shows the class of a Parish Council we have," Mrs. B. says. She's still annoyed about the tea.

Not as annoyed, though, as tonight after the pubs close and old Eugene and his fellow storyteller Charles show up at the door. "The other lad is outside in Charlie's car," he says, "the one who can tell Deirdre of the Sorrows in English."

Charlie guides a wool-capped man who teeters up the dark path. Tea is made again and we draw in to the firelight.

"Fadó, fadó, long, long ago, there was a beautiful young woman, daughter of Phelim, the bard ..." He keeps slipping into Irish and has to be herded back. "It was told that ..."

At the end, we sit in silence, feeling the pain of the young woman doomed, even before birth, to the unendurable loss of her beloved.

"I'll say one thing for him," Mrs. B. says when they're gone. "There's none can tell a story like 'Better.'"

# March/Mí an Mhárta 1967

## Whose Map Counts?

Mrs. B.'s lasagne tonight! She's already sent pans of her improved version to others, including relatives up in her home place, Owenteskiny, and further afield into Kilcar. One is old Eugene and Eugene's son Conor, a builder, whom she says is a sweet "dote." Conor has promised to come tomorrow and decorate the bathroom. I know we speak the same language, but I'm related to builders and I've never known one to decorate anything.

Evenings in this house have been lively since Michael Boyle's visit, when I discovered the very different ways that he, James Mary Agnes, and The Perpetual Smile saw the same village main street. I've interrupted my farm mapping to ask other people to help map the street: the shops, houses, meeting places, occupants, and users. Shane, Willie John O'Donnell from Straleel, a woodwork instructor in the vocational school, James, and another publican have sat at the kitchen table with pencil and paper, the back of old wallpaper, to draw.

While people work alone, the relative size of various buildings differs from one person to the next. Each jabs a forceful finger on his drawing to show its accuracy. But whose is "right"? Whose "counts" for more? When people work together, the map is a heated compromise on issues such as where the village ends, who owned some of the buildings in the past, where the first tweed market was, even where the original "main" road and bridge were in the distant past. But what does the "group map" mean? I'm intrigued. Mrs. B. reminds me again that I haven't asked any all-women groups. She issues invitations.

So today seven ladies, including Liz in a back brace, tumble into Mrs. B.'s kitchen in a rush, laughing. "That's a fierce breeze, I'm perished in this light frock"; "It would flay you, sure."

"I'm no scholar," Margaret Cannon warns me. She pulls me to one side. "Many's the time Mrs. B. rapped my knuckles when I was in school. They still hurt when it rains."

They decide to work together, sketching the road over the bridge, then the Bridge Bar, Gallagher's shop and pumps, Gildea's pub, and the Garda barracks. Now they'll run out of paper so they skip to the other end of the village and draw the church and graveyard. Houses and house-shops in the middle are squashed in and then erased through to the bare table. They decide each will draw the middle on smaller sheets and pick the best to transfer to the big map.

I can imagine these women as the schoolgirls they were twenty or thirty years before, serious, careful, hair hanging down in their eyes, absently rubbing one foot against an ankle. Noreen slaps her hand on the table, finished, and soon they all edge their maps to the middle.

"What's this wee building?" Margaret asks Étaín, a student.

"It's Gallagher's, I think," Étaín says. "No, I tell a lie, that's McGinley's pub."

"And on Margaret's map it's twice as large as the wee scrap of a thing I've drawn," Liz says. "But she has Carr's pub very small."

We look at the other mini-maps. None agrees on sizes, except for the post office and the church.

"I see it now!" a dancing teacher, Emer, says. "We're supposed to show what shops we use and what pubs our husbands drink in, right?"

Silence. Then, "No, we're supposed to draw a map of the town," Noreen says.

"Well," Mrs. B. says, "whatever you thought, you've done just as Emer said. The pub is an important place for a woman. She can't go in herself, but her family's money can disappear in it and she can be holding supper till midnight, waiting for himself to come home. She can be sending her child, begging him to come home, or she can be lying in bed, his pajamas beside her, wishing he was there with her instead of up in that place."

The women wait, wide-eyed. Some of the older ones look down. I think they feel Mrs. B. had some experience of this.

"I'm not saying it's true for all of ye," she says, "but you know what I mean. The pub is bigger than it should be for women, who won't go in it. And the shops, sure most of us go to a few shops but you might prefer one because they don't gossip or your mother before you went there. I never went near one shop when I was first married because they were only interested in why I wasn't pregnant."

"That old bitch," Étaín says. "One time she asked my mother why there was so much space between me and my little brother."

"And for pure badness," Emer says, "That pair in the other shop, I don't know who's worse, him or her. I suppose it's him puts her up to it."

"Not at all," Liz says. "She makes the balls and he fires them."

Now each seems embarrassed by her own map's social insights. They exclaim over Mrs. B.'s embroidered napkins, "serviettes." "Lovely," Noreen says. "God forgive me, I sew like a monkey, myself." Over a tea of dainty sandwiches, the talk switches to the hospital closing in Killybegs. Now the nearest one is more than an hour away in Donegal Town.

Emer turns to Mrs. B. "My sister said she thought she saw you going into a shop in Donegal Town but I said no, why would Mrs. B. bother with Donegal Town?" Emer's sister, a dedicated gossip, is known as The Flycatcher,

"Serviettes! I didn't set out enough!" Mrs. B. cries, pulling more napkins out and sending them around the table in a flurry. The women turn their talk to someone named "Betty." "Well, I suppose it's for her own good ..." Noreen says, but looks doubtful.

That evening Mrs. B. says, "Maybe you need young people to do maps for you, too," so over the next few weeks we have visits from groups of children, plus a few elderly people, some newcomers, and a scattering of those who live further out. With teenagers, I explore what occupations some of the boys hope to have. "Welder," "mechanic," "pilot," "doctor" ... I ask them to draw "maps" of the steps involved in reaching their goal. "Learn to fly on one engine," the would-be pilot writes, as his only step. None knows that it's impossible to enter most of the professions with a vocational school education. The few children who go away to secondary school know their steps, even if their parents don't.

Brian Vocational wrings his hands over this, as we draw a different kind of map. I know the village has no official limits, no mayor, and not even a Parish Council at the moment. He shows me that every other unit in Ireland, the county, the school district, the parish, the district electoral division, the barony, even a field, has a boundary. Confusingly, though, for people who want to compare figures, one type of boundary can partially overlap with another type, so, for example, the outlines of the school district and the health district don't match. Our map looks like a messy Venn diagram.

But the village is unbounded, and on people's maps even the buildings are malleable; they start and end in each participant's mind, yet each could recognize the village in a photograph. Most of the children's maps feature their friends, "Máire's house" or "where the twins live" and details of the sporting field, plus a house where a "very cross" dog rests on the doorstep, as evil as a troll under a bridge.

Later, Mrs. B. says, "Sometimes when I asked my students to draw pictures, I learned a lot more about their lives than I wanted to." And that's why I'm doing it, too – to get another sightline, learning from these imaginary maps that contain people's lives.

But am I straying too far from my thesis topic? I put this to James when he arrives at eleven.

"Your thesis topic is just a small star in a galactic cluster. You won't know anything until you get the bigger picture, past and present. Some of it will be relevant, some not."

"Anyhow, your study isn't just about what you want to know. It's also about what we want you to know, and then what we'd like to tell you," Mrs. B. says.

That's me told, as people say here.

## "A Banned Book before I Die"

"A telegram!" Mrs. B. hands me the yellow envelope. I hesitate. Words I'll never forget might be inside.

"CANNOT REACH YOU WOULD YOU EVER GIVE US A SHOUT?" It's signed by the Gaeltarra Éireann official in Dublin, Micheál de hAl. I phone him only to be told by a distracted woman that no one was there, they were moving, would I ring back when they were settled? I know they're moving next year to Furbo, *Na Forbacha*, in Connemara.

I put it aside because there's a tentative tap on the door, and I usher in a reluctant, sheepish-looking group of teenage boys. The younger half are vocational school students, commandeered by Brian. Others are already working and, if they're over eighteen, on the dole at times. I picture this scene ten years from now: some of them will be Americans, some

Australians, some working in England. "A fine soft day," one boy says politely, while another is saying, also as a conversational opener, "That rain would cut the eyes out of your head."

Pleasantries over, I show them the task. Not having to speak to me is a great blessing, and they set to, drawing the buildings rather mechanically. But one young man, Jackie, a house painter in color-splashed clothes, is a slightly older charmer who eggs the others on about their courting haunts. "Show her the ditch where your mother found you with Colette and beat yis both out of it." Bit by bit, like an archeologist brushing sand away to reveal buildings, he brings forth most of the places each thought was secret: in bushes, behind haystacks, inside ruins. They giggle delightedly, since most of them are still working on holding a girl's hand and merely hoard this information for future reference. Most couldn't expose any of Jackie's secrets because he's too canny. But one vocational school student, Felim, catches him.

"You do your courting behind the dancehall in Killybegs," he crowed. "I know, my cousin told me." Even though the dance admission age is fourteen, most of these boys have neither the money nor the social skills to attend, so a lot of what they know is hearsay.

"I don't know your cousin."

"Yes you do. Sheila. Last week in the car to Killybegs, you nursed her," Felim says.

The painter flushes. This is a new one on me. Nursed? The others shout over each other to explain it. "Yes, we club together and hire a taxi to take us to a dance, and if too many pile in, the lads hold the girls on their knees. That's nursing. Jackie nursed Sheila last week."

One boy, younger than the others, weedy-looking, smirking, has said nothing so far. Now, in an adolescent squawk he calls out to Jackie, "Did you get your hand?"

The others are mummified with horror. He's broken so many rules, trying to equal the sophistication of an older, far more charismatic boy, not even being 100 per cent sure what his words mean, saying them in daylight in a neighbor's kitchen, and worst, in the presence of a woman, older, an outsider, maybe even a teacher. It's not possible to mend the situation. After ten minutes of pretending to work on the map, they scrape their chairs across the floor and tumble out the door in a jammed mass, shoving the miscreant roughly from one to another. All because a gentleman, a Catholic gentleman, does not advert to the private place between a woman's legs, let alone talk about touching it, in polite company. Jackie lingers to apologize, and to say he might not be able to "attend" again; he's trying to apprentice to Conor. He says "Conor" with a hushed reverence.

But for all the maps' physical appeal, rolled-up scrolls with meticulously drawn plots and features like fairy rings added in, their real value for me is in the discussion while they're being made: the rationales for choices, the disputes in the group, the resolutions, the memories that attach themselves to buildings and places. Why is one owner considered an "outsider"? How did "Delia" in Chicago get land in Carrick Upper rather than the local heirs? Stories of love, trickery, disputes, triumphs over adversaries all come out.

"But perceptions aren't objective," "Mr. Slippers," the junior manager of the Kilcar factory says when we meet on the street, I with a fresh roll of wallpaper under my arm, he with a shiny briefcase on his way home. True, perceptions can't be quantified, but money can; I don't mention I've heard his landlord overcharges because he doesn't like him.

"I see they haven't run you out yet," he says.

~

Mrs. B. reads in Irish to me, and we finish the night on our knees with the Rosary in front of the Stanley. She knows I'm not a believer, or maybe she doesn't believe I'm not, but saying the prayers gives her comfort, so why shouldn't I join in? She slips in a request for Eugene's son, the elusive Conor, to come and decorate the bathroom.

"Listen till I tell you what I was just thinking," she says rising. "I'd love to read a banned book before I die."

I remember my conversation with my pal from the Trocadero, Seán MacRéamoinn. It doesn't take much to get a book banned in Ireland: one irate person ringing the censor's office. Mothers of ten, priests, people with strong political views, all have a go. The works of Frank O'Connor, Ireland's pre-eminent short-story writer, are on the list for political reasons; others are considered obscene, such as Aldous Huxley's *Brave New World*, Eric Cross's *The Tailor and Ansty*, and Edna O'Brien's *The Country Girls*. The odd thing is Irish-language books are rarely banned, although both the language and its ancient culture are more amenable to forthright speech and ribaldry. Fortunately, as MacRéamoinn explained, many potential complainants don't know their native language. For example, Máirtín Ó Cadhain's Irish-language novel *Cré na Cille*, rejected by his publisher in the 1940s as obscene, was serialized in the *Irish Press* newspaper a year later.

"Which book would you like?" I ask.

"Oh, any one."

I'll send a note to my Trocadero comrades. They're well able to help: I was only in Ireland a couple of weeks when one of them showed me some French photographs that were both shocking and instructive. They think I'm cosmopolitan, almost a Manhattanite. I should carry a U.S. map and a picture of my father wrestling with the raccoons that raid our garbage cans, so they can see my exact geographic and cultural position.


## Enter Conor, Exit Bathtub

Mrs. B. whips a disgruntled-looking fish from her shopping bag and guts it. "I'm having the builders in," she announces as she sweeps entrails into the pantry slop pail.

I've been in Ireland long enough to know that other than news of mortal illness or death, few words are as likely to elicit pity and consolation from the listener.

"Aoife and the children are coming for a holiday in August," she says. I've heard many times about her daughter Aoife's immaculate home. "So I said to myself, 'Why stop with the bathroom?'"

But of course she hasn't started with the bathroom; it's mid-March and Conor never appeared, despite several entreaties. "I need him to fix the taps and get new linoleum for the kitchen floor. I want that underground water pipe checked, I think it's leaking, and the front gate is rusted shut. And someone will sprain an ankle in the drive if I don't get more gravel."

"Who are the builders?"

"Conor. He said he'll come this evening." I take her out to see a friend in Glen, and return to my factory questionnaire. It's seventeen pages, a bit long. But by the time I shorten it and get the results back, I'll have known the area well enough to know what they may mean when they answer the questions. One reason anthropologists stay in the field so long is to learn about the people themselves. Surveys of unfamiliar people, no matter how careful the questions, can lose context and meaning.

At 9:30 a.m., Conor appears. "I'm not really here," he says. He's my age or a little younger, dark blond, with a rosy complexion and the shoulders of a baseball player.

"Hello, Conor," I say.

"Not so bad," Conor replies. "Yourself?"

"Grand," I say.

"Mrs. B.'s been begging me this long while to tackle a few things, but it's only now I have a minute's peace. A woman in Donegal Town has me murdered doing bits and pieces, but I'll give the bathroom a go today."

In less than an hour he's removed the bathtub and some wires preparatory to "doing up" (painting) the bathroom. He calls from above.

"Would you ever see is there any lad going the road could help me take this bath down the stairs?"

I look out.

"James?" I ask.

"God no, he'd spend an hour calculating the angles of the banister."

I look again. Only the young twins across the road who would love the chance to bang a bath down the stairs. Then three fishermen approach in an old car, towing a boat toward Teelin bay. I hold my hand up.

"Could you help Conor McGinley take a bathtub down the stairs?"

They edge the boat to the stone wall and come in. Most men here seem happy to give a hand, but these look glum. I've already heard a bit about depression in this region, and Teelin features in some of the mentions. The men study me closely as they come in, probably not seeing many new faces.

"Good man yourself," Conor calls to the first up the stairs, and after mumbled exchanges they wrestle the bath down and into his van. They leave, and Conor continues working. Like the few other Irish tradesmen I've met, he whistles a vague tune whenever I pass nearby; this is a courtesy to ladies who might have forgotten the presence of a man.

At around eleven, he, like Mattie the plumber, appears meekly in the doorway of the kitchen.

"I met Mattie on the road," he says, rubbing his hands. "He told me that when he was here, it was his first time meeting you." A long pause.

"And?"

"He said you were a lovely girl. Of course."

"That's nice."

"But ... mind you, I wouldn't pass this on, but seeing as it's yourself, I've heard you want to get on here. Mattie said you never asked him had he a mouth on him. He was parched for the drop of tea."

I make tea. Over Conor's second cup he explains a tradesman has to be fed and watered at regular intervals.

"None of this old guff. 'Oh, you'll have a cup of tea, Mattie' and he says, 'No, not unless you're having one yourself' or 'No thanks, I'm just after my dinner,' and you think you've done your duty. No. You say, 'Well, surely you'll have a wee cup in your hand.'" Conor acts out both parts, playing Mattie quite well and awarding me what I think is a John Wayne impersonation that he thinks is an American accent.

"Not at all," he continues. "You shout, 'Your tea's ready, Mattie.' Bread and butter, biscuits, even an egg or a ham sandwich are what's wanted."

"I had a bit of salad I could have ..." I said.

"That wouldn't suit at all. There'd be more goodness in yesterday's newspaper."

Over the third cup, I ask about depression in Teelin. It's good to get local perspectives.

"Depression? You'd have to beat those people down with a stick. They're all day doing nothing but leaning on their spades, singing."

"Those three fishermen didn't seem too happy."

"Why would they? You ruined their day's fishing. They can only fish legally between April and August 18 and they pay Gael Linn thirty pounds a year to do it."

"It's March now," I protest.

"No odds. I said 'legally.'"

"It just took twenty minutes."

"It wasn't the *work*," Conor says. "It was your hair. A red-haired woman is very bad luck for a fisherman. If he meets one on the road, he goes home. That first fellow up the stairs asked me was your color real. They debated it the whole time. The young lad put a shilling down it's dyed."

I try to get enlightenment on another issue. "You said you were going to 'decorate' the bathroom. Decorate?"

"Paint it, what else? I've left a bit of a mess but don't bother your head, I'll be back the day after tomorrow. I have to plough my old lad's field for the potatoes. He won't turn a sod till March and then he'll be out like a demon, wrecking his back if I don't get at it first."

He goes out, but a minute later sticks his head back in the door. "For God's sake," he says, "Never go near Teelin pier when the fleet is going out." I promise. "Or else go at midnight. It's bad luck for fishermen to set foot on that pier at midnight."

I miss talking to people my own age. What must it be like for a young person working on the old parents' moldering patch of farm?

Mrs. B. returns from Glencolmcille just after the postman knocks at the side door with a parcel.

"Here are your banned books," I say, producing *Fannie Hill*, *Lady Chatterley's Lover*, and *The Woman's Home Medical Dictionary*. She leafs through *Lady Chatterley*. "Mmmm," she says once or twice. After an hour or so, she shuts the book. "Well, I can't see what got *that* banned."

## It's a Lonely Washing That Hasn't a Man's Shirt in It

St. Patrick's Day! But it's likely it was our own Niall of the Nine Hostages, on a foray into Roman Britain, who kidnapped and enslaved the young Patrick. "Better" told me this last night when he called to Mrs. B.'s to fill me in on some of Niall's romantic escapades, including having two co-wives. I'm learning a lot, especially that it's better to stay upwind of "Better."

I expected green decorations and later, surely, a parade. Eventually I see James Mary Agnes wearing a sprig of shamrock. He says Kilcar's famous pipe band will perform there later. We'll have something more sedate in Carrick: a dance down in the hall, the only break people get in Lent. "But really, it's only you Yanks that have all that carry on. You can see there's not a sinner out on the street here."

Another telegram when I get home, the same plea for A Shout. I ring Gaeltarra in Dublin but the Galway Irish speaker who answers doesn't understand my American Irish, or, more surprisingly, Mrs. B.'s Donegal Irish. "Better" delivers a huge sack of potatoes and listens, transfixed. When Mrs. B. is in the kitchen, he whispers, "Will you get me a phone for my shop?" He lays a finger alongside his nose, meaning it's not something to be mentioned, and scuttles out.

Later, Mrs. B. says, "He asked was I absolutely sure you're married. I nearly took the umbrella to him." After the wet dog incident, I've noticed the umbrella seems to be reserved for attack; she rarely takes it out in the rain. "And he wanted to know if you were ringing Moscow."

Moscow?

She has a gift of freshly made butter, sent down by old Eugene, who got it from a neighbor. Perhaps this is by way of apology for his son, the missing Conor? "Go you over the road with this to Margaret Cannon. Séamus Twin loves anything I send over."

Most days Margaret's oven sends out a flow of cakes or buns: Queen cakes, fruit scones, sugar-dusted tea cakes, rock buns and chocolate biscuit cake for Shane and the five children. One, Pádraig Twin, is eyeing a tray of shortbread. She hands him the butter and says, "Go up you, and see if Willie John O'Donnell is above in Egan's shop. He'll like this butter on a bit of bread for his tea."

While he's gone, she mentions she hasn't been well, so she slipped up to Father Devlin, the curate, who has a special blessing, an "office." She produces a sealed envelope. "Blessed salt. He puts on his stole and reads something from his missal over it." It's also useful for safe travel in a car or a boat. The fishermen give him a salmon for luck, and he'll give them an office. They'll put it in the bow, with a bottle of holy water.

"Why Father Devlin? Wouldn't you go to the parish priest?"

"Oh, no. It's Father Devlin has the blessing. And every priest who has a blessing has a curse, too. He suffers for the gift."

"And Father Devlin's curse?"

"Drink."

Pádraig Twin returns with the parcel and the butter. "He's not at Tom Carr's, Mammy." Margaret nods. "And I looked at Seán Gallagher's too, and Egan's, but he wasn't there." Margaret's face brightens. "I didn't look at Michael Gallagher's, though," he adds.

"You didn't, of course," she says, satisfied. Pádraig runs off. "I shouldn't say it about one of my own, but he's not the dimmest one on the go." She, like most mothers here, wouldn't rush to speak well of their own young children: "That Johnny of mine, he's a right wee maggot" would be more common. She notices I'm confused, and laughs.

"Willie John would be found in front of Tom Carr's pub, or maybe by Egan's or shopping at Seán Gallagher's, or he wouldn't be found in the village at all. Pádraig didn't look at Michael Gallagher's because he knew he wouldn't be there."

"Why not?" I ask.

"Let me think now. Actually, no one ever explained it to me, no more than I did to Pádraig, but it's because the people from different townlands stand in front of different shops or pubs. Willie's from Straleel. Maybe because some Straleel people used to shop at Seán Gallagher's or drink at Carr's and today they stand there out of habit. You have a good chance of finding somebody if you know where they're from."

"Last Sunday after Mass, in front of James's, I heard some men say to Liam from the vegetable co-op, 'What are you doing here? Go across to your own place,' and they all laughed, James included."

"That's because the group you heard are from Teelin, and Liam is from Glen."

"But when I'm up on the street I might meet James Mary Agnes or Michael anywhere."

"Yes, but you're walking, and you stop to have a chat. I'm talking about people just standing. Men."

"Not women?"

"Never. Do I have time to be standing in front of shops? Do I even have time to go out? I have the boys going the road all the time, fetching my messages for me."

Since I do a lot of Mrs. B.'s fetching, I know a "message" is an item of shopping. I've also noticed that women must have a purpose to be on the street: shopping, going to church, seeing the doctor. Men don't.

I offer to take the butter up to Willie John's. He insists I give half to someone else, perhaps Eugene up in the far reaches of Owenteskiny, because he "has no woman." So I do, and Eugene receives the gift graciously.

"Why would Conor need to take out the bathtub just to paint?" I ask Mrs. B. when I get back.

"Oh, that would be like him. He's very tasty." "Tasty" means doing a neat, nice-looking piece of work. In the last published Census of this area five years ago, only a little over 10 per cent of people had hot water, and about the same number had a "fixed bath." At least we have a bath, but not "fixed."

Tonight I draw a diagram for my professors showing reciprocal exchanges among local people, babysitting in exchange for a lift in the car, and so on. Today, though, it was one way, Eugene to Mrs. B. to Margaret to Willie John to ... Eugene.

James comes in as I'm pondering the diagram. He wags a scolding finger. "I suppose you're thinking of comparing the butter episode to the Trobriand Islanders' Kula ring." He's reading my copy of Malinowski's *Argonauts* now. The islanders circulate symbolic items clockwise and counterclockwise among the islands until each ends up where it started. "I don't want to see any articles on "The Kula Ring of Carrick." I say it never occurred to me. But I can almost see it in the *American Anthropologist*.

He produces a fistful of notebook pages. "The nicknames of everyone in and around Teelin."

"Aren't they a bit personal?"

"Not at all. I sat down with a few of them last night. They want this in your book."

We go through eighty-six households, name by name, from Proinnsías the Bungalow to Doctor Kelly, who looked like a local Doctor, to Biddy Con Johnnie, plus a wonderful family that includes Mickedy, Franco, and Voucher. Some names are in Irish, others anglicized Irish, and others are English with an Irish flourish: the genitive "John a Phlumber," son of a plumber, pronounced "Flummer," from the Irish *an phluiméara.*

"I'm already in trouble with my professors for not sticking to my topic."

"Don't anthropologists think all aspects of culture are interconnected?"

Mine don't.

~

Conor returned three days in a row with his adoring apprentice, Jackie. He's re-plastered the pantry wall, cleaned the chimney, shortened a leg on the kitchen table to fix a wobble, and rewired the one-bar electric fire in the parlor. He didn't paint the bathroom, even though he had the young painter, Jackie, with him. The bathtub still sits in one of the many sheds behind his home place. But over tea and digestive biscuits, he and Mrs. B. agreed on the program of work: the driveway, the taps, the water pipe, the front gate, the bathroom, the new linoleum, the gravel, and they set a starting date of three days hence.

In the weeks since then, he's been as elusive as the Loch Ness Monster. Mrs. B. and I drove past him in Straleel doing a job he took on after his agreement with her. She takes this with equanimity. I miss my bath, or maybe just the idea of a bath, given the freezing bathroom and the need for a sweater in the tub, pulled off for the brief moment when I wash my upper body; or the towel and dressing gown rolled around a hot water bottle, or the leap into the bed previously warmed with hot water bottle number two.

We carry on, using the bathroom sink to wash. ("The Victorians said a true lady could bathe in a teacup," Mrs. B. says.) We sight Conor rattling past in his van with Jackie. One day I flag them down.

"The building trade's slow right now," he says, "so all of us, the sparks, the carpenters, the roofers, use the time to fix up the home place." He didn't say why, if he had so much time on his hands, he wasn't doing Mrs. B's work.

"We sign on for the dole and then start on the turf or maybe fix a stone wall, whatever the Da shouldn't be chancing his arm on. You have to catch the old fellas, they're devils for repairing the thatch or taking the cow to the bull and next thing they're stretched out at the fire with a broken rib."

Another time I find him clearing a drain down the Teelin road for two widowed sisters. "Would you ever look at me," he laughs, heaving shovels of muck. "I served my time under a master builder in Donegal Town. He could turn his hand to anything." But Conor can, too, apparently. Mattie told me that last year Conor built a house single-handedly, "down to the ironing board." But for a big job he draws on a spider web of plumbers, electricians, roofers, stonemasons, and so on, all of whom he refers to as "feckin' cowboys, excuse my French. Except Jackie, here, of course."

When I get home, Mrs. B. says, "Hughdie Phat passed away."

I remember him, a stew of soured tweed, sweat, and turf smoke. But she sounds sorry. Could she be regretting an old, thwarted love? "Is he the man with the big wart? Were you close to him?"

"Me and the likes of him? That one, he'd drink off a sore leg."

I see *The Women's Home Medical Dictionary* beside the breadbox.

"Now, I liked Fanny Hill very much," she says. "But *Lady Chatterley's Lover*! The descriptions! Wonderful. Lady Chatterley was a bit of a madam, though, and I felt very sorry for her fellow, that gamekeeper."

"And? The Medical Dictionary? That section on first aid seems very good."

"Didn't like it."

"No?"

"I always thought you couldn't get pregnant without an orgasm," she continues. "I had five children, so I thought ... But whatever I had, it wasn't what's in that dictionary. All I had was a wee cuddle." This isn't the first time she looked like a sadder, younger version of herself. "It's too late now, sure."

This might be the only time in her life she'll discuss this with some-one, and the person she picks is a disillusioned wife.

Over a late night supper, I say I've heard James thinks his wife Liz hung the moon and stars in the sky.

"Och, aye, and she's the one who brings the birds back to Ireland in the spring. And she thinks the same of him. Imagine him wasting away in a seminary."

"A seminary?"

"You don't get Latin and Greek in engineering. It was the mother's doing, but it was only a junior seminary. He ran into Liz before it took hold. They did a line for quite a few years. His mother wasn't that happy."

"A line?"

"Walking out together. Being nearly engaged."

We mull over this near loss to love. "Do you miss your husband?" I ask.

"*Is uaigneach an níochán nach mbíonn léine ann.* 'It's a lonely washing that hasn't a man's shirt in it.' Do you miss yours?" she asks, but mine is alive.

"I miss Seán," she says. "I missed him even when he was alive. He took a drink." This is the first time she's told me this, although other people have.

"At night, I'd go to bed and hold his pajamas in my arms, I missed him that much. It's something like an ache, it's hard to explain." She opens the door of the Stanley for warmth before we face into the freezing hallway, and in the light, her face looks like a girl's. "Do you know what I mean?"

I remember it, what she means, but I no longer have it. I envy her, a woman of seventy-three who can still feel it.


## Who Stands Where on the Street?

Just when I think I have a minimal grasp of the Irish language, I discover I don't even know how to greet people. This morning I heard Mrs. B.

greeting Manus McLoughlin as "*Awannish*," or something like that. Was it an endearment, something like "alanna" or "asthore"?

"Merciful Hour!" she says, later when I ask. "Me and Manus?" although I know she's tickled when I suggest romance. But she explains she was simply saying his name in its correct form for addressing him. "For Séamus, you say 'A *Shéamuis*,' as I do with James when I speak to him. We use the letter 'A' like the English use 'O' – the way you'd say 'O Lord.'" She then outlines the rules for forming the name, the vocative case, and by the time we finish the table is covered with notes.

If you're lucky enough to have a non-Irish name like Tiffany, it's simple, she says, just put "A" in front of the name. For Irish names, gender counts. For a woman's name beginning with a consonant (except "l," "n," "r," "sc," "sm," "sp," or "st"), you say "A," then insert an "h" after the first letter, so "Maíre" becomes "A Mháire." The fun begins with men's names, but by then she's lost me. I think of the Irish Americans who say, "Oh, you bet your boots I can speak Irish," and then offer something like "Faith and Begorrah!" or "Top of the morning!"

I decide I'll just nod when I meet someone. And the next person I meet is "Better." He wants to talk about the evils of Russia and communism. For many years, worshippers prayed for the conversion of Russia at the end of every Mass, until a recent Papal decree ended it. "Better" says it's clear the poor Pope is in the hands of Moscow's communists, and he's written to the Bishop about it. He's also written to the Department of Posts and Telegraphs about getting a telephone for his shop. They fob him off. But here's an Irish speaker, just trying to make a living. James says he's heard that "Better" mixed up the two envelopes, but even so, shouldn't the government take an interest?

~

Another day, another telegram. I try to phone Gaeltarra again, but in putting me through to himself, the woman cuts me off and from then on the line is engaged. I ask in the factory. They shrug.

It's a long trip to Dublin, but I know Mrs. B. worries about the phone bill, seeing the telephone not as an instrument of communication so much as a potential source of bankruptcy. She's stiff with fear as the seconds tick away, and although I leave money beside the phone, we know an inexplicably complex and stupendous bill will arrive.

For now, though, I reflect on people's kindness, even if I can't address them properly. Word goes out that I'm collecting cures. Máire Beirne of Teelin, Máire Johnny Johndy of the long black hair, tells me "Put spit on your eyebrows to stop 'pins and needles.'" A Kilcar man gives me a toothache cure: you bite a live frog's leg until it squeals. And Mrs. Doctor says when people here are sick they send for cream crackers, then the orange drink, Lucozade, then a healer, then the priest, and finally the doctor when it's almost too late. In between visits from a bonesetter and a seventh son of a seventh son, I talk to so many farmers in Kilcar and Carrick that a new word goes out: I'm from the Agricultural Advisory Service.

~

I'm still intrigued by the insights maps can produce. One night when Shane and James arrive, I display a large map, primitive, but suited to my needs, that I've drawn of the village street.

"I need to know who stands where in the village," I say.

"That's difficult to answer. We have an obvious leadership vacuum at the moment. Leo is too careful and nice, and Owen, well, a fine man, but he can get a bit intoxicated by his own grandeur ..."

"*Níor bhris focal maith fiacail riamh,*" Shane says. A good word never broke a tooth.

"I mean who stands where on the street," I say. "Margaret told me groups of people tend to stand in front of different places. Can you show me this on the map?"

James's interest is piqued: my question throws the old, familiar street groupings into a new and exotic anthropological light.

"The hotel." James takes my pencil and marks a corner. "Men from Teelin stand in front. The owner's ancestors are from Teelin." He moves the pencil further along. "Tom Carr's Undertakers and pub: people from Bogagh and Straleel. A Bogagh man married into that pub."

Shane moves the pencil to the other side of the street. "Mona Gildea's: people from this side of Straleel and from Carrick Upper. Michael Boyle stands there. And this one, Michael Gallagher's, people from the road out to Glen." Slowly, we fill the spaces.

"And I saw people standing in front of Joe Gallagher's shop," I say.

"They're buying something. They could be from anywhere. Otherwise, they stand where we told you. It's like an extension of their own community, like the way a tourist might visit his legation when he's abroad."

"And they don't change?" I ask.

"No, unless someone wants to talk to a man in another group about something concerning him or his people. Or maybe a man might see a distant connection stepping out from his group and go to speak to him ..."

"As a visitor in a friendly camp," Shane says. "But he won't stay long."

"What are they doing while they're standing?"

"On Sundays, the pubs are open from twelve to two, and they're getting news, putting the world to rights, setting the cat among the pigeons, waiting for their dinner at home, or recovering from the dinner, because the pubs open again from four to ten. They talk about things they might not talk about at home."

"What about weekdays?"

"You wouldn't get so many, except on a Fair Day or a funeral. But if you're looking for someone on the off chance he's around, you'd go first to the place he stands on Sundays," Shane says.

"What about those old fellows in front of the Central Bar every day?"

"Just waiting to see who gets off the bus," James says. "Or waiting with someone who's waiting for the bus. There's three a day."

"Now," he says, flipping the paper over and starting a new map. "You'll want to record where they stand when they leave Carrick."

"All I know is where people go when they can't buy what they want in their own village. Glencolmcille people come here to Carrick to shop, and Carrick and Kilcar people go to Killybegs, and Killybegs people go to Donegal Town. If all else fails, they all go to Donegal Town."

"Exactly. But where do they stand when they get there?" James grins and jabs the map with the pencil. "People from Carrick go to a particular pub in Killybegs, and people from Kilcar go to a different one. When they travel further on, to Donegal Town, Carrick and Kilcar people go to the same pub. This isn't unusual. The same thing probably happens to people a little north of us, say in the townlands outside the two villages of Ardara and Glenties. And by the time Ardara and Glenties people finally reach Donegal Town, they might end up in the one pub, too, just as we and Kilcar end up together in ours." James sketches a sort of flowchart, with branches fanned out among the townlands, and coming together as they move away from home.

"And when all of them, all the people from southwest Donegal go to Dublin, they go to the North Star Hotel." Shane slaps the table. "You know, I never gave much thought to this before. And then when Donegal people go to London ..."

"Yes, and by the same token, when they go to America, they go to Butte, Montana," James says, since that's where Shane was born, to Donegal parents. "Well, a lot did, anyhow, and some to Mauch Chunk, Pennsylvania, and to Illinois and ..."

"I wonder where people up in northern Donegal, say in Gweedore, go when they go to Dublin."

"We don't know," James says, irritated. "They think they've got a little paradise on earth up there; they don't leave it except to work in Scotland." Gweedore is resented here because it's a favorite with the government, speaking Irish non-stop.

Shane looks tired. "I know all this, I do these things myself, but *how* do I know them?"

Once again: the thing about anthropology is that it unearths things that people know but don't know how they know.

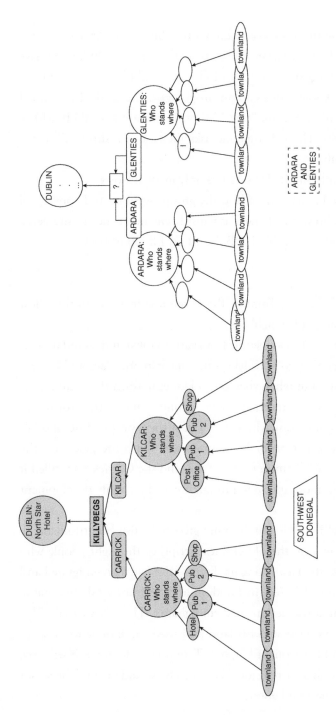

Figure 1. Divisions and Alliances: Affiliation and Association Patterns of Two Donegal Areas.

Note: The diagram on the left shows general socializing and shopping affiliation patterns for Carrick and Kilcar. Ardara and Glenties would show a similar pattern, although their destinations would be different. A diagram showing boundaries of parishes, school districts, medical and postal services, and so on, would not usually correspond to the boundaries shown here, so if an issue arises in relation to one of those units, the affiliations will be different.

Where I come from, everyone knows the difference between a small tree, a bush, and a shrub, even if they're all the same height and all have flowers. These categories don't exist in botany, and it's difficult for us to explain how we know. But as an anthropologist, I've worked it out: if I see a central trunk, I'll think "tree." If not, I decide if it's wild (bush) or cultivated (shrub). Then if someone asks me to buy a shrub, I'll come back with a shrub.

I share this with Shane. He says I've only made it worse.

As we sketched a diagram of how the groups separate and converge, I had a hunch. Who would I check it with? I remember the county development officer, the agreeable Pat Bolger. I say I'll report back.

I also arrange to meet big Tommo, the warehouse manager in the Kilcar factory, and some of his neighbors.

They agree that in Kilcar, people from various townlands stand in separate places. When they go to Killybegs they meet in one place and Carrick people in another, but when they get to Donegal Town they join forces. In Dublin, they tend to meet, as Shane Cannon said, in the North Star Hotel. They may stay somewhere else, but if they want to find another southwest Donegal person or leave a message, that's the place. It's the same story Margaret Cannon first told me, and the Carrick men filled it in. Now I'm even more interested in talking to the county development officer.

After his neighbors file out, Tommo gives me a list, beautifully handwritten in *Cló Gaelach*, the old classical script, of the eight people who left the factory in the past two years. Four of the five men emigrated and are conductors and laborers in London, and Séamus, a talented handweaver, works in construction in Birmingham. "The last weaver of his line," Tommo says. "He sold his land and used the money to move to England." Two of the women left, too. Tommo says he himself will stay, although he hates his current job. "No one else would take it," he says. I wait, but he says he's said enough.

Before bed Mrs. B. and I exchange the news of the day. I mention "Better" is writing to the Bishop about communist spies.

"Aye. He thinks you're one."

# April/Mí Aibreáin 1967

## The Archbishop of Canterbury Embraces the Pope

A note from my father about the Morris. He's not happy about my tappets. They should be twelve-thousands of an inch. And another scrawl on the back from Patrice. I've heard she's saved for weeks to go on a school field trip, but the other kids laughed at her orange poncho and no one would sit with her on the bus. I'm not to tell my mother.

I look up to see Conor outside, picking at the paint on the pantry door.

"Hello, Conor."

"Mighty," he says.

I wait.

"I hope you won't be offended if I ask you something," he says. "Would you give the cow a shot?"

"What?"

"It's just that I'm stuck, everyone's out cutting turf, and I can't stand to hurt an animal. I can't even get a shot myself. So I thought, you being a doctor," he says.

"I'm not ..."

"I know, I know, you're not a doctor yet. But surely to God you must have learned *something* by now. And the cow's roaring."

"What about Jackie?"

"Jackie looks up to me."

Well, we couldn't disillusion him.

He propels me out the door and into the van. "She's a wild lassie, she can get through most fences. There's an old saying: '*Bíonn gach duine go lách go dtéann bó ina gharraí.*'" He waits while I struggle to work this out: "Everyone is nice until a cow gets in his garden?" I get a thumbs up.

At the house, he hands me a syringe. "She kicks. I'll stand by the legs." He points to a spot. "Just slip the needle in." He faces away and strokes a flank.

I jab the syringe into the coarse brown hair. It bounces back. I try again. And again. "What is this?" I demand.

"Cowhide, what else?"

Finally, he grimaces, eyes squeezed shut, and grips my elbow. Together we force the needle in.

"A skilled butcher would have got some briskets off that animal with less to-do," he says, rubbing my palm, then soothing the cow, hushing its lament.

"You're aglow," Mrs. B. says when I get back.

"It's sweat from cow-wrangling," I say, but I can see that sounds unlikely.

She stands barefoot, halfway in a lilac watered-silk dress, with hat and veil to match.

"For the wedding," she says. "I had it made in Donegal Town. You can do nothing here only someone sees it. My son Fergus is getting married to a Belfast girl. A Protestant."

I know. Margaret said Mrs. B. came to her, weeping, at the news.

"I was so mithered, all I could think of was what people would say. But Father Devlin put it right."

"How?" If your family escapes those great stigmas of illegitimacy, tuberculosis, mental illness, or your son leaving the priesthood, there's still disgrace if one of your kin marries outside the church. In my family, a beloved uncle was considered dead by many of the adults when he married a Protestant.

"By the time Fergus arrived from Dublin for a visit I was resigned. I said, 'You must go up to the priest for your Letter of Freedom, you need that from your own parish to marry.' Fergus doesn't have much time for the church, but up he went anyway and said, 'Father, I'm getting married. Unfortunately, it's to a Protestant.' And Father Devlin said, 'Man dear, what do you mean, 'unfortunately'? Did you not see the photo in the *Donegal Democrat*? The one of the Archbishop of Canterbury embracing the Pope?'"

"So it's all right now?" I ask.

"Yes, she's a lovely girl, I couldn't ask for better. You're invited to the wedding."

In the shop a few days later I meet The Flycatcher. "Fergus marrying a Protestant!" she cries. "I hope you're not going. People wouldn't like it."

"But Mrs. B. says she's very ..."

"Well, it won't work. My niece was engaged to one and he actually converted."

"Well, that was something, anyhow."

"No. The devil, he stopped being a Catholic on the honeymoon."


## The Irish Word for Homesickness

Revolution!

To the innocent, Carrick and Kilcar look like storybook villages, but they were once Irish Civil War battlefields, and who knows, they may be again.

Unbidden, two elderly brothers living only doors apart, Manus McLoughlin and his brother Eoin, tell me their stories of fighting on opposite sides in the Civil War, 1922–23. Each insists I talk to the other, too, and in fairness, also to a nearby shopkeeper who served in the Royal Irish Constabulary, the British-administered police force that preceded today's Garda Siochana. All three would have been enemies at the time.

Manus joined the Republican Army, fighting for independence for all thirty-two counties in Ireland. Eoin belonged to the Free State Army, which accepted the British offer of dominion status for twenty-six. Manus was captured, injured, in Dublin. His brother visited him in hospital and begged him to quit. Later, while Manus was imprisoned, his house in Carrick was burned by Free Staters, but a Republican group burned down the landlord's lodge and the Coast Guard house. The landlord's big hotel had already been burned down in the earlier pre-Civil War "Troubles."

The two main political parties today reflect this division, the Free Staters usually in the Fine Gael political party, and the Republicans in the Fianna Fáil party. Carrick is almost evenly divided; Kilcar leans more toward Fine Gael. Kilcar's own elected Dáil member, Fine Gael's Miceál Óg McFadden, had a major role in bringing the factory to Kilcar. Even so, anger festered: the factory's opening, with its nine employees, a mix of parties, was marred by riots and burnings over "political" hirings.

As I try to plot out the possible political leanings of a new Parish Council and any implications for development efforts, a new revolution occurs. Like many coups, it came about in a deceptively simple way, or else an elegantly complicated way. An unannounced meeting was held and it was decided, by whom it isn't clear, that instead of having a Parish Council, the group should be a Post-Primary Education Headmaster's Committee. The only post-primary education institution in the area is the vocational school, so that ruled out the headmasters of the various primary schools, except it didn't: some were invited, others not. Some people were teachers, others weren't. By the end of the third meeting, the group was no longer a Post-Primary Education Committee but a Development Committee. However, it was still teacher heavy.

"What do teachers know about development?" an attendee, Shane, one of the primary school headmasters himself, complained to me the next day. But officers were elected, including Leo McLoughlin as chair, the role he held once on the Parish Council. This committee now represents the community.

I go to see James, who has bits of anchor strewn across the bar. He issues a shocker: "I'm re-forming the *old* Parish Council and people can be on it or the so-called 'Development Committee,' but not both." He looks rather imperial.

Later, Shane says the new development committee is intended to have a broader area representation in addition to the usual suspects, so some non-locals were invited last night. "It was very democratic."

"How? It was a closed meeting."

"Well, a vote was taken. But why wasn't James included?" he wonders.

"And why weren't you?"

I'm torn professionally between the desire to be involved so I can see how things develop and the realization that not only would I be studying a village with an anthropologist in it, as anthropologists always do, but studying community development while being one of the leading actors. I point this out, loftily, to Shane. He leaves, perhaps to re-enter the fray.

Later, he returns, fraught.

"James has demanded the minutes of the new development committee meeting. He says he has a hotline to the secretary of the Department of Finance, T.K. Whittaker, 'Ken' he calls him, if you don't mind. He says they have an agreement to inform one another of new developments." He darts off.

Out of pure mischief, I ring Brian Vocational to ask what's happening.

"I can't talk," he says. "I'm painting with fast-drying paint."

Within five minutes, he slips in. "It wouldn't do for me to be heard on the line. What's this I hear about the secretary of the department? It's very worrying. The secretary takes his summer holidays here and it could be he takes a drink in James's pub."

"James says he's also a friend of the new Minister for Industry and Commerce, Mr. Colley," I tell him. "He may involve them both."

Brian stubs out his just-lit cigarette and lights a new one.

"I suppose he should be on the committee, then?" I ask.

"No! If we want lessons in anthropology we can get them from you with less blather," he says. "That reminds me, would you ever think of giving a talk to the vocational school students? You could explain anthropology. Most of the poor devils will be emigrating to England soon enough; you can prepare them to deal with the natives."

Things degenerate and divisions abide: one committee member refers to another as "the community eunuch, always trying to do things he can't," while the latter describes the first as "never letting his left hand know what his right hand is doing." They both describe a third as so hapless he could "mess up tuppence."

It's not right to be as fond of a Parish Council/Post-Primary Education Committee/Development Committee, and so on, as I am. I think they're brave, true, and steadfast. In the old 1940 Parish Council minutes, not only were the issues and discussions the same as today's, but the names were, too; Manus McLoughlin, the Civil War veteran, was elected chair. Today's group contains some of their identically named sons and grandsons.

One morning after I harvest more versions of the committee saga in Gallagher's shop, Seán apologizes for giving me four pounds nineteen shillings in change when I buy a newspaper.

My stars have realigned: the public phone box is empty, it's free of drunks' pee, the vandalized cord has been repaired, and for once I might have enough coins to phone home.

"What's wrong?" my mother shouts in her real voice, not her phone voice. She says everything's fine, really. My father has a "little touch" of emphysema, but he's doing good.

Willie John over in Straleel has emphysema. I've heard his wracking cough. I don't think emphysema comes in touches.

"Is it bad?"

"Just the one lung. A bit in the other." My mother comes from a tubercular family and even a wheeze is bad news. "When he goes back to work he hopes they'll give him something lighter."

The old clock in the dining room chimes. I realize it's six a.m. there. "I'm sorry I woke you."

"It's fine, I was almost out the door. I've been doing a little work in the school cafeteria."

"I'm coming home," I say. The pips sound. I'll be cut off soon. The street outside looks alien.

"You can't. He's so proud of you, his friends come over for coffee just to hear about you and that car. They're worried about your tappets. And he's got all your maps on the kitchen wall. I think he'd die of shame if you gave up."

The final pips go. I step out of my mother's dining room and back into Ireland and *cumha*, the Irish word for homesickness.


## The Mapper

There's a phrase in Irish, *trí na chéile*; even people without any Irish use it: "treena kayla," they say. It covers a variety of brain fogs: confused, all over the place, unable to focus. That's me since I talked to my mother. My mind is like a trapped bird, never settling. I phone again. She says she loves working in the cafeteria. That can't be true: she believes it's a "privilege" to stay at home, the first woman ever in her family to be able to.

I ask Mrs. Doctor about emphysema. She a plain speaker; it's progressive and shortens the sufferer's life. As I leave, I try to break the mood by mentioning that my mother believes tuberculosis or any lung disease increases sex drive, although she wouldn't use those specific words. Mrs. Doctor says it's true, but the poor devils deserve some kind of distraction.

Now what? The development committee loses some of its fascination. I turn to land tenure.

People here don't talk openly about land or stock or yields, which is why the agricultural sections of the Census of Ireland are worked out by the Gardaí. Everyone is happy with that except, perhaps, the Census officials. In my many discussions with farmers, I've asked about farming, but not their own farms. This is how I got my name as the best agricultural advisor around.

But it's taken me this long, three months in, for Michael Boyle to find time to talk to me about inheritance. He's an extraordinary man, intelligent, generous, and intent that anything in my thesis about local farming will be correct down to the last rood and thruppence. He's already volunteered detailed information on his own farm: for example, his income from the sale of wool and the few "beasts," cattle; his wife's income from knitting and egg sales; his income as one of the stewards for part of the estate; and his dole income ("Not the 'soap money,'" he says, which is the dole some get by eating soap and then going to the dispensary for a "sick letter" saying they can't work.) It's a living, but not much left over.

What I need to know now, though, is whether people are passing their land along to heirs or selling it once they get a chance to work at something else, just as the government hopes. If they are, it's far more likely to be happening in Kilcar, with its factory jobs, but I need Carrick for comparison. Kilcar is only three miles away, but for hiring purposes, it could be the other side of the moon. And are there any heirs who are just "stuck" with the farm? Can they sell? Do they?

Michael arrives late one night after a day's work. James is with him, "to keep me honest," he jokes, but I suspect James is really there as a witness to Michael's discretion, should anyone accuse him later of passing on private information. I want to begin with the eighteen plots in the townland of Carrick Upper where Michael lives, because he and his father know the histories of each in great detail. But James points to my notebook, indicating I should take dictation, and pulls out a brown envelope with inky scrawls on the back.

"The Ideals of Land Inheritance," he recites. "One: The family should provide the means of acquiring a living: land, money, or education for every child of the household. But the land itself goes to one heir.

"Two: Land should go to an heir who will actually work it or use it as a part of his livelihood. The eldest heir who can do this has preference.

"Three: The land should not 'leave the name': preferably, the heir bears the family name, or the farm 'keeps' the name."

He puts the envelope carefully into his top pocket, perhaps thinking others may want it in future.

Michael looks at him, flummoxed. "I said these were the *ideals*," James says.

"Maybe in Tipperary, or where Eileen comes from, but not here," Michael says. "My own Da, 'a stranger,' married into the farm. He was young and still able when his oldest boy was grown, so I got it. I'm the youngest. Fair enough, though; a man who marries late might pass the land on to the oldest."

Some plots are what he calls "wee stripes";[1] long narrow strips containing some arable, some grazing, and some rough land. Once a man who had a very long stripe was summonsed for making poitín but pleaded that he could not possibly be held responsible for others' mischief on a farm a mile long. He was fined six pounds, nonetheless. Michael points to one small patch marked "Likely to Flood" on the ordnance survey map. It's owned by sixteen people: three, including himself, own two-thirds of it, and the others own the rest. A man usually has rights to bogland, too. Now it's clearer that every one of these types of land might have its own history, bitterly contested perhaps, as well as heirs with their own complicated histories. My simple table is useless.

---

1 "Stripes" comes from "stripping," the word used in Donegal when an earlier settlement and land-use pattern, rundale, was replaced with these "stripes." Map 4 shows a stripe pattern.

So a "plot" and a "farm" are not the same thing: a "farm" can consist of a number of scattered plots or holdings, and each bit could possibly have been acquired in a different way – say, inheriting some parts and buying others. Or the bits could have passed down together. Today, the eighteen plots in Carrick Upper are held by sixteen owners, each from eight to eighteen acres. Not all are farmed.

And I have to analyze many more than these sixteen, for both Carrick and Kilcar. If I had stayed with my husband, right now I could be making suburban party canapés of Ritz crackers and pineapple chunks with little flags representing American football teams stuck in them.

But the two men continue calmly, marking each plot with a number, knowing which one is the heart of the farm and which one is merely a wee stripe of grazing. They list the various occupiers today, and if each is not the official holder, their relationship to him, although a couple of owners are women. To see if today's pattern is unusual, they work back to previous generations, at least two, and sometimes as many as four, spanning a hundred-year period. I could go back even further if I visited the Irish Valuation Office in Dublin, but their records won't explain the relationships between owner and heir, so I'd still have to ask these men to tease them out.

We work until 12:30 a.m. Mrs. B. had given us tea at eleven. Afterward, James watched her nervously, thinking we might all be corralled onto our knees, but she's retired to her room, Rosary in hand.

"I'm off, so," Michael says. "Long day. I've the whole mountain land walked, looking for new lambs to bring in, and the ewes brought down to build them up."

"No cows out yet," James says.

"Not for another month, thank God. Still in the barn. I'm out cutting turf all day but at least I've got the spuds kibbed, and the onions and cabbage."

"Kibbed?" I ask.

"A word from the old days. It means the potatoes are planted with a *cibín*, a flat blade with a wooden handle. But I use a regular spade because

I'm planting a half acre. I saw Con Cassidy down in Teelin using a *cibín* the other day because he's not putting down as much."

"I know Con," I said. I'd seen him digging his plot and asked him to explain the potato cycle. He spent hours giving me the history and the practice. I show them some sketches Con's drawn now, the ridges made by running a spade along a length of string, the seed potatoes set down and covered, page after page of notes and drawings illustrating a year of growing and storing.

"Con? You asked Con to tell you about farming? That's a good one," James says.

I feel I must defend Con. It's a pity about these local rivalries.

"That's like asking Picasso for a discourse on how to change a fuse," James says. "Con and his cousin Frank are famous fiddlers. People come from all over the world to hear them and interview them."

So I'm dragging men out of the bog after a hard day's work, and hounding internationally known musicians about planting potatoes.


## The Ruined Poet

My head feels like it's been put through a pencil sharpener, and I think I've swallowed a rasp. I'm packing for Fergus's wedding in Belfast when Mrs. B. comes in. "Child of God! You can't go out and you with a throat." I'm disappointed; the wedding was to be the bright spot of my time here, a happy release after the dark winter. And I know my company meant a lot to her, cocking a snook at the local gossips. She goes off on the bus, a brave lone figure with her new dress and our wedding presents in a little bag.

Ladies visit my bedside with cream crackers, Lucozade, and an envelope of blessed salt from Father Devlin. If my research on local cures is correct, I've skipped a step, so the next event should be a visit from the doctor, and right enough, when my fever reaches 103 over a few days,

Margaret, who's tending the Stanley, gets Mrs. Doctor. "A change in the weather is what has you as are," Mrs. D. says. At 104, a Navaho curing chant takes over:

My body restore for me,
My mind restore for me ...[2]

On the sixth day Tommo sends a boy. "He's says he's got a few of the old lads to do your maps, Miss. They want to hear what you're doing from your own mouth."

Margaret is shocked; "Does he know the lady has a throat?"

I've explained my work many times now, but so often "the lads" and everyone else here have explained their situation to politicians and academics who arrive with preconceived notions and leave with the same ones. These men want to make sure I understand.

So I go, making my way through the Fair Day crowd, calling in to the once-a-month bank to wire money home.

Happily I walk.
Feeling light within, I walk ...

A purple-faced, apoplectic figure appears before me. "Get back into your bed!" James hisses. "Back!"

In Kilcar, Tommo says he's told "the lads" about the government's plan, but they don't believe him.

Soon we're joined by a bulldozer of a farmer, a six-foot-something brick. The Fear Ruadh, The Red-Haired Man, shares his official name with a quarter of the parish but can be distinguished by his wiry stand of hair. Immediately behind him is a gaunt, wary-looking old man who is introduced as "A." I'm curious: how is that spelled? "A-o-d-h," he says. "A."

---

2 William A. Lessa and Evon Z. Vogt, 1958.

I explain the government's plan and my study. "Do those boyos in Dublin think we all came down in the last shower?" The Fear Ruadh roars. "The factory's been here years, but all these government factories make a loss. It could go wallop and then where would I be if I'd sold?" Aodh agrees. This is yet another example of government stupidity.

Tommo waves us to the big kitchen table. Clothes dry on the line above the grey cast-iron stove. I spread out the ordnance survey maps of Crowkeeragh, Crowanrudda, Bogagh Glebe, and many of the other townlands in Kilcar. Cracked voice, I show how Michael and James filled in the Carrick maps, which land is being farmed by owners, and which has been left fallow, rented, or sold. I remember Michael's reaction the first time he saw the maps, checking them with exquisite care and finally marveling over their accuracy. The Kilcar men's reaction is different: if a man like Michael Boyle thinks the maps are genuine, it's good enough for them. They choose two townlands and set themselves the task of bettering his speed and breadth of detail.

An attractive young woman comes in from the pantry and leaves a tea tray with thick white mugs. "My daughter, Bríd," Tommo says. She motions me into the kitchen and gives me a powerful hot whiskey.

She's a trained teacher, twenty-seven, and until recently she taught in London. She's the only daughter in a family of brothers, and although they live in Kilcar, she was expected to come home when her mother broke her hip. "So this is where I've ended up."

She slips upstairs and returns with a biscuit tin of odd scraps and pieces of paper. "They say you're writing a book. Would you look at these poems and tell me if they're any good?"

I start reading and she cries out, red-faced, "Not here! I'd be too embarrassed!" But I can't stop. They're filled with longing, desire, waste, self-reproach. I shouldn't ask but I do: "Are they written for a particular person?"

Yes, she says, they're written long after the event, about a man she'd once thought she might have been in love with but had been too shy to return his attentions. She'd been nervous of local gossip. She slips the tin under some ironing.

"Nervous?"

Yes. She says a long time ago she and Cáit in Carrick had formed a group, a club for young single people like them, teachers, nurses, civil servants. "We went on little excursions to places like Donegal Town and Sligo. We met to listen to music. Then word got around we were 'loose.'

"They say Cáit and I let our names down. It's not forgotten, but I still can't see what we did wrong. I felt ruined, and this place was ruined for me." London had come as a longed-for release. She warns me to be careful.

A shout from the other room. "Bríd!"

"Maybe you could teach here, anyway?" I ask.

"And be like Cáit? She works part time, nursing, but her father still stands on the doorstep at six, waiting for her to make the tea."

"A lot of 'strange names' moved into Kilcar in the last twenty years or so," Tommo says when I go back in. "Some of them married local girls and live in the village. Or farmers sold them little bits and pieces for a house site." But the big sale of land the government hopes for hasn't happened as men went into the factory.

As we finish the map, Tommo shouts again for Bríd. "Will you clear this clatter of mugs away, there's a good girl."

When I get home, Mrs. B. is back from Belfast, delighted with the wedding. I've missed a telephone call from Gaeltarra, she says. After the most recent inexplicable bill, she's convinced she's paying for incoming calls as well as those we make, so I ring from the public phone box. The woman tells me to ring back when someone's there.

"You'd nearly need to go up to Dublin yourself," Mrs. B. says. We spend the evening parsing the wonderful wedding. She glows with happiness: the bride's people welcomed her with open hearts.

Tonight in bed, bits of Bríd's poems drift in and out of my sleep. I wonder if the loved one even knew of her interest.

# May/Mí na Bealtaine 1967

## Blessing the Parish Priest

This morning Mrs. B says, "Well, that's a relief. The fire's still going from last night. Our lives are saved."

"Saved?"

"The first person to light a fire today, May Day, *Bealtaine*, will die within the year."

Spared for another while, we walk up to the village, she to brazen any wedding gossip and I to get more Lucozade, because "You're just after recovering from that throat."

The Flycatcher pounces as we round the corner to the street. "You were seen going away," she says to Mrs. B. "Yes, I went to Belfast," Mrs. B. says. "Won't you congratulate me on my new daughter-in-law?"

"Indeed I won't," The Flycatcher says, her overpermed hair vibrating with indignation. "Couldn't he have married one of his own? He let you down. He let Carrick down. He let Donegal down." We march on, admiring people's front windows with May altars to the Virgin Mary, decorated with the mayflowers and marshmallow stems that little girls have gathered.

Mrs. B. insists on braving her walk alone, and I return to find Conor and Jackie in the house, cutting a large square of linoleum from the pantry floor so they can match it.

"You washed your face in the morning dew today," Conor announces. I'd forgotten; the early dew of May 1 is supposed to give women a radiant complexion. I turn away and straighten the framed picture of the Sacred Heart in the kitchen.

"It's crooked," he says. "You have a parallax problem."

"What?"

"*Nigh do chluasa*! Wash your ears! The apparent displacement of something caused by the actual change of the observation point," he says. "The angle." Jackie looks weak with admiration. He takes the sample to the van.

I may not have explained to Conor that, mathematically, I've never advanced beyond that tedious algebra pair, "a" and "b," forever swimming upstream and down. I wait.

"In layman's terms, you think the picture is straight but when you move to a new spot it looks crooked. Parallax. See?" He stands behind me and moves me a few feet away.

I adjust the picture a little. A lot of anthropological research depends on observation.

"But don't detain me, I'm off to mound the Da's potatoes and cut the turf before he can get dug into it. He's like a bag of weasels this weather." Thanks to Con Cassidy, I don't have to ask. Mounding involves piling manure up around the young plants on the neat ridges to protect them.

"Would it be cheaper to buy potatoes?" I ask.

"To *buy* potatoes?" he cries, and he's off. I write down his words: "The apparent displacement ..."

Today, I phone Gaeltarra Éireann again and the same woman asks if I don't remember she's just after telling me to wait until someone's there?

I've decided it's not my fault Dublin has become part of my field now. I'll give Gaeltarra "a shout" in person. And I have a note from Alf MacLochlainn at the National Library saying he's holding some interesting material for me. I'll call in to Dónall Ó Móráin at Gael Linn, too. Mrs. B. would like some new banned books.

James arrives, ostensibly to discuss the latest news from the development committee. He's not a member, but he seems to know more about what's going on in the meetings than some of the members, which is still very little. As he's leaving, I assume he might apologize for shouting at me on the street, but instead he winks and leaves some blueprints for what seem to be the anchor he's inventing. I can see he's an engineer.

Mrs. B. is excited enough about my trip to suspend her fury at The Flycatcher. "I'll go part of the way with you and visit my daughter in Cavan," even though she now has the throat I had and "a head." To save time tomorrow we'll cross east into Northern Ireland, then across the border back south into the Republic. We'll return the banned books she's finished, but just as she's about to retrieve the last, Lady Chatterley's Lover, kept under the cushion of her armchair for easy re-reading, she's startled by a noise.

"It's the parish priest!" she cries, looking out. "Saying goodbye. He's retiring back to his home place in Gweedore tomorrow. And the Holy Water font is dry!" She darts into the pantry, rustling in a cupboard and muttering until she finds a bottle and refills the font by the kitchen door. "Do you think he'll know I have that book under my cushion? He will," she decides.

She'll be sitting on it, and I can't see him searching under a lady's backside.

We shepherd Father Bonner toward the parlor, but he insists on sitting in the kitchen: "No priest should expect special treatment in this day and age," he thunders. Mrs. B. waves him to the best chair, her own, as all good Irish women would.

"Will you have a cup of tea, Father?"

"No, no, I'm just after my dinner, I won't have anything."

"A wee cup in your hand, just? You will, of course!" She waves me toward the Stanley. "Eileen makes a lovely cup; she's more Irish than the Irish themselves now." This is news to me; usually she won't let me near the tea. I always omit a crucial step: either I haven't stored the empty teapot on the Stanley to keep its ceramic belly properly warm or I don't measure the tea correctly or I take the boiling kettle to the teapot rather than the other way around, or I forget to let the leaves brew, stir once, and then brew it a little more without letting it get bitter, or I forget the little strainer ...

Mrs. B. cat-watches the priest. Will he reach under the cushion to remove an uncomfortable lump? She distracts him with an uninterruptible update on her children's recent activities.

Finally, he shakes our hands and at the door, Mrs. B. sprinkles him generously with holy water. She wishes him Godspeed. "*Go n-éirí an bothar leat.*" He makes his way up to the three old men at the bus stop.

"Do you think he noticed anything? He must have felt it?" She flaps about, pulling the book out and giving the cover an angry little slap.

I'm in the village getting petrol for our trip when the parish priest breaks away from a cluster of well-wishers. "Is Mrs. B. all right?"

Could the things some people believe about priests be true? What could he possibly have noticed? She talked a lot, but most women's response to a priest is to talk too much or too little.

"When I was going, she sprinkled me with white spirit." Turpentine, to me.

I want Mrs. B. to have a good rest before the journey, so I won't mention the parish priest's comment.

~

I drop James's blueprints back to the pub. On the bar, the anchor's long flukes are closed and it's very similar to the blueprint. It's being used as a bookmark on my copy of the *Trumpet Shall Sound*, which bristles with slips of paper.

In the morning Mrs. B. and I settle ourselves into the still heater-less car, even colder now that the seal on the door has crumbled.

"You were seen talking to the priest after he left here," she said as we drove away. "Did he say anything?"

"He said when he left the house you sprinkled him with white spirit."

"Merciful Hour! Me with this head and throat, I didn't get the smell off it!" And then, a look of pure glee. "Well, those ones in his home place in Gweedore will have plenty to talk about this night."

About a mile out of Carrick I realize if we go the short way, into Northern Ireland and back out, we'll be going through Irish customs on the Republic side. The officers seize contraband: televisions, liquor, contraceptives, groceries, anything that's cheaper in the North or forbidden by the Catholic Church.

"I forgot customs!" I say. "The banned books!"

"Don't worry, I've it all planned, I wrapped the books in my nightdress at the bottom of my case. Nobody's going to search through an old woman's nightdress."

At customs, some cars are already directed to the side and officials are pulling out alcohol, dralon sofas, cameras, and other oddments. I roll down the window and Mrs. B. pushes across me to speak. "I'm Nellie Brennan, ex-national teacher, and this is my American niece, the doctor, nearly." She looks at them with a doll's pursed simper, her hair escaping its bun in the excitement.

We're waved through.

"I still can't see how *Lady Chatterley* got banned," she says. "It would probably do those lads good to have a read of it."


## The Irish Telephone System Wasn't Set Up for the Irish

After a great welcome at breakfast in the guest house in Dublin, I set out with the telegrams, but Gaeltarra Éireann's street is blocked as a large funeral cortege makes its way to St. Andrew's Church. I park instead on Grafton Street and go to Gael Linn, to Dónall Ó Móráin in his aerie at the top. He's on the phone, speaking in Irish, English, and a mix. He listens for a bit, then covers the mouthpiece. "I'm on to Posts and Telegraphs, trying to get a phone installed in the flat of an artist who's composing music for our record company," he says. "He only rings when it suits him, usually from a pub when he's stocious." He uncovers the receiver. "Yes, ask him to give me a ring immediately he returns."

He explains that P&T don't want people to have phones. "The bastards would love nothing better than to hook two tins together with string and have all us plebs roaring down the lines."

I mention "Better" and his quest for a phone. "He's a small businessman. Should I try P&T?"

"God bless your innocence. The average waiting time for a phone is seven or eight years."

"What's your own strategy?"

"Step one is to pick my man in P&T, someone who has a common interest, the language, or perhaps someone I was at school with or, even better yet, a fellow who owes me a favor or who might be on the lookout for one in future."

"Or maybe you might have something on the person?" The girl leaves Youngstown, but Youngstown never leaves the girl.

"No, if he knows I have something on him, then a friend should make the call, just glancing on the fact that it's on my behalf. Much more effective that way." It's clear I'm a novice.

"Then I must establish the urgent need for a phone. I thought of the old medical angle, doctors need phones, but I think that's a non-starter here. The maestro has an honorary doctorate, but P&T knows it's in music."

"What, then?"

"There's no urgency. He's not elderly, he's only incapacitated when he's well-fluthered, and he's certainly not living alone, although you didn't hear that from me. So I'll find a like-minded person in the department."

The phone rings. His assistant has connected him to step one, and he takes the call. "*Éist*," he mouths to me, pointing to the phone. Listen. He speaks in Irish in a low, intimate voice until he worries I might not be appreciating the finer nuances.

"No, I got off," he says, changing to English, "I suppose you didn't get arrested yourself? No, *shíl mé nach*, you're around too long for that. The same guard himself, the bastard, will be up on charges one of these days, with that caper he's at." He chuckles at this obviously delicious notion. I assume the bastard under discussion has himself fallen afoul of the drink driving laws, the tax inspector, or a sexual misadventure of some sort.

"Who do I talk to to get to contracts about the musician?" A pause. "*Ceart go leor*," he says: right enough. A call is put though to a second Irish speaker, a sports enthusiast who went to Ó Móráin's brother's old school. The man knows someone who plays Gaelic football on Saturdays with a guy in the contracts department.

Two more calls and then, "Ó Móráin here," he says finally in a confidential tone to the contracts man. "Your friend told me you were the man to talk to about our musician friend, yes, the very one, you've heard of my trouble with him? But have you ever seen him with a football? No? Magic. Could have played for Ireland. But right now, I'm trying to get a recording out of him, and the phone is my only hope. Your friend says you might keep me in mind. Sound man, *go raibh maith agat*, thanks."

He puts the phone down and leans back, a lion replete. "Job done." But I sense a slight disappointment; perhaps he might have relished a tangle with a more battle-worthy opponent?

"Have you ever seen colonial maps of the train lines in Africa?" he asks. "They go straight to the sea or the borders, moving goods out. They're not laid out in networks that help the natives travel within their own country. The same is true of the telephone system here, set up by the British to serve their own ends. We're free now, but the system still can't deal with the needs of the public. So a shadow system has developed alongside the official one. If you want a phone, you use the official channels only *in extremis*."

His explanation triggers a kaleidoscope of images. I think of the ordnance survey's triangulation points, which originate on the coasts of Britain. I think of the Kilcar factory workers; almost all say you need pull to get a job there. (The same men say they didn't use pull, themselves.) I think of the Mafia in Youngstown, who are the folks to approach if you want to join the police force.

He offers me "lunch," but my constitution won't take it. Instead I ask about his development efforts in Carrick. "Those lamps the furniture workshop made? People say they were sent to Dublin by the lorry load. So they sold well?"

"We sent the van to collect them for scrap. Seriously substandard." He hands me a paper-wrapped parcel, grinning. "For Mrs. B., *mar dhea*, as if." He winks. I ask him to give the first set back to his comrades, *mar dhea*. I leave with a perfect picture of two sound men, one in contracts, one himself.

Gaeltarra Éireann is closed for lunch, so I go to the Dáil library, looking for more of the mysterious exchanges I stumbled across a few months ago when I was reading the parliamentary proceedings. In them, an opposition Dáil deputy had denied he had a man's death on his hands. Now all I find is a reference to Kilcar and fiery debates about the appalling state of Gaeltarra's tweed accounts in the late 1950s and early 1960s. Should the taxpayers' money be handled so carelessly, the opposition party asks? Why is a Gaeltarra agent giving big discounts on tweed to a few selected companies around the country? Also, 20,000 yards of tweed went missing. The deputy is apoplectic: how did the parties involved escape criminal convictions? Why is the governing party protecting this agent? I find nothing more.

Is this why some Gaeltarra people were reluctant about my choice when I mentioned my plan to study the Kilcar factory?

Over in the National Library, Alf MacLochlainn gives me copies of many letters written by John O'Donovan, the scholar who worked for the ordnance survey in the 1830s and early 1840s, researching place names. The few letters I glance at now are so fresh it's almost impossible to believe they're over a hundred years old. Alf repeats what the clerk in the Ordnance Survey Office told me months ago: O'Donovan seems to have gathered this information at risk of life and limb, "much like yourself," Alf says. I save them for when I need a little boost.

⁓

"I have a telegram," I tell the thin, frumpily dressed woman at Gaeltarra's front counter.

"They're devils for sending the telegrams and I'm left here to deal with the brouhaha." She says all of this in Irish except for "brouhaha." "There's none of them here at the moment."

"It's just that a telegram seems important. I've never had one."

"You get a fright, all right. I suppose it's about what they were discussing for the last while ..."

"What?" I forget anything I've learned about subtle probing.

"Well, maybe they want you to do your research someplace else."

"Someplace else? Where?" Repeated bleating of *where?* gets me nowhere; she's told me all she knows. Mayo? Galway? Japan? But Cuba is the only other place supporting small rural industry, and my passport forbids it.

I think of all the people who have helped me, Mrs. B., Michael Boyle, James Mary Agnes, Tommo, Margaret ... and is my questionnaire, now cut down from seventeen pages to ten, just scrap paper? Is Gaeltarra worried I'm investigating possible crimes? The September 1963 issue of the *Saturday Evening Post* describes my hometown as "a shame to the nation." I'd hardly travel this far to look into a little shady bookkeeping.

## One Line in a Thesis

I distract myself on my final day by going to the Valuation Office, an elegant eighteenth-century Georgian building.

I lay out my maps and their plots' histories for the expert in charge, Mr. Boland, who brings out records going back to 1857. He warns me that when a holder dies, a new heir might not bother to notify the office. But I have a bigger problem: Biddy Con Johnie, Bríd Pat John, and Brigit John Tommy Seán, from three different families in Kilcar, are all "Brigit Byrne" in official records. Franco and Voucher from the Carrick area are Donegans with ordinary first names in the eyes of the law. Mary Anne the Miner, Boots, Ice, and Stickil all have official names, but what are they? Even locals get confused: James told me he went looking in vain for a Michael Doherty, one of several, only to be told eventually the man he sought was "Mickey Hooter."

Before the turn of the twentieth century, many of the people listed as holders weren't actually owners; they were renting from landlords, Connollys, Musgraves, Murray-Stewarts, all wealthy outsiders, some deeply hated, as I now know from bitter songs. Sons usually had rights of tenure, but the rent might be raised.

Over tea, Mr. Boland's small, bald assistant gives me a little history of their street. The gracious four-storey building we're in was once the home of the Countess of Clare. And Number 3 was the town house of the writer George Moore, who lived there at the turn of the twentieth century.

"Moore was my grandmother's landlord. She was a Stanton, a tenant on the estate in Mayo."

"Fancy that," Mr. Boland says. "Did she ever talk about him?"

"She says one of the Moore ancestors was a Spanish woman who brought a chest of gold as a dowry. The coins were packed so tightly it took tweezers to pull out the first one."

The small assistant fetches an ordnance survey map of Moore Hall and its surroundings, plus the ledger that goes with it. Until now, I've seen maps as part of my study. But here is my grandmother's family land, a small plot on the shores of Lake Carra, and the road leading away, the one she took on her journey to America. And in the ledger, I see my relatives: my great-grandfather, Thomas Stanton, fated to die in a Youngstown mill, his father Patrick, and more, going back.

"Stanton is a real Mayo name," Mr. Boland says. "Most of the Stantons are there in the one tiny spot."

"Did you ever hear the story of the Red Earl of Ulster?" the small assistant asks.

"Never mind this fellow," Mr. Boland says. "He's a bit of a historian."

"Yes, sorry," the historian says, "pay no mind to me. And anyhow, the sins of the fathers ..." he flicks his hand.

By the end of day two I have dozens of records, including all the plots Michael and Tommo traced. After a final tea break, Mr. Boland says, "We have a little bonus for you. The historian has little enough to do, so he's been in the back room tracing the holdings in the rest of the half parish of Carrick for you." He produces a chart. It covers 215 holdings today, some of them farms, but also the village center, with tenants or owners going back to 1857.

He promises to send the same for Kilcar. I feel light-headed, remembering what it's taken me just to study the eighteen plots in Upper Carrick.

But nothing in the Valuation Office shows whether holders, mainly men, are sons, sons-in-law, other relatives, buyers. I can look at parish records, or the originals of the 1911 Census, where relationships show up, giving me a pre-factory picture. In the end, though, it's only local people who will be able to help with some of my questions: some of the owners' names Michael Boyle has given me don't match the records. Who, for example, is this Lucy McLoughlin in the ledger? Why isn't she on Michael's map?

I try to act as if all of this will happen, that I'll be talking to Michael, and asking the new parish priest about parish records, and sitting beside Mrs. B. at the Stanley, and it would even be nice if we were saying the Rosary. For the first time I forget for a moment about how bad the Donegal weather is, and how cold the bathtub, and even about the fact that we don't have a bathtub ... Gaeltarra can't stop my study, of course, but they could make the factory off-limits. And just when my professors have begun to warm to my study.

~

On our way home from her daughter's house, I pass Mrs. B. the banned books. "These are from Dónall Ó Móráin," I say. She knows him; he calls in when he comes to Carrick to look at the trout farm and interrogate the Sultan.

"The brave Dónall. I knew he wouldn't let me down."

We're taking the long way back, entirely through the Republic, so we're not passing through border customs again. She opens the package: Frank O'Connor's *The Common Chord*, a set of short stories about love; a pile of detective magazines, banned for emphasizing crime, and one of the most recent, John McGahern's *The Dark*, for its depiction of rural Ireland as it well may be.

Home at last, and a restless sleep. I'm shocked awake at six: *what* "sins of the fathers"?

~

I've been thinking back to graduate school and how painstakingly detailed anthropology is: language sounds, evolutionary eras, ethnographic details. Now I count how many days I've spent, how many people I've talked to, how many resources I've drawn on, just so I can write one line in my thesis: whether land inheritance and sales have changed or not changed as a result of the factory. One line.

Mrs. B. hands me a letter from my mother.

Pentecost Sunday. Dad's medicine helps the emphysema and he has a job
lined up. He says thanks for the maps of Kilcar – now the kitchen walls
are covered from the refrigerator to the Sacred Heart. He and Jim are up
to something, but I don't have time to listen these days. And I'm knitting
Patrice a new poncho – she lost the old one. Green and a nice magenta.

I don't know most of my father's friends, but at least he's got something to do.

## What's Not on Record

The word "farm" is a cornucopia of confusions.

"Who is this Lucy McLoughlin?" I shout at old Máirtín Boyle, sounding, even to myself, like a wife confronting a philandering husband.
Máirtín takes no notice; either he doesn't hear or he relishes my unin-
tended suggestion of shenanigans.

His son Michael is away for that rarest of events, a small farmer's
holiday. Today one of his daughters graduates from secondary boarding
school and the family has traveled there to attend the ceremony. She
qualified as a proficient Irish speaker in primary school, so secondary
was "free," but even so, for many families the other expenses are a bar-
rier. Like my father and mother, Michael and his wife go without to get
an education for their children.

"Lucy McLoughlin?"

Máirtín laughs. "What about her?"

"Up in Dublin she's listed as the owner of this land." I point to Number 12 of the eighteen on the ordnance survey map Michael and I are
working on.

"Condy's place?"

"There's no Condy on anybody's map."

"Of course not. That's the *name* of the farm. What we call it here." He seems surprised I don't know this. "It's Charlie McLoughlin's place."

"Well, Charlie's name isn't on the Valuation Office maps. It's Lucy."

"Lucy died in the 1920s," Máirtín says. "What kind of people are they up there at all?"

"Who's Condy?"

"Her husband. They were both national teachers. Had thirteen in family, they all lived."

"Here's the map showing the people who hold the land, officially, right now," I say. He helps me to write in the "farm names" under the legal owner's name, who may be dead and simply never reported to the Valuation Office or retired and holding on to the legal title. I also have the current farmer's name, usually a son who is likely to be the legal owner, eventually.

I make a chart of the names. This is the first half:

| Holder's Name | "Name of Farm" |
| --- | --- |
| Patrick McGill | James John Brídín's |
| Bridget McLoughlin | Francie Jo's |
| William Byrne | Johnny Anne's |
| Con Doogan | Con Doogan's |
| Michael Burke | Burke's |
| Tom Carr | Tom Carr |
| Mona Gildea | Tommy's |
| Francis L. McLoughlin | Mary Phelim's |
| Danny Ward | Pat O'Donnell's |

Máirtín stops. "And here now," he says, pointing to a different townland, "Malachy John Beag's farm is a case for you. Malachy John was a McLoughlin. The farm belonged to his sister's husband's ... let's see ... his sister's husband's brother. Malachy farmed it, but only after he died did it pass on to his children."

"So he never owned it, but his name is on it?"

"Yes."

"And a McLoughlin is on it now?" I ask, searching among Michael's map for another McLoughlin.

"No. Pat Doogan. And look you, now, at Danny Ward on the map. He has another farm we'll come to in a minute. One of the farms is called by his name, but the other one, this one here, is called 'Pat O'Donnell's.'"

My notes are unreadable.

"What name have those people in Dublin put on my land here?" he asks.

"Michael Boyle."

"That's right. I passed it over to him."

"So what's the farm's name, then?"

"Máirtín Boyle's, of course." The farm might be called that for two or three more generations, if Condy's is anything to go by. Michael has already told me when he shears the sheep in June, he'll brand their horns "MB." He assures me the "M" is "Máirtín."

We move on.

| | |
|---|---|
| Charlie McLoughlin | Condy's |
| Michael Boyle | Máirtín Boyle's |
| Peter Ward | Peter Ward's |
| Danny Ward (same as above) | Danny Ward's |
| Charlie Doogan | Mary Condy Harley's |
| Charles O'Rorke | O'Rorke's |
| " | " |

O'Rorke is a "blow-in," an outsider like me.

So we have the eighteen plots, sixteen owners, forming bits and pieces of twelve farms, and historically each one could have three names: the recorded legal holder, the "farm name," and the person farming it. Or four, if any of them uses a nickname the Valuation Office never heard of.

I marvel at my naiveté in assuming that a city person, someone whose only previous knowledge of agriculture was "Old MacDonald Had a Farm," could ever understand this. But how lucky I am to have, perhaps, the only person who has a complete command of the situation. As I leave, Máirtín clasps both my hands in his. I'm moved; I don't have any relatives as old as Máirtín. My grandmother is a decade younger, but they both have the honed, dignified faces of people who have done all they can, know it was enough, and want nothing more.

In fact, what he wants is my pen to write out his full name, in case I don't know it, "Máirtín Boyle," in a fine hand. I suppose he wants to make sure I know his name, since I'm so confused about everyone else's.

We part, agreeing Michael had done great work on my maps but is still too young at sixty to know everything.

I already knew that fine hand of Máirtín Boyle's. I've seen it on his 1911 household Census form. "Máirtín Boyle," he'd written at the bottom of the form, after a young Royal Irish constable from Tyrone, aged twenty-two, filled it out as part of his local duties. The policeman lists Máirtín as "Mick," but Máirtín, in a hand identical to today's, reclaims his dignity.

Ten years later his new family was flourishing. He and his wife, Anne, were thirty-five, with six children, all living (see Table 1). He had, according to himself, taken over his wife's family farm somewhat reluctantly. He preferred boot making.

If Máirtín had been a peer of the land, or a professor, there was a space where he could enter his titles and any important posts, but he was a farmer. The tables continue: On a line for occupation, his schoolgoing children are listed as "scholars," but the Census gives strict instructions about women working in the home: they don't have an occupation, so the line for Anne must be left blank. Not "domestic duties" or even "housewife." Michael, the youngest son, is listed as "can't read and write"; reasonably, because he's three, but next year he'll become a scholar. All the family can speak English and Irish.

Máirtín had a "second-class house," which is good; no one in Carrick Upper had a first-class house, and three of the twelve families had a third-class house. The class is calculated by the number of windows (Máirtín

Table 1. Residents of House 5 in Carrick Upper (Glencolmcille, Donegal), 1911 Census

| Surname | Forename | Age | Sex | Relation to Head | Religion |
|---------|----------|-----|--------|------------------|----------------|
| Boyle | Martin | 35 | Male | Head of Family | Roman Catholic |
| Boyle | Anne | 35 | Female | Wife | Roman Catholic |
| Boyle | Patrick | 6 | Male | Son | Roman Catholic |
| Boyle | James | 5 | Male | Son | Roman Catholic |
| Boyle | Annie | 4 | Female | Daughter | Roman Catholic |
| Boyle | Michael | 3 | Male | Son | Roman Catholic |
| Boyle | Jane | 2 | Female | Daughter | Roman Catholic |
| Boyle | Mary | 1 | Female | Daughter | Roman Catholic |

had three) plus the walls, the number of rooms (three for ten people in Máirtín's case), and the type of roof. His house is thatched, which reduces his score a little. But what kind of picture does this give? Who taught Michael his careful husbandry, his farm organization, his immaculate tidiness? Máirtín and Anne, undoubtedly, and whatever the size, it must have been a pleasant, well-run place. The tables don't show this.

What's missing on Censuses is not just the interpretative element but also the names of those who were gone. The differences between the Censuses of 1840 and 1850 are large enough to fill another Census, which they did, in Britain or America or Australia. When I found Máirtín in the 1901 Census, I thought of looking for my own people in County Mayo, too, but they'd left eight years before, appearing instead in the 1900 Census of Youngstown, Ohio: my grandmother and her sisters are maidservants in a boarding house. By 1910, she's married, at home, and three of her five children have been born. On the next Census, her eldest boy is missing, dead of cancer, but there's a new child, not on the Census, because her husband, my grandfather, fathered it elsewhere. On the next Census, she's listed as a "janitress"; he's gone. And in the next one, two of her daughters are missing, both in a long-term tuberculosis sanitarium. One remains there for nineteen years. So I wonder what stories lie beneath Máirtín's Census entries.

# June/Mí an Mheithimh 1967

## A Stranger Comes to Town

James rarely uses anything more than an elliptical reference, a wink, or a sideways glance to convey news. This time it's a door.

He's hanging his shop door the other way round because his butter "is moving faster than it used to." I've heard a prominent lady has been pilfering it from behind the door. Rather than moving the butter to a safer place, or God forbid, saying anything, he sends the message this way. "She's not herself lately."

He tells me "The Long Fella," Gaeltarra's MacGabhann, is down at Mrs. B's. and waits for information.

I could say something like "Wouldn't you know?" and force him to reveal a little more before he's entitled to the lowdown.

"Ah, now," I say, instead, winking. I hate to do this to James, my dear friend, but it's he who taught me. I wonder, though, if people will be as nice to me in Japan.

Cathal MacGabhann sits in the parlor before the one-bar electric fire with tea and an enthralled Mrs. B. The contrasts are striking; she, a tiny

lady with a bun and wire-framed health board spectacles; he, tall and
thin, with his high crew cut and fashionable glasses. But I suspect she's
rethinking her decision to steer him toward the parlor. This is the kind
of man she could sit with in the kitchen.

"The very woman," MacGabhann says, rising. "You're a hard person
to find." Mrs. B. goes out for more of the pastry he's just said he couldn't
eat another bite of.

"I was here to have a look round the factory and hoped I could catch
you in," he says.

Do I really need Gaeltarra's cooperation? Can I concentrate on the
land issues, instead, enough for a more modest thesis? "I got a few telegrams from you, and I went to Dublin last week to see ..." I begin.

"Sorry. We're having a bit of a wrangle. You'd think Galway County
Council would be delighted we want to move our offices to their Gaeltacht," and he nods to Mrs. B. in the doorway, "*Ach tá sé an pholaitíocht
céanna d'aois.*" Same old politics. "We wanted to ask if you'd administer
your questionnaire someplace else, too. In fact, we'd like you to give them
out in all our factories, thirteen of them. We'll only want the analysis. I
just want you to figure out how to adapt our factories to rural life. Like
Driver is. We'll pay you, of course, and all expenses."

Japan fades a bit. My Kilcar questionnaire is now eight pages, but I'm
still wondering how to analyze the results. Magnifying the logistics by
thirteen is impossible.

"I'll have to think about it," I say.

"Fine. Mmm, what is this pastry?" MacGabhann asks, wiping syrup
from his hands.

"Baklava," Mrs. B. says.

MacGabhann leaves with some baklava in a biscuit tin, saying someone named "Joe" will be in touch with me. This I understand. "Joe"
sounds suitably undercover, even Youngstownish, since everyone else in
Gaeltarra has a name like Cumhaí Ó Caorthannáin or Séafra Ó Maol-
chluiche, prompting even some Irish speakers to say, "In the name of
God, what's that in English?"

"By the way," he says in the doorway, "I might also be pushing for you to do five or six studies like the one here, if this one works out." He puts his arms up in front of his face as if to ward off an attack and goes out laughing, into the long evening light.

I'm numb. A year ago I'd never heard of Gaeltarra Éireann and now its general manager thinks what I'm doing has some practical use.

Mrs. B. is annoyed. "You're like a dervish up in that bedroom. If you got some help with the simple tasks you could manage to do your own work *and* take on his offer. You need a nice young, lively Irish speaker who has gone to the vocational school, not looking for much money ..."

"Name?"

"We'll go down to Teelin one of the days. There's a family that always enjoys a visit from me." Mrs. B. is entirely free of false modesty.

The glow fades as I remember I've worked weeks to get what might end up as that single line on farm inheritance and consolidation.

This evening James comes by. He compliments me on my "Ah now" this morning. "Except for the wink. Women don't wink."


## The Love Affair

I must be in love. I read his letters obsessively. But it's hopeless, the usual story: the guy's handsome, charming, intelligent, funny. Married with nine children. But a real soulmate with a great understanding of my kind of work. Dead 106 years, which makes it even more poignant. They say there's someone for everyone, but what if that someone lives in Asmara and you're in Amarillo? Or you're mid-twentieth century and he's mid-nineteenth?

My man, of course, is John O'Donovan, whose letters Alf MacLochlainn showed me in the National Library. I read a few each night. He worked out local place names for the first ordnance survey maps in the 1830s and 1840s, drawing on local knowledge, geology, botany, history, archeology, etymology, and sometimes quirky speculation. The letters are written to his boss in Dublin, and I'm reading the ones for this time of year from landscapes like these.

His encounters are a combination of high adventure, humiliation, and discovery; his deprivations were daunting and his tongue acid. My sweater-clad dips in Mrs. B.'s former bathtub are piffle to O'Donovan's damp, flea-ridden beds, indigestible food, and perpetually sodden clothes.

He did much of his Donegal work on foot, using quill pens on damp paper in wet shelters, questioning old people, drunken fishermen, poets, shepherds, drawing on his extensive knowledge of ancient and modern languages and scholarly works, often short of money. "Our money is run out again, we want our pay as soon as possible," he complains on September 3, 1835, because he can't leave Dunfanaghy, Donegal, until he pays for his scrofulous lodgings. His pay arrives thirteen days later.

My luxuriantly warm bed is delightful as I read about the day he sprang ashore from a marooned ferry only to land on a rock and sprain his ankle. He then walked the five miles to his final destination, Glenties, although it became eight because to ease his pain he'd taken a mile-and-a-half "shortcut" road that ended at a steep mountain, forcing him back to the original road.

In October 1835, planning to go to Dungloe, he and his assistant ignore local warnings about flooded mountain passes and a dangerous bull. O'Donovan is upbeat: "No matter, said I, the morning smiles and the sun looks beautifully bright ... what care we, such practiced travelers, about puddled roads or mountain forests, or mad bulls guarding their herds in the gorges of glens? ... Should you place the sun on my right hand and the moon on my left and crown me with the rainbow I would not be diverted from my purpose!"

Soon, showers roared down the valley. They took shelter in a public house in Fintown, where they had "a biscuit and a pint of beer as sour as vinegar and sickening, too." As they proceeded toward Dungloe, night fell with nothing in sight but a forked road. Choosing one, they eventually met a solitary being who told them they had made the wrong choice, they were on the road to Glenties, six miles away behind the mountains, whereas

Dungloe was more than twelve, across flooded glens. They pushed on to Glenties in the rain and dark. O'Donovan consoled himself with the words of Pope: "better this than sit on the richest sofa when anxiety wastes thy frame, and the absence of new pleasure renders life monotonous."

The next day the road to Dungloe was blocked by a tide, and they ended up two miles out of Fintown, where they had had the biscuit and beer the day before. This allowed them to engage with the bull they'd been warned about. All for place names.

He's been criticized, rightly, for "anglicizing" his results: after the place names in 63,000 Irish townlands were established, he converted many of the Irish names into the English phonetic forms that appear on the maps. Quite often the names had no connection to Irish at all, being hodgepodges of possible root words. But the survey was a British military operation, and perhaps his decision was personally expedient, although damaging to the Irish language.

O'Donovan was not simply a good-time boy, though; he also translated seven volumes of the seventeenth-century *Annals of the Four Masters* and produced works on ancient law, culture, and literature, plus a grammar and dictionary, aspects of which have been analyzed critically by later scholars.

But all I can say, as a fellow fieldworker, is *bail ó Dhia ar an obair*: God bless the work, because a century later, and at his age, I'm working in only two tiny communities to his many, with a hot water bottle, and I'm exhausted.

But his spirit lifts me. I decide to take MacGabhann's request to carry out my questionnaire in all thirteen factories.


## The Midnight Dancer

The shortest distance between two points is a straight line, but how do you describe the longest? A scientist might study James's maneuvers when he's trying, once again, to get information without asking. Today, he begins, not by asking about MacGabhann, but my father. What is his background? Training? I say he left school at sixteen to support his mother.

He pulls the anchor from under the bar, opening and shutting it like an umbrella. "Genius. I couldn't have done it without him."

"Who?" I'm sure there's a MacGabhann trap here. But once I see my father's beautiful calligraphy on an envelope on the bar, I know. "Jim O'Donnell, Carrick, County Donegal," it says.

"I rang your mother when you were so sick; I had to, Mrs. B. was away, but it was your father I got. I told him not to come, just to hold himself in readiness. The next time I rang, we got talking. You never told me all the things he's invented, real patents on them! I told him about my anchor, knowing he'd be interested. He sent me his blueprints. Now we write all the time." So those were the blueprints I saw.

"'Jim,' he calls me. Everyone here calls me 'Jim,' now."

What else am I missing while I'm fussing about plots and holdings? But I'm overwhelmed by James's concern for me. Also worried he might think patented inventions are always moneymakers.

This evening Mrs. B. and I go down to Con and Mary Kate Cassidy's thatched cottage above the bay in Teelin. Along the road, people take advantage of the weather, mounding the potatoes again, watching for disease. The fat sheep on the hills are ready for clipping, the few cows are out, and the golden hay is bright against the electric-green fields. This must be the one day the Tourist Board can take photos. The fishermen in the bay are dressed the part, thick sweaters and caps, but I doubt they're thinking about posing.

An old man waves us over to say they've been out since early morning. Now, around eight, five boats come in, three men rowing in each and one aft, dragging an oar to steer. A two-man, two-boy boat belonging to a Kelly family has caught five salmon. The old man says the first boat to see a salmon leap will row fast and throw a *dul*, a "go," or a "take," using a circular net. If they get a catch, they must move on, and another boat may take its place. The best spots are one at the end of the pier, another a "pool" in the shelter of the pier's arch, and a third at Derrylahan across in Kilcar.

The old man, shrunken into a sweater he might once have filled, explains how the fish are divided among a crew. Several piles are laid out on a floor. A crew member turns his back. Another man, sitting, points to a pile and says, "*Cé leis é seo?*": "Whose is this?" The man facing away names a crew member and eventually each pile is given out.

Beautiful music floats out over the road beside the Cassidy house, punctuated by young female screeches. Inside are Mary Kate; her elderly aunt, Maggie Ruadh, Red-Haired Maggie, in long skirts and a shawl; and Mary Kate's two girls, late teens, darting around the house. Maggie Ruadh draws Mrs. B. up beside her to the smoking fire.

The females participate in the drama of getting Annie, the elder girl, ready for a dance. Maggie and Mary Kate do it by jeering and sly innuendo, Sally, the sister, by putting her own best items of clothing out of Annie's reach. Despite this, Annie now wears Sally's shoes and stretches a leg out, admiringly.

Annie explains the ritual. At about 9:30, John Eddy's car will start out for Foresters Hall in Killybegs or the hall in Glencolmcille with perhaps eight others in the car.

"Last week we had six in the back seat, one nursing another."

"Nursing?" The teenage boys who helped me with the village map had used the word. "To get us all in, the girls sit on a fellow's knee, but I told one last week if he tried any more of his capers I'd tell his sister and she'd tell his mother and the mother would be the woman, all right, who'd lock him in the shed for the next dance."

Her mother laughs. "Where did we get her at all?"

Annie pays three shillings for the car, and six or seven for the dance, depending on the place, either Glencolmcille or tonight's venue, Killybegs. "We'll chat and primp in the hall cloakroom until about 11:30.

What I have on me now is what most wear": a tweed shift and sweater. "The odd time a few stuck-up Mod dressers with long hair and earrings might turn up from Killybegs."

"But the hall really opens earlier, around 9:30?"

"Yes, but most of the fellows are in the pub until around midnight, so we dance after that, until the hall closes at two." The parish priest says all dances in Carrick must be over at 11:30, but Killybegs town is more worldly.

"What happens at the dance itself?" I ask.

"There'll be Killybegs girls, very forward indeed, always preening and throwing shapes. The Carrick teenagers are considered good mixers, and the Kilcar ones are snobbish: they're better dressed and better dancers. People say Glencolmcille girls are the nicest. The Teelin boys must think so because they go for the Glen girls." She pulls some hair back from one ear and holds it with Sally's clip.

"We start by facing each other across the hall, usually the same number of fellows and girls. Not facing, really, because if girls are talking about a particular boy, we'll pretend to look around. But if boys discuss a girl, they turn their backs to the hall. When they turn around again they're such *amadáin*, fools, that they can't help looking straight at the very girl. All the girls laugh. The boys get very red in the face."

Eventually, a lad, pushed by his friends, ventures across to ask for a dance. I know from talking to young men that this is a torment, because girls sometimes refuse and they have to walk back again.

"A boy will have a set of comments, always the same ones." She lists the choices:

'The hall is big.'

'The band is good (or bad).'

'It's a big crowd.'

'Are you enjoying the dance?'

'Do you work?'

'Where do you come from?'

'What's your name?'

"I might give my name or not, but either way I'll ask his. He might give me a false name, but I'll find it out sooner or later from my friends, and if I dance him again, I might say, 'Do you know John Byrne?' That's his name, and he'll say something like, 'My God, you're sharp.'

"If a boy dances you two or three times, you can be sure he'll pop some kind of question before the night is over. First, he'll ask, 'Would you like a mineral?' If I let him buy me a mineral, his next question will likely be, 'Can I see you home?' If I say no, you can see him looking at the mineral as much to say 'There's my ninepence-worth to loss.' That's why I like to pay my own way in and buy whatever I want myself; I can do whatever I please. One girl, somebody's cousin who comes here for her holidays, she takes a mineral or sweets or cigarettes from two or three lads and then goes off with someone else. She's a real wagon, that one, no one should dance with her at all."

"She's well got, that one," Maggie Ruadh says. "Her mother and grandmother were the same."

"Well, after that second dance," Annie says, pushing her fringe back to see if that looks nicer, "the action begins. The boy takes a limp clasp of your hand. Then the fingers become intertwined, and from there to the arm around the shoulder, then to the waist, then both arms loose around the waist. If he's a brave lad, he puts both hands around the neck at arm's length."

"And?" I ask. This sounds familiar: I'm only eight years out of high school.

"I say, 'One arm will do, thank you.'"

Mary Kate and Maggie Ruadh howl. "'One arm will do,' would you ever mind her!"

"And," Annie says, "if you're sitting down, he might hold your hand and before you know it his hand and yours are on your upper leg and then his hand on your knee."

"And then?"

"Then he takes his hand away. It seems like he only wants to feel you, that's all. Boys think girls don't even notice these things, but I could draw a map of the moves they make."

Mary Kate shrieks and orders her not to say another word: she doesn't want to miss anything while she's outside fetching water for the tea. Maggie Ruadh and Mrs. B. go to the pantry.

When they're out, I tell Annie what the weedy boy asked when the other boys were making the map: "Did you get your hand?"

"Indeed, he would not have got his hand! Not unless it was a striapach of a girl from someplace else, maybe Donegal Town. The idea!" The women return with bread and butter, Christmas cake, and a bottle of whiskey. Sally spoons tea into a teapot and pours boiling water from the kettle hanging over the fire.

The women are still laughing at Annie's primness. "Wisha, you wouldn't be laughing if I landed back here with a wee babby," she snaps.

"Where's the fun? In my day ..." Maggie Ruadh says.

"In your day, the men gathered in a house to tell stories and smoke pipes and the women to sew or knit, and what kind of fun was that?"

"Yes, but later, in my day," Mary Kate says, "we had rake houses, almost every night in somebody's house, a widow or widower, where you'd dance, too, and some, men and women both, took a drink, none of your old minerals, and told stories and laughed and roared, and one old man would keep a bit of order, because a fellow might try to sneak a póigín ... and then the fellows walked the girls home."

"And what better did you get out of that?" Annie asks, as she drapes Sally's scarf across her jumper.

A knock. Silence. A little later, another knock. "The Red Hammerer!" Maggie Ruadh laughs at the prospect of the fearsome local phantom, but we all shrink in a little – not Mrs. B., of course.

Con Cassidy, celebrated musician, father, my potato advisor, comes in. Everyone relaxes, but he winks at me and says it could have been the

Red Hammerer, he's often heard him. Con is a strikingly handsome man. "I got this," Mary Kate says, and pulls Con down on her chair.

"You could do worse, I'll give you that," Annie says, and strides out with the cut of an ancient priestess, an invisible jeweled cloak trailing behind her, out through a whiplash gale to John Eddy's honking car and the chance of a magical night.

On the way home, Mrs. B. says, "That wee Annie is your helper." I agree. Her observational skills are formidable.

What surprises me is Mrs. B.'s placid reaction to the discussion tonight. She reminds me it's much more respectable to say "racy" things in Irish than in English.

"That's one of the beauties of Irish," she says.

"But they were speaking English. For me."

"Oh, but it was really Irish, underneath," she says.

## No-Hope Joe Arrives

Today, June 9, is the feast of St. Colmcille, and tonight barefoot people will make prayerful rounds, "stations," over rough terrain to recall events in his life, like the battle he had with the Devil.

Is Mrs. B. going?

"Indeed I'm not. I said to Our Lord, 'You know I'm old and tired now. I'll bet You when Colmcille was my age he wasn't hopping around barefoot on sharp stones in the dark.'"

Thinking about battles with the Devil reminds me of my quandary. "What do my professors *want?*" is a question every student obsesses about. Certainly they want your conclusions, the big picture, but as in math they also want you to "show your work." So how much? Thanks to the Valuation Office, I have 109 years of history, needed or not, on my map's eighteen plots. The only people who can help me now are locals. Who inherited? Was any land sold and consolidated?

I tell myself that O'Donovan researched thousands more villages and townlands, without a hot water bottle or a car, even one like the Morris Minor. I'll mention that to my mapping helpers.

But both Michael Boyle and James are avoiding me these days, pleading the need to finish the turf and support their families or attend deathbeds or some such thing, but with the legendary persistence of all graduate students, whose shared motto is "Me, Me, Me," I beg. They trudge in around 11:00 p.m. James mentions Liz's back is right as rain now and he had hoped to take her for a wee moonlight stroll. I harden my heart.

"Look at them," Mrs. B. scolds from the pantry. "Their tongues hanging out of them and you with those blessed maps and lists out all over again." The men sigh, relieved, as they hear cups being banged down on the counter.

I present them with the 109 years. After an hour, they've worked out 98 per cent of who did what and why for all the years between then and now. Between 1857 and 1967 in Carrick Upper, the men helped me traced 115 land tranfers. Only seventeen were sales, outright or to family. The eldest son or the widow inherited, but that declined around the turn of the twentieth century, long before the factory opened. Today, there's one eldest son on the twelve farms. The median age of holders is sixty-three.

Selling land is rare. And my eighteen plots, now consolidated into twelve farms, are far too small to be even one of the "ranches" the government wants. So, there have been some sales, but none leading to someone going into the factory. The future is even less promising: some holdings will end up with distant relatives abroad and even if sold, will be too far apart and too small. Some farms will lie fallow.

"I don't know how this 'ranch' notion came about," Michael says.

James says in the 1890s the British Congested Districts Board tried it, but even they gave up in this area because the land was so bad. Later, the Irish government suggested it, too, but retreated.

Annie comes in. Teelin people are just thinking about getting started at this hour, she says. She'll help me with typing, copying records, and interviewing in Irish. The idea of interviewing intrigues her. "One thing, though" she says, "I won't ask anyone what they eat."

"Eat?"

"Never ask anyone here what they eat. They won't like it."

People have more money now, and traditional food, big steaming bowls of buttery potatoes, stews, and homemade bread are not for visitors. Tinned food, store bread and cakes, processed cheese and meat slices are what I'm given if people invite me to tea, and that's how they want to be remembered.

She hands me two torn-out copybook sheets. One is a map of the lineup in the dance hall. Another has the outline of a girl's body, and numbered spots on it.

"Where the boys try their hand," she says. "For you that loves maps." The men are speechless but clearly delighted.

It's long past midnight now, and first light is around four. Michael has a day's turf-footing in front of him and says goodnight.

A torchlight bobs alongside the house. Shane Cannon and Brian Vocational come in, accompanied by a neat, cheerful-looking man, introduced as Seosamh Ó hÓgartaigh from Gaeltarra. All are delighted at the offer of tea. "Just to keep ye in the picture," Shane says. "We saw your light on.

"Chairman Leo McLoughlin invited Gaeltarra Éireann here to interrogate them. Why doesn't Carrick have a factory? And what about that new industrial estate?"

Mr. hÓgartaigh sits like a schoolboy, hands folded, peaceably awaiting his tea.

"And Brian here showed him the woodworking program in the vocational school. It's urgent that Gaeltarra support a new furniture factory, to make chairs for the hotel trade in this region."

Mr. hÓgartaigh beams.

"The chairman also pointed out the lack of tourist accommodation here was a disgrace and Gaeltarra should build a good-sized hotel," Brian says.

We all look at Mr. hÓgartaigh, nibbling a biscuit. He looks like the kind of person Mrs. B. calls a "wee pet."

"Well," he says, shuffling closer on his chair. "I mentioned to the Chairman, An tUasal McLoughlin" – the honorific "An tUasal," with its glancing implications of nobility, seems a good idea right now – "that Gaeltarra doesn't build hotels, you might consult Gael Linn, although I understand they already tried to buy a local pub and build a hotel, but ..." James pretends innocence.

"And the furniture idea, well you know a local man, Manus McLoughlin, already supplies chairs to all the hotels in the region, so ..." Manus is a relative of Chairman Leo, and I see a wee twinkle in the wee pet's eye.

We sit like birds on a wire, alert, expectant.

"Of course, we must support all the Gaeltacht areas, not just one." He looks around agreeably. "So that's why we're starting an industrial estate up in Gweedore in northern Donegal and another down in Connemara." These two are the strongest Irish-speaking areas in the country."

As he's leaving with Brian, Mr. hÓgartaigh pumps my hand. "Joe Hogarty. I came up today to talk to you about doing seven more community studies but I got hijacked. Another time, soon."

~

James, Annie, and I dip biscuits into the last dregs of tea before I drop her home. "So the committee might approach Gael Linn now?" Annie, Miss Innocence, asks James.

"No. I had a ring from them this morning. They're selling the estate for forty-five-thousand pounds to the first buyer and investing the proceeds in what Dónall Ó Móráin calls 'a real Gaeltacht.' It's 'the black breast' again."

MacGabhann's mysterious "Joe" is not the fedora-hatted Mafioso I pictured. And the development committee's future is not what they pictured, either.

Later, the committee sends a letter of complaint to the local newspaper about Gael Linn's plan to sell the estate: "This is the greatest single attempt to wield a fatal blow against the area since the coming into being of the freedom of the State," it says. To me, the bigger surprise is that this area, with the most promising factory by usual economic standards, isn't getting anything.

When I next see Brian, I remind him Ó Móráin says he's lost £30,000 on the trout farm/piggery, when you take overhead costs and the rest into account.

"We know all about overheads. We know all about porous rock, too, and we told them not to build that trout farm on it. But would they listen? No. Did the advisors from Dublin let the vegetable co-op lads store the potatoes in pits, as we do here? No, and they rotted. Did they listen when people here told them the potatoes, 'Pinks,' wouldn't grow in sandy soil, and 'Banners' were the only ones that would? No."

This evening in the shop I meet Chairman Leo, who says the Kilcar Parish Council refuses to send representatives to the Southwest Donegal Regional Development Committee. No one will come from Glencolmcille, either, unless elected by their village.

"What's the Southwest Donegal Regional ...?" I ask.

"It was going to be our new name."

## "Farmers" Don't Farm

Tonight a horizontal rain skates across Slieve League and slaloms down Mrs. B.' s chimney, dousing the sitting-room fire that welcomed a newly ordained priest earlier today. Probably about a nine or ten on the Beaufort scale, and who better than an Irishman, Thomas Beaufort, to devise such a scale? He must have seen every kind of gale at his mother's knee.

By ten, rain almost drowns the sound of the pantry door opening and Michael Boyle's quiet "God bless all here." A less resilient man might have been flattened against the frame, but he's well used to snagging turnips in storm-scoured fields and dragging sheep carcasses across mountain scrub in winds he could teach Beaufort something about.

"A right fierce one," Michael admits. From his sodden overcoat he produces the ordnance survey maps, perfectly dry; rain has no chance of getting through Irish tweed. He fields Mrs. B.'s offer of tea, maybe confident that it won't be the last tonight. Shane appears. "I don't like to miss the fun," he says.

I'm surprised at their visit: last week I mentioned I have records for the bigger picture, the 215 holdings in the half parish, the ones the "historian" in the Valuation Office gave me. Some are farmland, some aren't. I thought, at best, that we might look only at the farms, but they ignored me and over three nights, in rapid-fire Irish, they took on all 215.

After tacking back and forth between maps, timelines, unregistered land, single owners of multiple plots, and single plots divided among multiple heirs, they presented their findings. The pattern is similar to that of Carrick Upper's eighteen plots. The eldest son is no longer the most common heir, and some land has been sold but not consolidated into bigger farms. Most relevant: those who sold haven't gone into the factory.

"Months of work to be able to say this about Carrick," I say. And the Valuation Office has just sent me the bigger picture for Kilcar. "I have to do that, as well."

"*Tusa?*" Shane laughs. You?

Tonight the two men return. Michael has the map of the eighteen plots-sixteen owners-twelve farms we first worked on, those in his own townland. The ones I'd assumed we were done with.

"I was talking to the Da. He says we've gone astray here," he says, tapping the map. "But he put me right. The Tillage, the Census, has these fellows down as farmers. And we talk about them as farmers."

"Why wouldn't we?" I ask. "They own farms, they know every stone and blade of grass, people call them farmers, they talk about farming."

"But they don't farm."

He agrees the holdings in Carrick Upper form twelve "farms." Only four are used full time now, and of those only two are being farmed by the people who live on them. One is Michael. The other two holdings are rented, farmed by one man who lives on a farm elsewhere. He'd be the government's ideal, consolidating land, but no one has left farming to work in the factory because of what he did. Some holders are retired. Some plots are idle or used for crops for home consumption or rented out for hay. Three of the holders have other jobs, but they hold on to the land. Except for these three, all are called "farmers."

So "farmer" seems to be a courtesy title, like the "Madame" bestowed on older unmarried French women. Official records won't tell the whole story.

But some of the cynics in Dublin are right? The men on the village street aren't getting market information, even for the small market they'd be involved in? They're just hanging around, yet resisting factory work?

"I wouldn't say that," Michael says. "Two of the fellows *are* factory workers, in the seasonal vegetable co-op. Probably talking about tickets to England right now."

"*Oíche mhaith!*" Good evening, James calls, swiping water from his eyes.

"C'mere to me," Michael says. "Are the fellows she sees standing on the street just lazy hoors?" James, startled, edges back toward the door.

"Have a look at this. Your woman here" – me – "thought all the people who owned these farms were farmers, and when they stand on the street

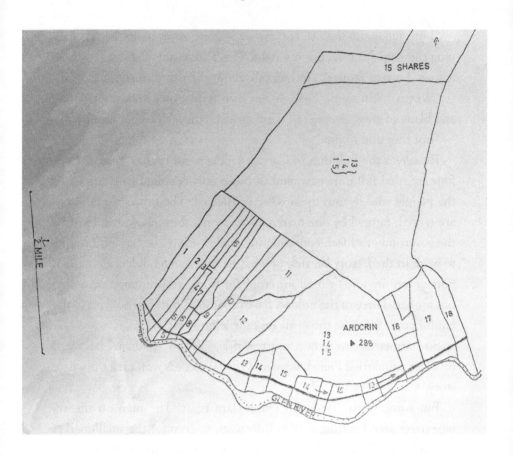

Map 4. Map of Carrick Upper. The map shows the eighteen plots. Most of the
long "stripes," reaching up toward the mountainous, rocky terrain ("fierce wild,"
Michael calls it), are arable. The numbers refer to holders, some of whom have
scattered plots, such as number 13, 14, and 15, who also has number 10,
and grazing. The "15 Shares" are commonage. Numbers 17 and 18 are rented
out to the farmer who lives elsewhere. (When Máirtín listed the owners, he
matched them to their holding numbers. I have omitted this; even today, a land
dispute might arise as a result. I speak from my own local experience.)
Source: An Forus Talúntais / The Agricultural Institute, Dublin,
unpublished document.

they're on the lookout for any news about what's going on. Who's sold what and what way prices are going and ..."

"Well, of course they're farmers," James says.

"But they're not farming," I say.

"It's a fallback. If you're not working at something else, keeping a shop or teaching or whatever, and you live on a few acres, or rent a few acres, you're a farmer, even if you don't plant a stick. You'd always plant potatoes, of course. But I'll tell you this, their fathers farmed! *They* had to live on what they grew."

"That's right," Mrs. B. comes in from the pantry. "But today, if an outsider came in here and bought a piece of land and didn't keep animals on it, or sow something, he wouldn't be a farmer. In fact, not even if he farmed."

"What would he be then?" I ask.

"An outsider."

"True," Michael says. "We wouldn't say 'farmer'; we'd say something like 'That fella there, the one that's fooling around with the tractor' or 'Your man who's going to go broke with them pigs.'"

"What if he buys a shop, instead?" I ask.

"He's still an outsider," Mrs. B. says.

"Be fair, Nellie," Michael says. "Some might say, 'Sure he's the only real farmer around here, he makes a holy show of the rest of us.'"

Mrs. B. goes out and returns with settings for a late supper. The men hasten to shift the maps.

"*I* only come from Owenteskiny, and I'm an outsider." She lays the table: milk pitcher, sugar, plates, napkins, cutlery, a little pot of butter, and two jars of homemade jam.

"What about factory workers?" I ask. "Suppose they live on farms and keep the same stock and grow the same crops as someone who's seen as a 'farmer'? What do you call them?"

"Insane," Michael says. "You can't do that and still work in the factory. Something will give, the factory job or the farm."

I go back to James's point. "Okay, the ancestors had to farm because they had nothing else, so why aren't the sons farming? What do they have?"

James moves a salt cellar to the center of the table. "Some have a job, year round or seasonal. A shop. A pub. Teaching. Construction work. Fishing, working in the vegetable co-op. The doctor. The nurse. The social welfare officer." He moves the salt cellar near the center of the salt table. "All of that is paid employment."

"But what about the rest? The farmers who aren't farming?"

Michael pulls the little butter crock over. "Growing some of your own vegetables." He puts a fork beside the butter crock: "Cutting your own turf." A knife, "for keeping a few beasts and sheep." The blackberry jam jar goes down beside the knife: "Older children emigrate and send money back. Some youngsters get local jobs in hotels, shops. The wife knits and sells eggs." He moves the other jam jar into the mix.

James takes the marmalade. "Poaching fish." He rakes in the remaining items, like a poker player sweeping up his chips, and puts a pepper pot beside the jam. "Using your car as a hackney, a taxi." Michael lifts a dessert spoon from James's hoard: "Renting a room to a guest."

"Money from the government," Mrs. B. says. "The pension, old age, widows. The Gaeltacht grants for keeping the children who come in the summer to the Irish College. Our own schoolchildren with good "school Irish" can get fees for secondary school. Grants for eyeglasses, children's shoes, dental work, maternity benefits, free milk depending on the number of children you have." She puts down a thruppence.

"Farmers get grants for fertilizer and odds and bobs." Michael takes a cup. "And some folks get a council house for a low rent, maybe thirty shillings a year."

James takes the largest item, the milk pitcher. "The dole, for any man who isn't employed. Thirty-eight shillings a week if you've no dependents. But if you're single, it's cut off from June to November. You're meant to be looking for farm work." I know from the Central Statistics Office that most local men on the dole are over forty, with no dependents.

Mr. Redington told me people who are in the official labor force for so many weeks can build up "stamps," and if they're out of work they apply for Unemployment Benefit, paid if they have enough "stamps," based on a required number of workweeks. But the number of people here who can claim this kind of benefit is the lowest in Donegal, because so few work in qualifying jobs. The majority here are on Unemployment Assistance, "the dole," which is means-tested.

"No woman can get the dole, except for unmarried mothers, and they get less than a man." Mrs. B. brings in a round breadboard with a home-made loaf. "The Irish Constitution says we have a special place within the home and we're employed there. But I say any work that pays nothing is a poor enough job."

"But the Children's Allowance ..." I say.

"*Fathers* get the Children's Allowance," she says, reaching over to re-set the table with the cutlery and the other sources of income. "Not mothers."

"Stay your hand a minute, Nellie," Michael says, gently.

"No! The man can drink the whole lot away if he likes. I say the woman should have a little money of her own. Some knit sweaters for an agent, maybe three pounds a week, but they're too heavy to hold for an old woman like me, so I knit caps. For less than sixpence an hour."

James stares out at the black landscape. Michael shifts in his chair.

A question occurs to me. I've seen dozens of older men at the Garda station collecting the dole on dole day. "Are they farmers?"

"Most of them," James says.

"Is anyone farming who doesn't get the dole?"

"One man," Michael says. I know how hard Michael works, so I assume ... "and it's not me." He names the man: Finbarr Doherty. So one farmer lives off the land. He rents it from plotholder 17 and 18 and has more land in his own area.

"Give us a loan of that breadboard, if you please, Nellie." The salt, pepper, jams, fork, butter, all go on the round board. Some get more space than others, "slices." "There you have it. A family's economic pie. Most people have a combination of those, very few have the whole lot. If you lose one of the smaller ones, maybe a couple, depending, you might still be okay. More, you could be in trouble."

It's a fine balance. The factories could close since most of them are only here because of the current language policy. So people like Tommo go into the factory but keep the farm, thinking they'll have something to fall back on.

"But they'll find it hard to farm if the factory fails. Their networks are gone," Michael says. "You'd need to have kept up with things and maybe get some new angle on farming. After being in a factory, you might be inclined to invest in new farm machinery or fertilizers, but I can tell you right now it won't pay you back." I know that, too; I've seen a summary of a recent survey by the Agricultural Institute; they say, in words close to this, that the land quality, the farm size, and the climate here are hopeless. Beautiful, but hopeless.

So they're not farmers. I'm amazed at how words can blind one to the obvious. When did "farmers" living on "farms" stop being farmers here? I remember James's comment a while back: "When agriculture was a way of life here it worked; when it became a way of earning a living, it didn't."

I repeat that now. "So this is fairly recent, having to combine a lot of sources of income?"

"Not at all," James says. "What do you think all the Coast Guard stations in the area were for? In the 1820s we got six, right in this little spot. We lost a good source of income when they came."

"Why?"

"Smuggling," Mrs. B. says, rather proudly. "They were built to stop people smuggling poitín and tobacco. Teelin had two." She sees my surprise.

"Aye, it was Teelin that was important in the old days, and it wasn't just for fishing. The road to Teelin goes past this house today, but in the old days it bypassed Carrick village entirely."

"But Glencolmcille had four lighthouses," Michael says, perhaps trying to take the bad look off Teelin.

"Carrick is landlocked. How did people here benefit?"

"You're confusing production and distribution," James says. Not surprising; I'm still confused about "farmers." "Remember I told you the people in Carrick were the middlemen. They distributed what Teelin produced."

We reassemble the tableware into conventional patterns and have a supper of toast, scrambled eggs, tea, and cake. Michael laughs. "You must think we're quare people around here. Your own people, your father, he has a regular job."

"Her father is off work betimes," James says. Maybe my father told him.

"He is." I take a fork. "This is my mother's sister Mary, she has a job and buys clothes for my brothers ... Mary can't drive, so this knife is my mother, who drives Mary to church and the store. Mary pays their other sister, Louise, an invalid, to do her ironing, she's this marmalade, and my grandmother ..."

"Is that the Stanton grandmother from Ballyglass?" Michael asks.

"Yes, she's a priest's cook, with no pension; domestic workers don't qualify for Social Security. Neither do agricultural workers."

"You'd wonder," Michael says, tapping the knife, fork, and marmalade. "Was it worth her while to leave here?"

I fall asleep thinking I should write to the little historian in the Valuation Office. The Stantons? Those "sins of the fathers"? But at 3 a.m. a more urgent question bolts me upright: if the Valuation Office's records don't show ownership unless people report it; if a farm can have three names or even more; if a "farm" is, in fact, a hodgepodge of plots; and if "farmers" don't necessarily farm, how will the Irish government monitor the success of its plan? And my thesis ...?

A line from Ireland's greatest playwright, Beckett: "I can't go on. I'll go on."

## Another Way of Planning Development

Conor is across the road on Margaret's roof. A *scréachóg reilige*, he says, a barn owl, has made a nest in her chimney.

Mrs. B's bad gate swings shut on my finger.

"Will I kiss it for you?" he shouts.

I take the high road. "Brian asked me to teach anthropology to the vocational school students."

"It's all Irish they speak there. Your own seems to be getting worse."

"I just have trouble with some sounds. Like the difference between *súil*, 'eye,' and *siúl*, 'walk.'" I spell the words.

"They don't sound alike at all. Look." When he says one, it looks like a kiss, and with the other, I see four upper and lower teeth. I study his mouth. I can do it! Margaret looks out, surprised.

"So tell me again what Brian asked you to do."

"*Mún*," I say. "Teach."

"Holy God. I hope it was '*múin*.' '*Mún*' is 'piss.'"

~

Where is the blasé Youngstown girl who continued shopping for a poodle skirt while a Mafia don was shot dead a few yards away? Today she's swooning over a draft report from the county development officer, Pat Bolger.

Pat is here to meet the development committee, now back to its old name, no "Southwest" anymore, about his draft county development plan. Afterward, he calls into Mrs. B.'s.

On a map he plots where Donegal's development might be focused.

"Who complains about the place that's chosen?"

"If you put a clinic in Kilcar, they'll want one in Carrick. If one village gets a sign, the village beside it wants one."

"So when something new is introduced into an area, you can predict where the complaints are likely to come from?"

"Certainly. They'll come from the twin of the successful place, village against village, town against town, region against region. No one understands if a library is built in one town, it's for the area. So the nearby town will want a library, too. If people had their way, every village would have a library, a clinic, a factory, a football stadium, a handball court, a swimming pool, and anything else that's going."

I think of Gaeltarra's planned industrial estate up in Gweedore, northwest Donegal. "Who will complain about Gweedore?" I ask. Not surprisingly, I know at least part of the answer to this.

"On the local level, the village nearest Gweedore. On the Donegal level, the southwest area; the whole of the peninsula down here will be up in arms. On the regional level, a truly Irish-speaking area in Galway, Carraroe. Probably that's why Gaeltarra is going to put the other estate there. Almost all the cardinal sins are involved: pride, covetousness, anger, greed, and envy."

All of this sounds familiar. I mention my study of where men stand on the village street in Carrick and Kilcar, then in Killybegs and then in Donegal Town. Everyone's together in Donegal Town, and working backwards, I can predict where they'll stand, down to the village level. I show Pat the diagram that James and Shane worked out.

"Does this reflect how people come together or divide when they're competing for good things?"

He studies my drawing and his map of Donegal, sketching small and big circles. "You might send me a copy of that," he says. "It matches my imaginary map, the one I use to predict where the complaints will come from."

It's clear to me, too, now who will protest a development, like a factory, and even how the successful community decides who can use it. For example, who's entitled to work in the Kilcar factory?

Later, James arrives with my copy of Evans-Pritchard's *The Nuer*, in Sudan. I notice that Evans-Pritchard's diagram of Nuer lineage and political organization illustrates the pattern that James, Shane, and Pat Bolger explained. I don't mention this to James for fear he'll forbid me to compare the Irish to the Nuer.

And I think about the anthropologist George Foster and his theory of "the limited good." In peasant societies, he says, people believe that the world has only so much of a good thing to go around, money, fame, whatever, and if you have more, I have less. The Irish don't qualify as "peasants," but from what I've learned today, their concept of a limited good is dead right.

## Make neither Big nor Wee of Priests

This morning a gentle local boy was ordained in Letterkenny. This evening we'll be treated to a gloriously medieval pageant, thanks to the community's ignoring a direct order from the new parish priest, Father Shiels.

Mrs. B. shares her ideas on the clergy: "Make neither big nor wee of them." She's a great woman for the chatty confession and the Novena, but she keeps priests to their sphere. And a priest is judged on his ways, not just his position, so she has a soft spot for the curate, Father Devlin. Some past priests are remembered fondly: A swallow-tail-coated canon, for example, who got the area court to sit regularly in Carrick in 1932 because he liked to play poker with the judge. "A real gentleman," James says. "In fact, so much of a gentleman he was almost a lady."

The new parish priest is concerned, reasonably, that the festivities will deteriorate as they did a few years ago in Kilcar. Drunken ordination revelers damaged property, leading, according to James, to bloodshed and "nearly litigation." At Mass today he said no celebrations can be held except in the parish hall. The faithful sat looking suitably meek, and once out the door they hurtled into action. Men strung colored lights across the street and banners saying, *Fáilte Roimh Abhaile*, "Welcome Home," and another in Latin, *Ad Multos Annos*, "For Many Years."

At the bridge, they build an arch of heather and lights, and timber is cut for torches. House-decorating begins in earnest: a big lighted cross upstairs in McGinley's shop takes the whole day to get right. Shrines appear in every window. When I ask what the priest will say, one lady laughs. "Yerra, the priest!" she says dismissively.

While it's still dusk, every car in the village goes out The Line. At 10:00, about fifty men and boys march out as far as "The Rock," *An Charraig*, after which Carrick is named. The Kilcar bagpipe band arrives. Soon the keen of ancient music echoes back across the river, and hills and mountains are alight with bonfires. The young man's entrance, escorted by the silent men bearing their tar-pitch torches, is like one Colmcille might have known. Car headlights come on at a signal, and the river's line seems strung with beads.

People whisper, "He's coming!" A banner stretches across the way as he enters his village: "Thou Are a Priest Forever." From every townland people flood in to stand in each other's traditional places, a wild, heady departure, and into houses and pubs to drink, dance, and celebrate a great day.

Afterward, everyone agrees it was a grand night; we won't see the likes of it again. The parish priest is gracious and relieved.[1]

---

1 For an extensive account of religion in the same area, see Lawrence Taylor's *Occasions of Faith*.

# July/Mí Lúil 1967

## The Woman with the Beautiful Eyes

A letter, from "Your father, Arthur L. Kane":

> I can't take my eyes off your mother, she's been so good to me over this emphysema. It's like a second honeymoon. I feel like I've buried a graveyard and planted a rose garden.

I've heard that's lung disease's upside, a high libido. His poor lungs. And my poor, prim mother.

Downstairs, visitors arrive and hushed voices share news. I go down hesitantly; maybe I'm not supposed to hear it? Margaret Cannon sees me from the kitchen door and waves me in. The conversation shifts to a newborn baby, and the length of its mother's labor.

"I had all my children at home. I never had any trouble until the last," Mrs. B. says. "I got a long tear and had to have eight stitches. I said to the doctor, 'Couldn't you make a decent seam of it? I could have done better myself.'"

"They don't care," Emer said. "When my mother had my youngest brother, her seventh, she was damaged but she didn't get fixed. A few years passed and the priest asked her why she had no new baby. She explained she couldn't. The priest said he wouldn't give her absolution until she promised to get herself repaired. So she went to a local doctor, and he did such a bad job she couldn't walk for a long time. She had years of misery; I remember it well. When I grew up I got hold of a specialist and he said she was lucky to be alive. He fixed her up in no time."

"I was 'churched' after each of my babies," Mrs. B. says. "To be 'purified.' These days they say it's a thanksgiving ceremony, but it didn't seem like that to me. I couldn't attend Mass at all until I was churched."

More horror stories, and tales of how little they'd been taught about their bodies. "I asked my mother why she never told me anything before I got married and she said she never told her other children anything and they did all right," Emer says.

Deirdre, a clerk in the post office, looks surprised. "I thought you younger girls knew more."

"No, I think most are told very little before marriage. If a girl's lucky, she knows enough to get by. If not, she's in for a terrible shock."

"I told my children whatever they asked," Mrs. B. announces. But I remember her son Fergus telling me how he learned everything from sifting through the encyclopedia in the parlor. He fled from his first sexual experience. "She had me in a clinch on a sofa, chewing on my ear, and I said to myself, 'Hold on here, amn't I supposed to be on top?'"

They tuck into tea and a tart Margaret brought, then swoop out like starlings, calling out about collecting children or, in Deirdre's case, being murdered for slipping away from the post office.

It was an odd, hurried assemblage, and I ask Mrs. B. why they came.

"I think they feel more welcome after some of them came over to help you with the map. They wanted to talk about poor Betty.

"Betty had a baby a long time ago. He must be nearly twenty now. She wasn't married, so her brother threw her out. After she had the baby I saw her on the road in Killybegs, freezing, with only a thin shawl for the baby. She couldn't go back to the brother.

"I helped her to her uncle's house in Killybegs and the devil, he wouldn't have her, but his wife said she could stay until the baby was stronger. After a while, the brother let her and the baby back."

"Well at least ..."

"He only did it because she'd got the special dole for unmarried mothers. Just for the first baby, not for more. But now, after all that, she's having another baby and Emer says they've taken her away."

"Who took her?"

"The brother, maybe, or the County Council. But I know where she's gone: the County Home in Stranorlar. It used to be the workhouse. It's a terrible place, they work all hours scrubbing and cleaning up to the last minute, and this is her second baby, so they'll take it away and then she'll probably be sent to the nuns in the Magdalen laundry in Galway. You could be there for life unless someone takes you out."

"Like who?"

"Your family, some relative. I knew a girl, Joan, her family took her out because she was getting the special dole, but they wanted to put her back when the second baby came along. I'd been her teacher and I brought her here as a maid. I knew the baby's father. *He* got the full dole all his life. Under Brehon Law in ancient Ireland, there was no concept of illegitimacy. You could say there still isn't, for the father."

"Where's Joan now?"

"England. The first baby is here, a grown man, single. He was never really accepted and he won't find any wife here, I can tell you that."

"And her other baby?"

"Who knows? The nuns adopted some babies out to Americans. For a fee. But Betty, she's a nice wee woman, a bit innocent maybe. Those eyes, you'd want to hug her ..." Betty must be the lost-looking little woman I've met a few times, the one whose eyes speckle with glints of azure and violet. I remember her soothing the child who fell on the parish priest's steps, and the angry look its mother gave her.

I go out into a wild, skin-lashing wind, but a bright sky, nothing between me and a sliver of ghost moon above. How can Betty, who knows the sweet heather on the mountains and the corncrake's rasp, survive in what sounds like a prison? And the father or fathers of her children, they're free.

Depressed, I go to Carrick Upper to see the farming I'm told is not being done. Map in hand, I talk to old men and to glum teenagers dumbstruck to hear American English coming out of this ordinary woman's mouth. I ask questions and later check the answers against the ones people gave on an Agricultural Institute survey last year. I've been warned people don't tell the truth on surveys, although a recent survey in Connemara asked people what they did "at night before television came in" and some were quite forthright. The answers I get today, and what I see, match the Agricultural Institute results.

From this and information from other townlands here and in Kilcar, I create a composite picture of the men on the land:

Seán Carr, sixty years old, will be the last representative of his line in Donegal. All of his siblings have emigrated to Long Island, New York; Butte, Montana; Glasgow; and Birmingham. Four of his five children have followed to Britain, and the youngest will join them when he completes the local technical school course. This son and one daughter who is a nurse are the first in the Carr family to have been educated past primary school; the girl was sent to a boarding convent school whose status implications are considered well worth the substantial drain on the small farmer's income.

Seán's farm clings to the edge of the sheerest seacoast in Europe. The scene, idyllic to the casual observer, is violently dramatic: the tiny, manicured, fluorescent green fields within neat mortarless fences of blue-grey field stone, and the whole park-like scene encompassed in the roar of the raging ocean and the incessant winds. Tourists congratulate Seán on the most impressive landscape in Europe.

The Agricultural Institute has worked out the average annual income for a farm like Seán's is £138; this includes the value of farm produce consumed by the family household.

Annual net farm cash income: sixteen pounds a year.

The farm, inherited from his father, has passed to Seán because he was the only child left at home. It's five acres in three fragments, each one nearly a half mile apart, plus commonage for sheep. Four acres are under grass; the remaining is divided equally between oats and potatoes. The farm has two cows, two calves and a dozen sheep; Seán's wife keeps ten hens. The only farm building is a derelict house built by Seán's great-grandfather. The family has no car, television, or farm machinery except a cart, a plough, and a harrow. His land is so rugged only a scythe will do for cutting hay. Most groceries and small household purchases are made from a traveling van sent out by a shop in the next town.

Seán Carr has no hope for his farm. He has never used agricultural credit; he does not know where to get it and fears taking on a debt he could not repay. He feels no sensible agency could give credit to a poor older man without heirs like himself. He supposes he would use credit for fencing and manuring; he would not apply it toward new land, stock, machinery, or farm buildings.

He works on the county roads when he gets a chance. His grown children send money home, his wife knits, and Seán gets the dole.

Michael has more land, eighteen acres in three separate parcels, twelve arable, six grazing, and a shared hundred of commonage. He has more livestock. His farm machinery is the same as Seán Carr's, except that he hires a tractor to cut the hay. Except for hay, everything he grows goes to feed his family. He attends every local rural science class he can. With this, the dole, his part-time work as one of the stewards of the Gael Linn estate, and the hard work of his wife and children, the family has managed to send one son to university, a daughter to nursing school, and the other children to secondary school as they become old enough. And still, he makes time to help sort through my maze of land records.

## A Trip to The Mental

"A wee bit slack, that poor creature," Mrs. B. says one morning as a young man passes by. "God laid a heavy hand on him." People make careful distinctions when they talk about mental handicaps: a person may be "innocent," "a wee bit simple," "not the full shilling," "nervous," "on tablets," or, oddly, "religious."

I'm satisfied urban skeptics are wrong about rural people being lazy, but a second possible stereotype is that high rates of mental illness make it hard to find and keep good workers. Is it true? And do people who live here think it's high? (The quick answer: yes, in every village except their own.) I want to see if rates are indeed high and if yes, why? Outsiders often blame inbreeding; life in closed, small-minded, suspicious communities; and lack of sexual outlets.

Yesterday James nabbed me at the petrol pumps. "You wouldn't be going to Letterkenny anytime soon?" He's opened his gambit correctly, making a negative statement rather than asking a direct question. He said he wants to see the county engineer, but "some gobshite" has smashed into the back of his car/taxi. The mental hospital is in Letterkenny, too, so I decided to visit it and I offered him a lift.

～

Before dawn, Annie and I collect James. The village is asleep, as still as a stage set, but out along the road some of the farmers, real and part time, are setting out to save the hay. James says we are in for a treat: the mental hospital, now called St. Conal's, was built in 1866, one of twenty-nine built under the British. "It's one of the finest buildings in Ireland. Neo-Georgian, built by a famous architect ..." As he settles in for a learned discourse, we're flagged down in Straleel, a few miles out of Carrick, by Willie John O'Donnell on a bicycle. James gives him a jerk of the head and a wink, which is the correct thing to do when one male passes another on the road.

"Is Willie John a relative?" I ask.

"Not at all," he says. "He's a different O'Donnell. He isn't even a friend. He isn't even a distant friend!"

"A distant friend?"

"A distant friend would be someone like a far-out relative of your mother's or father's."

"Surely, one of yours, too?"

"No, no. Look, here's an example: a second cousin once removed that you didn't really know very well might be called a 'friend.' Someone might say to me, 'Sure, you must know Bridget Hegarty, she's a friend of yours.'"

"But wouldn't she be a friend of your mother's, too?" I ask. James never mentioned these categories when he was helping me with local genealogy.

"No, Bridget would be closer to my mother, pure second cousin, so my mother would say, "Bridget is 'three and three' to me.""

"'Three and three.'"

"Exactly. See, it's simple: let's say I have a first cousin, Paddy. So Paddy is 'two and two' to me."

I pass my notebook to Annie in the back.

"Paddy and I are first cousins," he says, very slowly. "'Two and two.' First I work out who connects Paddy and me; it happens we have the same grandmother. So then I count down from my grandmother to me: my mother is one and I'm two. Then I go back and count down from my grandmother to Paddy. His mother is one and he's two. So Paddy is 'two and two' to me, or 'four of kin' to me."

"Uh huh," I say. He sketches it on the fogged windscreen.

"That's in English, of course. Here we'd say *a dó agus a dó* – 'two and two.' Or we *could* say *col ceathrar*, which is the same as 'four of kin.'"

"Right."

"Now, if Paddy has a child, that child is 'two and three' to me, *a dó agus a trí*. So that's a second cousin once removed. *Col cúigear*. Five of kin."

Annie murmurs agreement.

"Just as if I had a child, that child would be 'two and three' to Paddy."

"And if Paddy has a child, as well, the two children will be 'three and three' to each other?" I ask. It seems like a neat, elegant system, better than our own saying: "He's some kind of cousin, I think."

"Exactly!" James beams at me as one might at a dog that's finally learned the meaning of the word "sit."

In 1966, the anthropologist Robin Fox did an excellent study of kinship as part of an examination of land tenure on Tory Island, in the far north of Donegal, and I doubt he was roared at like this.

"So," I ask James, "What are you to your mother? 'One and two'?"

He sighs. "Where do you get these ideas? Your mother's always your mother, isn't she? Sometimes I don't understand Americans. You're very cold-blooded."

We drive on.

In Letterkenny, the original part of the hospital could be mistaken for a palace, with stepped immaculate lawns and farm fields extending over what must be a huge acreage.

The chief psychiatric nurse, Eddie McDermott, gives us an outdoor tour. "All these national hospitals were built on the philosophy of that time – beauty, good housing, fresh air, and plain good food were important in helping what they called 'lunatics' to recover."

Inside, vacant-looking men sit around the perimeter of a lounge. We go through a corridor lined on one side with heavy-doored cells, grates at the bottom and a few sight holes at eye level. Mr. McDermott says they haven't been used as lockups for a dozen years; today patients with money can furnish them as their quarters. Some areas get brightly painted when the County Council has the money. The "New Building," seventy years old, has recreation rooms and dormitories. Men and women are segregated, and as we come into a sunroom we see, through the windows, women working in a laundry.

Mr. McDermott introduces, in a kindly way, a man "who is the young English Queen's father," and then we move on to the "farm," where men work in the afternoon. They grow vegetables for various outlets, including the factory in Carrick. Before a man leaves the hospital for good, he might work for a farmer, who keeps him and pays him two pounds a

week. Others might go out on a daily basis. McDermott says it's difficult
for people leaving here to get work, and until the 1950s it was considered
a shame to have a family member in the hospital. Even now, some long-
term patients have no visitors. They send out Christmas cards and get
no reply.

I've noticed the hospital seems "open" and I ask if a patient could simply walk away. "Yes, if he has somewhere to go, but often the young single
fellows and the geriatrics go back to such poor conditions, no money or
food or fire, that they get worse. At least here they get a little comfort and
sixty cigarettes a week."

Mr. McDermott says the hospital has about 500 nurses and leaves us
in the occupational therapy room with one, a handsome young nurse/
therapist, Noel. Men are making rocking horses, cane chair seats, coat
hangers, fiber mats. The average hospital stay is about ten weeks, but
Noel says most of the workers we're seeing here have been in the hospital
five to thirty years.

Behind Noel's back, a man with a radiant smile holds the blade of a
five-foot, two-handled scythe only inches from Noel's neck. One of the
handles is broken. Noel sees our terror and turns. "Have some sense,
Jimmy. That's a dangerous object you have there. Take it to the carpenter."

As we part, Noel explains that four psychiatric workers travel around
the areas to help patients who have been released. Also, the psychiatrist
visits Killybegs once a month.

We stay the night, Annie and I at Gallagher's hotel, James with a
friend, distant or not; he didn't explain.

~

This morning we record details of patients from Carrick, Kilcar, Teelin,
and Glencolmcille from 1873, shortly after the opening, to the near present. (I avoid the latest; I might know the people.) Despite the pleasant atmosphere, the neat records show, line by copperplate line, this has been
a place for luckless wretches, some just bewildered, others doomed, past

hope and beyond recall. In earlier days, one, Robert,[1] was admitted for "loneliness"; Bridget, single, twenty-three, suffered from mania because her brother "lost his position"; and Con, an old laborer, was confused by "privation" and died in the hospital after seven years. Page after page, the elderly, the unemployed, the homeless, the bereaved, and anyone else not accepted elsewhere. As we moved through the years and into the early 1960s their diagnoses, such as "idiot," "melancholy," "depression," and "dementia," were the same. Some came, left, and returned, but "repeats" aren't distinguished from first-timers. Sometimes I'm able to tell repeats from the name, location, and age, but often shared common names, first and last, make it difficult. It isn't possible to form numbers or percentages of the communities' populations.

The causes of these complaints were often similar, too, reflecting "physical failures" such as alcoholism or masturbation, and "moral failures" such as poverty, homelessness, or the most serious, "religion." In Carrick and Kilcar, this last category was seen as the most serious even in the mid-1960s. But in the early 1960s, I saw blanks in diagnoses and causes. Why?

"A new system was coming in. We were waiting to hear," Mr. McDermott says as he shows us out. Most cases today, he says, are coming in for depression, followed by geriatric cases, and the 20 per cent who are schizophrenics. "Many people are suffering from these major complaints because they're old and isolated. Others, when we come to know them, are just lonely. You won't see that in the records because what you see is the initial diagnosis when the person was admitted. The comments don't tend to get updated or fleshed out afterward."

I'm worried I didn't compare the figures we've been recording with those of patients from the rest of Donegal, including more urban areas. But the records aren't kept that way: villages are mentioned, but a village isn't a Census unit, and the next level up, a district, is a Census unit but

---

1 All names are changed.

is too big and can contain both rural and urban areas. Eddie waves these concerns aside.

"Mental illness is worst on the southwest coast," he says flatly. "From Killybegs on out the peninsula, Kilcar, Carrick, Teelin, Glencolmcille. The causes you've read about, poverty, remoteness, lack of social life, all make life more precarious out there." Just as Mr. Redington said.

## A Bit Irish

James seems pleased with himself as we leave for home in the late afternoon.

"So Willie John in Straleel isn't a relative of yours," I goad.

"No! Yet he claimed there were offerings on me when his mother died."

"Offerings" are taken seriously in this area, the last in Ireland to observe the custom. Relatives, friends, and neighbors of the deceased pay carefully calculated amounts at the priest's house, after the funeral, or at the graveside. Later the priest or a parishioner reads out each name and amount publicly. The money is part of the priest's salary, possibly as a legacy of the Penal Days when priests had to function secretly and had no formal income. Someone with little connection to the dead person has no obligation; in fact, paying offerings unnecessarily may cause a chain of resentment lasting for years.

"Willie is being mischievous. And stupid, because if I paid offerings for his mother, he'd have to pay offerings for me and anyone in my family when we died."

We get back late. All curtains are drawn. Mrs. B. is staying overnight with a friend.

This morning I catch sight of James in the shop, his face like thunder. It's too early for more kinship lessons so I continue on to the post office.

"You've heard?" the clerk says. "You that knows everything."

"What?"

"James Mary Agnes is red raw with anger! You know the Sultan."

I do. I've gone to the trout farm a few times now. His poor hearing isn't a big obstacle: between us, we manage.

Most nicknames I can figure out. "Birdsong at Eventide" is an exuberantly "operatic" off-key singer; the woman called "A Little Knowledge" has an opinion on everything. I don't know how the Sultan got his name.

"Boys oh dear, the Sultan's a terrible man for Irish," she says, because he refuses to speak English to the locals. "Two days ago, while ye were away in Letterkenny," she says, emphasizing the plural ye, "the Sultan went to the Gardaí and gave out yards of abuse to the sergeant. 'If you ever speak English to my wife again on the phone,' says the Sultan, 'I'll shoot you.'

"Well, you know his Irish, he's so fast it can be very hard to understand. Everyone was confused, so the Sultan made shooting motions. 'Ah,' the sergeant says, 'It's the Humane Killer he wants.'" The Humane Killer is the gun kept above the door in the Garda station, to be lent to farmers when there's an animal to be put down.

"The sergeant hands the Sultan the gun." She acts out the parts. 'There you are, good man yourself. Bring it back when you're finished.' Of course, the Sultan's hearing isn't great and he thought the sergeant was challenging him to shoot. He was raging. He took the gun out behind the station and let off a shot in the air."

"And ...?"

"Then he brought it back. You know him, he's a real pet."

So. Nothing to do with James.

"Well, James was away, the village saw you going that morning, but someone from Straleel came down and couldn't find him. On his way home he met another fellow who said he'd heard the Sultan had shot someone, that it had to do with the Sultan's wife."

"That's ridiculous."

"The next thing, Willie John got wind of it and hopped down to leave funeral offerings for James at the presbytery. Then others did. The priest is away, or he could have straightened them out. This morning James heard about it and went up to the presbytery to see what was what. All the offerings came from Straleel or beyond."

"Did you think of sending one?"

"Sure nobody here in the village thought he was dead. Didn't we all see you go off?"

I turn in at the pub to get James's version.

"Only one offering came from this village, and to be fair, that one was just wishful thinking. But," and his face flames, "Willie John, the hoor, he *knew* I was away and yet he paid huge offerings, knowing well the priest will have to give them back to him, me not being dead. So Willie's lost nothing but I ... I have to pay offerings forevermore for *his* family, *and* some of the others, people we've never had to give offerings for." He grasps for words, trying to put the situation in its proper perspective. "You know what it is," he says finally. "It's a bit Irish."

Maybe this is why the Catholic Church is abolishing funeral offerings.

When I get home, Mrs. B. is back, indignant about the fuss. "You'd think people would have learned sense after the time McGill of Glencolmcille died. People thought it was McGuire of the Glen of Kilcar and flocked to his house. And the time the post office put out word a man from Muckross was dead when he was off playing cards."

Late this afternoon, I ask James what he meant by "a bit Irish." "It's ..." He sits down, makes a few spluttering starts, and then, "It can't be defined. As such."

This doesn't sound like James.

"Well ... here's an example. 'Pat The Clock' is the electrical repairman in Kilcar but doesn't have electricity in his house. *That's* a bit Irish. Of course, once you're in the know it makes sense. He's wired the house but he won't connect it to the grid because the rates are too high. Quite right. Or here's another: someone runs over one of your chickens and appears at your back door, selling you a fresh chicken."

"So is that different from someone being 'More Irish than the Irish themselves'?"

James reflects. "'A bit Irish' can mean a bit outrageous, or over the top, a contradiction in terms, the worst in us coming out maybe, *but* ... a little admirable, nonetheless. People like stories like this about the offerings. You wouldn't have heard about it if they didn't. It could easily have been hidden from you."

I ponder this, for good reason.

"But 'more Irish than the Irish themselves' isn't a compliment. We say it about non-Irish people. It plays on our secret worry that maybe the Irish people are failing to be sufficiently Irish. Or, possibly, a suspicion that too much Irishness is a bad thing. And maybe it is: like the capers you Yanks get up to with your St. Patrick's Day parades; that's just what we call 'Paddywhackery,' cartoon Irishness."

My grasp fades in and out. What seems clear is only the non-Irish can be "more Irish than the Irish themselves," and only Irish people can do things that are "a bit Irish." But of course there's an underlying question: "What's Irish?"

## Mental Illness Caused by Tea Drinking?

Mrs. B. is making a version of my mother's pierogies. I open my notes on the mental hospital records, ninety-four years of them.

Thousands entered this hospital in the years for which totals are given. Over the years, 340 people from this area were admitted, almost equally divided between the two parishes, Glencolmcille and Kilcar. Kilcar people think there are more from Glencolmcille parish. But Glencolmcille parish includes three separate villages, Carrick, Teelin, and Glencolmcille, and some people (those from Carrick and Teelin) think there's a lot more mental illness in the isolated areas of Glencolmcille. I imagine the Glencolmcille people have their own views. But certainly the kinds of diagnoses for all three villages are similar.

Why so many, though? Probably for the same reason that the area is Irish speaking: historically, land in western coastal areas was too poor to attract colonizers. Poverty protected the language, just as it made life unendurable for some.

Until hospitals were built, the last refuge for the disadvantaged, particularly the poor and elderly, was the local workhouse. In the worst decade of the famines, 1841–51, almost 285,000 people died in workhouses, nearly half of them children under fifteen. Glenties, the workhouse closest to Carrick and Kilcar, was no exception. Doomed wretches, starved on watery rations, ragged, freezing, segregated, removed from their young children, were packed into sleeping quarters on dirty straw alongside those dying of dysentery. Before the famine of autumn 1846, existing workhouses were half full; six months later they were packed to capacity and turning away thousands.

My first records are from 1873, so all those horrors and more had happened only twenty-five years earlier. But as the British began building more mental hospitals in Ireland for "lunatics and idiots," they were quickly filled not only with the mentally ill but also with those who would have once been housed in the deeply stigmatized workhouses. Unwed mothers, the "simple," isolated bachelors – vulnerable people left alone and others needing help to cope with ordinary life all entered, some willingly, others not. Even geriatrics entered the mental hospital because few forgot that the new county homes for the aged poor and infirm were once workhouses.

Once built, local communities saw the imposing buildings and professional staff as badges of their own significance and as sources of employment. Outpatient treatment and community placements, popular more recently in Britain, haven't gone down well in these places: if people are treated outside, will the mental hospital close? Counting all those in Irish mental hospitals as "mentally ill" and comparing the rates of hospitalization in Ireland with those of countries that also have outpatient facilities raises the percentage of Irish sufferers, wrongly, to pandemic levels.

In the early records for the area, many more men than women were admitted. Almost all men were single laborers under thirty. Later, the ratio becomes 55–45. Only about half the women were single, probably because there wasn't much place for a single woman in this area unless she was caring for a brother or elderly relatives. Most of the women were over forty. A few years into the records, some women are shown as having occupations; knitter, sprigger. A few male weavers and carpenters appear. Numbers of older people, especially men, increase over the years.

Some cases stand out. Daniel, a twenty-two-year-old unmarried laborer, diagnosed in 1878 with "mania" caused by "poverty," died in the hospital eight years later, about the time William, same age and occupation, was admitted for "mania" caused by "masturbation." In 1909, James, thirty-five, another single laborer, suffered from melancholia, the symptoms of which are listed as "religion, etc." Michael, a married farmer of forty-one, was admitted in 1933 with no diagnosis, but his symptom, "brooding," had been brought on by "poverty"; Helen, a married woman of sixty-six, had "delusions" caused by "financial worry"; and Sarah, fifty-five, was admitted for "worrying about her marriage."

In 1960, international diagnostic categories are used and no more "Nervous" or "Brooding." A diagnosis of schizophrenia becomes more common now, and other diagnoses decline. Some possible explanations are a florescence of schizophrenia, better diagnostic criteria, a trend in psychiatry, or even a "ditto" effect, with some records showing a string of dittos for schizophrenia, followed by a string of dittos for manic depression. But none of those explain why some recurring patients received a different diagnosis each time. It's not unusual for someone much earlier entered as "melancholy" to be listed as obsessive-compulsive on a later admission, and even later, as schizophrenic.

Some local cases are repeats. John, a middle-aged laborer living alone, appears first in 1963 as a manic depressive, and then, in the first half of

1966, he's admitted and diagnosed three times: "neuro-reactive depressive" the first and third time, and schizophrenic the second.

Even though some of the patients are dead ninety years, the names read as if from a census of today's Carrick or Kilcar. But as I came closer to the 1960s, I didn't want to see names of neighbors. I blocked people's names and just recorded their other details.

I began this exercise to see if high rates of mental illness affected the supply of workers and the attractiveness of the area for investors. I started with early mental hospital records just to see the causes and diagnoses, but it's easy to suspect them. And much as I would like to tackle urban prejudices, I found it difficult to compare these rural villages with urban areas.

Enough. I rise, stiff, and glance out. Today is Fair Day. The street is full of happy people. Or at least I think they're happy.

# August/Mí Lúnasa 1967

## When You're on the Front Foot

When you see an old countrywoman shawled and shrouded in black, it's hard to picture the magic underneath:

1. *A flannelette petticoat with sleeves, blue or pink*
2. *A chemise or vest of fine wool, with short sleeves and a high neck, reaching below the hips, used to keep the clothes tight*
3. *Some sort of corset with steel stays, tied with laces or hooked. The suspenders can be cut off and garters worn instead. From the waist down, a white báinín or flannel petticoat*
4. *A red flannel petticoat*
5. *A black skirt, of coat-like material, some form of serge*
6. *A blouse in a black satin material*
7. *A black cardigan*
8. *An apron on top*
9. *Black woolen stockings and black cotton ones over that.*
10. *On top, for church: a shawl of black blanket-like wool with a fringe*

Maybe I'm off topic again, but who can say? Everything is grist to an anthropologist. Annie gave me this list. The first nine are what her great-aunt Maggie Ruadh wears every day.

"And the modern young American lady?" Mrs. B. asks, after I read them out. "Woolly socks, thermal underpants, knitted undervests, and a flannelette nightgown and dressing gown over all, and that's only at night."

But she's reverted to her current worry: what will her daughter Aoife and her family make of the cracked linoleum, the rutted gravel, the leaky water pipe, and the unusable front gate when they arrive in two weeks?

"Where's Conor?"

"He's abroad somewhere," she says, so I go looking in the rain.

He's alone at a house site, turning a hand-operated cement mixer. "It's a high-wire act every day," he says. "The suppliers don't have the stuff, or else it's the stuff you only need at the end, not the start, or they might order the wrong thing, glass too small for the window, so you have to start again with a new order and wait. If some of the crew show up, the rest might still be stuck on another job because it rained when they wanted to pour cement or another guy they needed didn't show up to help, so they can't finish, and there am I ... So I start with some block layers but then the plasterer comes early ..." He's drawing a rough flow chart in the mud. "And the carpenter is held up because they didn't send enough timber out, and the electrician wrecks the plasterer's work."

But I notice Conor is smiling, his face pink with pleasure as he reflects on the scenario. "So you wouldn't do anything else?"

We look around at the broken wheelbarrow, the battered bucket filled with hardening cement, a pile of boards warped in the rain, a mound of spent tea leaves and a mucky length of old carpet. He picks at a grimy bandage on his hand.

"Och, when you're on the front foot, like this, it's easy enough to love." What can the "back foot" be like, then?

"So still no *grá*, no love, for factory work?" I ask. "You'd get two weeks' paid holidays."

"I'm on my holidays this minute. Builders always take two weeks in August. Not a block to be laid. The suppliers are closed, too, to keep desperados from making their own home repairs. Not a pane of glass, not a bag of cement to be had."

"I meant a paid holiday." I see now Aoife's family will have to rough it at Mrs. B.'s, whatever season they come.

"Why would I go into a hot factory?" He waves his beefy arm at the sopping grey plot strewn with odd bits of metal and plastic. "Or why would I be laboring for someone else in the tunnels in England, taking shifts in a dirty bed in a boarding house, when I could be here ..." He trails off, laughing. "Here, where no one's shown up today, and I'm the one mixing cement by hand in the rain."

I point out that he's stopped, a bad thing to do with cement. He curses. "You always put my head astray," he says.

I see Conor as an unpredictable force of nature, a breezy enigma, his timetable something like the Sumerian calendar, but I've been surprised to find out most others don't. "He's a genius, that fellow," Brian told me one day at the vocational school. "He had no business leaving school here at fifteen."

I look around. For all I know, some of this rubble could be inventions-in-progress, leftovers from engineering breakthroughs, or, as it looks, some of the old pipework from Mrs. B.'s bathtub. When I turn back, Conor is immediately behind me, almost touching. I laugh, a false, merry tinkle, and move sideways.

"Just an experiment." He coughs, embarrassed.

"What experiment?"

"Did you hear what I said just now?" he asks.

"You didn't say anything. You're just standing behind me, like you're always doing lately."

"You can't hear," he says. "I tested it over and over, indoors, outdoors, shouting from Margaret's roof. You can't hear when someone's speaking, behind you. You must read lips or something because you seem to get by all right. Don't give me that look. Just turn around and put your hand up when you hear something." I turn.

"See, you didn't hear me."

"What did you say?" I ask.

"I'm not telling you."

I go back to Mrs. B.'s, subdued, and tell her I don't hear properly.

"I know. You never answer the doorbell. And your Irish got even worse since you were sick."

"Does everyone know?"

"You pay so much attention when people speak, they think you're a great listener."

I recall a comment of Father McDyer's: "Forgive me if I seem to be addressing you as if you're a public meeting." Maybe he has an oratorical flair, as some say. But maybe in my case it was a kindly gentility.

～

Back at the house, Gaeltarra Éireann's chair, Ivor Kenny, is on the radio. "What the Gaeltacht people want can be said in one word: work."

What the Gaeltacht people in Carrick and Kilcar want requires a few more words.

"Three-phase electricity," Chairman Leo says.

"An industrial estate," says Bláthnaid, a chilblain-cheeked teenager in Gallagher's shop.

"An advance factory," says an old man at the bus stop.

"What's an advance factory?" I ask James, who's behind his shop counter.

Three little boys approach and put down thirty-six ha'pennies (half pennies). "We sold lots of sunflowers," one says delightedly. "Please will you change these into eighteen pennies?" James does so, patting the boy's head and praising his ability to do sums.

"An advance factory is what it says. A company might want a factory, but it won't come here unless we put up a building first. And infrastructure."

"Advance factories sound like industrial flypaper," I joke. James frowns.

The little boys return and ask him to change their pennies into six thruppences (three-penny coins). He does. "Ah, the wee pets," he says when they scamper out, each clutching two coins.

I hear one woman say to another, "That's a bit Irish. Those boys got the sunflowers from James's garden."

~

James shows up at Mrs. B.'s during his pub's legal closing time, the "Holy Hour," daily from 2 to 4 p.m. He's carrying my copy of Worsley's *The Trumpet Shall Sound*, obviously well-read.

"You know about these cargo cults down in Micronesia?"

"Yes."

"And the warehouses?"

I nod. "In World War II," I tell Mrs. B., "Allied troops landed airplanes there and unloaded lots of supplies, razors, torches, toothbrushes, combs. The natives never saw anything like it and their hearts were broken when the Allies left and took everything with them. So they prayed and built bamboo warehouses, bamboo landing strips, docks, thinking it would attract cargo."

James raises a cautionary finger. "You asked me about advance factories. I sensed you might be taking a light-hearted tone."

I was.

"People here won't want you writing any anthropological articles on 'The Cargo Cults of Carrick' or any such nonsense. I'm telling you now." And with a little salute, he goes.

## The Prides of Kilcar

Kilcar is a fine place, industrious and, to me, it's almost more familiar than Carrick, with its factory workers and greater number of cars. A senior anthropologist might see it as the more interesting place, although what could be more interesting than Carrick? Carrick had the same Parish Council/Development Committee members or their children for twenty-seven years, seeking the same factory, not getting it, and going on regardless. But poignancy gets you nowhere in anthropology.

I've interviewed Kilcar people for months now, but much of what an anthropologist learns comes from informal encounters, and I wasn't part of Kilcar's day-to-day life. The young Kilcar curate finds me a place to stay with an older couple. Some rush to tell me the couple are "crabbit" and difficult, but I was forewarned about Mrs. B. and it worked out wonderfully. I listen to the priest.

Moving day is dry and hot, and the first person I meet in Kilcar is "Better," who's handing bundles of straw to a couple of men thatching a house. I ask if I can take a picture, and the thatchers agree, no bother, they say.

My hosts, Billy and Madge, are pleasant, obliging people. I have a bedroom and the parlor is set aside as my "office." People go out of their way to help. The McFadden family invites me to copy some letters from nineteenth-century Kilcar emigrants to the United States. Knowing their parents couldn't read, they sent the letters to Miceál Óg McFadden, a businessman, who read them out. Later, Miceál Óg was elected to the Dáil and the Seanad (Senate) and lobbied to get the factory.

The writers, most with a primary education or less, explored the issues such as the Gold Standard and the ethnic rivalries on the first transcontinental railway. The letters show how easily men traveled great distances, peddling goods, visiting people, seeking work. "I was in Butte, Montana, last week," a man writes from Chicago, "and I ran into Danny McBrearty from Bogagh Glebe, who has a fine wife now."

Tommo and The Fear Ruadh, The Red-Haired Man, spend nights looking at the plotholder records for the entire Kilcar area, village and countryside, just as Michael and Shane did for Carrick. They reach a similar conclusion, although more land is being sold or divided, not for consolidation but for housing, mainly for factory workers.

One day, waiting for the factory to open, I feel a gentle stroking on my coat. I turn to see a little girl about eight, with dark honey-colored hair.

"Are you the famous lady?" Her hand lingers on the strands and nubs of wool. She looks up, eyes wide, smile full of sweetly wayward teeth. "Miss O'Donnell?" she whispers.

Oh.

Kilcar has four claims to distinction, according to the many people who ask me to mention this in "The Book": its factory, its football team, its marching band, and Mary O'Donnell. Underlying their stories is a heroic resolve, feistiness, and a touch of magic.

Why write about Mary O' Donnell when eventually Hollywood will do a better job? She left school at fifteen and Kilcar at seventeen. In New York, she saw marvels: telephone numbers longer than two digits, teenagers on pink phones chatting for hours; beautiful clothes. Irish girlfriends got her a job in a restaurant.

"What would you like to be?" a favorite customer asked her.

"A fashion designer." The customer directed her across the street to an excellent design academy.

"A thousand dollars a year for tuition," the Irish-American manager said, more than half Mary's wages. You could attend Harvard for $500 more. But the manager said she could pay it off monthly and attend evening classes. She came second in a class of ninety-seven.

She took her diploma and crossed the street again, this time to the world-famous designer Mainbocher, who dressed princesses, film stars, and the Duchess of Windsor. She was dismissed: "We don't take trainees." But then real magic came into play, because as Mary was about to leave she caught the eye of an elegant woman and was given a week's trial. Weeks passed; she kept her head down and worked hard. The elegant woman disappeared into the higher reaches of couture.

Their next encounter came months later in the elevator. Her Exquisiteness smiled. "You're doing grand, Mary," she said in a thick County Fermanagh accent.

Now, in New York in her early thirties, Mary is an internationally known couture fashion designer, a celebrity in Ireland and a heroine in Kilcar. What inspired her? If you lift your eyes from the rainy street you see shadowed hills changing from fawn to deep purple to smoky blue, and the agate, foam-dappled Glenaraddagh River bubbling over the rocks. The view never left her.

Some girls, like Mary, followed their dreams; others followed the pipe band. Men in kilts! Sporrans! Spats! The firm legs, stockings fitting nicely at the calf. The glorious shivery sound as they practiced on the lonely roads by the light of the moon!

Band life hadn't always been so magical. In the early 1930s, pipers and drummers, instruments and uniforms, even people who could read music were in short supply. Three brothers and a couple of friends, along with four drummers, struggled on, practicing in Paddy McNelis's barn. Someone sent away for a book of Scottish pipe music and a man came from Derry to teach them. William Gallagher from Bavin got a legacy from America and bought six pipes. The factory donated green and saffron tweed, and Mary Carr and Columba Doherty made the kilts. Most of the men were farmers or weavers, and their surnames are still common among today's proud marchers, who know their legacy.

The band's first outing was St. Patrick's Day, 1934. "They marched up to the priest's house," an old O'Donnell in the post office told me, "where they played a few tunes and Canon McGinley gave them a pound. Then they marched out along The Line, maybe as a treat for the unfortunates of Carrick who had no band."

They've been at it ever since, sometimes with descendants of the first members, so long as they're male, all in stunning russet uniforms. They come into their own when Kilcar footballers play in a final.

The football team! In the early 1950s, emigration made fielding a team difficult, but the factory kept some young men at home. Players had to be nerveless: the football ground at Tawny Beach, possibly one of the most picturesque in the world, could put a man off his game. If a ball, often the team's only ball, shot into a calm sea, even in rough waters, a foolish player might risk a cold dangerous swim rather than give up play. Another problem was foot size; the team had only so many boots, kept in a box in a pub, and if a fellow found a pair that fit on the day, he played.

But within a few years, Kilcar had a star team. The big day came on May 13, 1960. People talk about it as if they were still up in Glenties, watching Dungloe being trounced – Kilcar 1-11, Dungloe 0-7 – to win the first senior county victory in twenty-five years.

A convoy of about sixty flag-bedecked cars awaited the heroes as they were borne out of the playing ground, led by the trophy-waving captain, Seán Doogan. Cheers, shouts, and horns followed the long procession home to Kilcar, where the band piped them in and hundreds of people, waving the Kilcar colors, carried them to the home field. Speeches, sing-ing, dancing, and drinking filled the evening; bonfires lit the hills.

The mid-sixties are darker. Kilcar lost five Glencolmcille players when Glen set up its own team. The players are older. But the younger team, the minors, are doing fine ... so maybe there's hope.

The last pride is the factory, giving employment to locals and involved in everything. If I hear of any non-local employees, I know it's because they're great footballers.

"If someone in the factory is suspended for something, the commu-nity thinks he's let down the name of the place," Mr. Redington says. "The good name, that's very important."

But the factory could close. Sometimes I wonder if the government, instead of designing schemes dependent on farmers selling land, would do better to insist on Irish being the language of the factory.


## A Lot of People Have Good Reason to Be Nervous

One afternoon outside Kilcar village I stopped because the car door wouldn't shut. From a field above me I heard a voice say, "Heeere's the pitch!" and a loud crack. I climbed up into the field.

A burly man with a mitt, presumably the coach, shouted, "You're sitting in the catbird seat now, Malachy!" Malachy didn't seem to know if this was good or bad. The coach was irritated at my approach, but when I apologized my accent got me welcomed as a baseball expert. He introduced himself as Peadar Malloy. People had said it was a shame I couldn't talk to Peadar, a great historian and sportsman who emigrated to Chicago years ago. Now he was back, retired, ready for anything.

But local interest in baseball wanes when Peadar gets a dislocated knee after a "collision at home base" and the boys drift back to their Irish games. Peadar gets a plaster cast and I visit him, bringing the requisite Lucozade. He's sunk into an upholstered chair, leg on an ottoman.

"How's the Blue and Gold doing?" I ask, knowing it galls him not to be down on the Gaelic Athletic Association playing field.

"Ah, sure, I wonder are our glory days behind us?"

A woman comes in and leaves a tea tray. Peadar sits up, groaning.

"You're well looked after," I say.

"She's a great neighbor, a saint. You've probably come across her son Huey, a *duine le Dia*." A person with God, a simple person.

I remember those other phrases I've heard people use. I list them: "A 'wee bit simple,' 'not the full shilling,' 'nervous,' 'on tablets,' and 'religious.' Is he a wee bit simple?" I ask, fishing for my notebook.

"No, 'a wee bit simple' is ... let's see ... a lowish IQ. A *duine le Dia* is someone who might be an imbecile but could also have a special gift, an insight or talent, a holy fool, a madman with a touch of brilliance. That's what Huey is."

"And 'religious'?"

"'Religious' is the most serious. For example, someone who goes in and out of church thirty times a day, blessing himself over and over. He can't stop, he'd be terrified of what would happen if he did."

"Obsessive-compulsive disorder?"

"Sort of. But our categories are more useful to us than the "proper" ones you'd see in the hospital. Different boundaries, even substance and symptoms, sometimes."

I say I know this from personal experience of using "tree," "bush," and shrub" instead of the "proper" botanical categories.

"Exactly. Experts might laugh," he says, "but how does a person end up in the mental hospital? Does a doctor go from house to house? No. We use our own categories to decide whether to approach the doctor. Take 'religious.' When the person isn't in church, he's at home scrubbing his sins. Maybe the family can't handle that after a while. They can't get through to the person that he's not sinful. They and the doctor agree he needs help.

"But not always. What's serious to a doctor may just be a wee bit eccentric to us. 'Nervous,' for example, is troublesome for the person, maybe, but not for the community. We can deal with that. So our terms include a dimension that the official ones don't. But maybe they should." He slaps his good knee for emphasis.

"Some of our local names might correspond to an official category, but others span more than one. And some of the official ones, we don't have names for them at all, we just see the behavior as extreme individualism. Of course, some of ours make a distinction you won't see in the records, like 'not the full shilling' as opposed to a *'duine le Dia.'* You know," he concludes, "I never thought this through before. Write it down."

~

Annie meets me at the Garda barracks in Carrick to finish copying the Census. The sergeant makes us a cup of tea and arranges Marietta biscuits on a little plate. "I haven't seen you this long while. Ye were off to The Mental, I hear? I'm there often enough, myself. The Gardaí are in charge of transporting the patient, unless he signs himself in."

"If he does, how does he get there?"

"He could go in a hackney." This seems very sad, so *purposeful*, hiring a local taxi to carry you to the mental hospital.

"Most of our cases are 'unsound mind' and 'no fixed abode,'" he says.

I tell him I'd stopped recording names of recent patients. I don't like the idea they might be people I know.

"Well, you were talking to one of them last week in Kilcar. He was out on parole, but we had to take him back yesterday."

I remember the young man's pale blue, black-fringed eyes. I'd met him before when I visited his elderly father's farm. He left school at fourteen because his brothers are gone and his father can't manage the six steep plots that make up the farm. "I'll have to see the old fella out, before I can leave," he'd said.

I remember Mr. McDermott's diagnosis of the entire southwest peninsula, and I recall some facts the Agricultural Institute has sent me. This area, they say, has always had the poorest land, the wettest weather, the poorest age distribution, and the highest rates of emigration in Donegal. Poverty drove people into the workhouse, and poverty drove at least some into its successor, the mental hospital.

Outside his rented house, I see "Mr. Slippers" in the jaunty hat of a country gentleman. "Haven't they thrown you out yet?" he says, smirking.

# September/Mí Mheán Fómhair 1967

## Malinowski's Mother

I'm bringing some nice tweed to Mrs. B. when James, who misses nothing, comes in with a book and a face like thunder. Even Mrs. B. looks a bit nervous. She grabs the umbrella, used only for unpleasant household situations, like the time "Better" came in, a little worse for the drink, and demanded a *póg bheag*, a "wee kiss" from her.

"Do *you* keep a diary?" he asks me. What, with a mother like mine? A billboard would be more private.

"No."

"Well, I hope not." He slaps the book. "I'm very disappointed in Malinowski."

I'd forgotten about my copy of Malinowski's recently published diary under Mrs. B.'s chair cushion, where we hide banned books. Ó Móráin sent it to me.

"Where did you get that one?" I ask.

"Ó Móráin sent it. He thinks it's hilarious. Typical of the Brits, he says."

The few Brits I know are quite restrained, and Malinowski was Polish.
"Well, I'll tell you this now, if this gets around, we're both in trouble.
I'll be a pariah for helping you. You can go back to Pittsburgh, not a
bother on you, but I ..."

Malinowski's second wife published A *Diary in the Strict Sense of the
Word* a few months ago, forty-five years after his death. It covers the periods when he was working in the Trobriand Islands and New Guinea.
In 1914, as a Polish citizen of Austria, he had traveled to Australia
with the intention of doing an anthropological study of New Guinea.
World War I began, and he would have been interned as an enemy
alien, but the Australian government permitted him to do research in
the Trobriands, and that study established his reputation. In a later
trip, he studied New Guinea.

James isn't the only one who's upset; many anthropologists are
disturbed by the *Diary*'s racism and sexual content. My professor has
sent me the September 14 issue of *The New York Review of Books*, in
which Clifford Geertz reviews the *Diary* with some disgust: "Preten-
tious, platitudinous, unsystematic, simple-minded, long-winded, intel-
lectually provincial, and perhaps even somewhat dishonest, he had,
somehow, a way with the natives." Seán MacRéamoinn, one of my Trocadero companions, also sent me an article by Konstantin Symmons-
Symonolewicz, from *The Polish Review*. In it, I read that Malinowski was
very worried about his "lechery," and also broods on his penchant for
reading "trashy novels," concluding that "I should read ethnographic
works."

Shouldn't we all.

Of course, we anthropologists like to be seen as dispassionate observ-
ers, measured, hovering benignly above the fray, non-judgmental, and
able to mix with anyone, at least while we're "in the field." There's a

theory, developed by me, that the more a professor seems unfit for human society, the greater the likelihood that he (I had only male professors) will be successful at doing fieldwork. Someone should do a study on this.

In Malinowski's time, almost all anthropological research was carried out among people who couldn't read the language that the anthropologist would use to write about them. Often they had no written language of their own, and even if they did, many might not be able to read it. This meant that most had no idea of how they were being portrayed in the anthropological literature, although by now, their descendants probably do. This is an issue for me; most adults in Carrick and Kilcar are more literate than I am.

Malinowski's *Diary* was written in Polish. The Polish term he used to refer to the local people is racist, although apparently slightly less racist than translations would lead us to believe. Still, racist is racist. He also appears to be fixated on his psychological state, although in the era in which he writes, there was a central European and British fashion among the higher born or higher educated for being psychoanalyzed. For students of British literature, you can find instances among the "Bloomsbury Set." He was also very concerned about his poor health, although the medicines he was taking, among them arsenic and extra large doses of milder cures, probably contributed to it. Rather endearingly, he read many British novels and magazines, and thought about "love" a lot, although, once again, in those days, both men and women of that higher class/educated group brooded about being or not being "in love."

What was Malinowski's second wife thinking of? His diaries show him longing for his first wife. What second wife broadcasts that?

Part of the Malinowski problem is that few career choices involve living for relatively long periods in societies very different from our own, always on the job, policing our minds to maintain a neutral stance, and taking notes of everything, no matter how small, since it might turn out to be important, for how can we judge in the moment? Every anthropologist can add something to that. Our training helps, our role models help, as does our yearning, perhaps even from childhood, to know more about the way other people live.

But I remember the strain I felt the first day I visited Kilcar, when the shopkeeper thought I had a New Jersey accent. My reaction surprised me and later I laughed, but at that moment, I felt that I was trying so hard to be sensitive and understanding to everyone but no one was trying to reciprocate. In the end, though, some of the local people probably understood me more than I knew.

"The *Diary* is shocking, really," James said. "Full of sex."

"Have you ever read *Lady Chatterley's Lover*?" Mrs. B. asked. "*Fanny Hill*?" Her eye wanders for a second to our library under the cushion.

"Certainly not! Novels? This *Diary* is the real thing."

It's late, and Mrs. B. cleverly edges him toward the door, like a dog herding a sheep, all beady, darting eyes, and a subtle wielding of the umbrella.

"What will happen to you, Eileen, if this gets out?" James cries from the door. "What will happen to anyone here who's helped you? Mrs. B.? Michael? Peadar? Me?"

"Am I a linguistically gifted Polish male anthropologist who's missing his mother, longing for his future wife, dosing himself with arsenic and enemas, taking Epsom salts and calomel, interned as an alien enemy, insulted by pompous official nabobs, and consumed with sexual longings?"

"Well, not linguistically gifted, anyhow," he calls over his shoulder. "You have to look down people's gullets to see how to pronounce Irish words." He winks, and he's off.

Ah, the bitter word, as they say here.

Mrs. B. retrieves the *Diary* from under her cushion and stokes the fire. "The poor wee pet, that Malinowski. He's missing his mother. It breaks my heart."

"He does go on a lot about her."

"*Is buachaill maith é!*" What? Malinowski is a good boy?

Anyhow, I'm keeping field notes, not a diary. No time for reflection. And as the famous Ohio author, James Thurber, wrote, "Leave your mind alone."

# October/Mí Dheireadh Fómhair 1967

## That Factory Could Go Down the Road Tomorrow

A letter this morning from my professor. Why am I recording an old lady's underclothing? But also, "Does that thing about biting a frog's leg to cure a headache work if the frog's leg is cooked?"

Today, Tommo and the fire-haired Fear Ruadh arrange a night to settle yet again the issue of factory versus farming in Kilcar. We meet in Tommo's kitchen, with Bríd between the Stanley, table, and pantry making a steak and kidney pie. The debaters, all men, sit on kitchen chairs against the wall. More are expected; they say some factory workers are worried that I'm getting a one-sided picture for "The Book."

"The first thing to write in The Book," Tommo says, "is Donegal people are the best workers in the west of Ireland, whether we're in the factory or on the farm."

"I'm not ..."

"Not long ago I had to go down to Connemara for a few days to do a job of work in the warehouse of a new seaweed factory. People are up to their oxters[1] in seaweed down there, but the factory couldn't get enough. Why? Because the local fellows took their seaweed down to a factory in Clare! They could have made two or three trips to their local factory in the same time."

"Why didn't they?"

"It gave them a nice day out and the Clare factory paid a bit more, so they were satisfied. You wouldn't see a Donegal man doing that. He'd have the wear and tear on the tires worked out to the penny."

"The Donegal people are very polite, too," I say, teasing. "In the factory, for example, as soon as people heard my accent, they spoke English."

"Why wouldn't they?" Tommo demanded. "The only people speaking Irish in the factory are the managers. They have to, to get hired. But it's 'book Irish.' They learned it from *books*. Madness!"

People trickle in. Pat the Clock comes in with Jimmy Condy, from the factory. Jimmy Condy says, "and a mini-survey I've just done shows that two out of three Kilcar workers live on a farm. They'll say they keep up everything, but you only have to look to see some don't." But they won't sell the land.

Jimmy Condy says when something has to go, it's the sheep, cattle, and corn (wheat) first. Last would be the potatoes and turf, although a few still keep cattle.

A pipe-smoking farmer looks disgusted: "That's not farming at all. How would I get the turf ricked in good time? Or the byres thatched? It can't be done." I've seen the ricks, huge beehive-shaped mounds of dried turf bricks, laid artfully. Their precision is a matter of pride as well as function. They're covered with a few sods, a *scraith*, to keep the fuel dry.

Pádraig the Post comes in and I move up one chair toward Bríd, who empties a churn of butter. Churning is unusual in the villages, but

---

1 "Oxters," from Old English, means "armpits" and is used in Ireland, Scotland, and northern England.

Tommo has a few cows. She starts on what may be a rhubarb sponge pudding. Tommo welcomes Dan Gillespie, the schoolmaster, and waves me up one more on the line of chairs. Three more men sidle in and we all move up. Nine people, plus Bríd and me, so more chairs are brought from the parlor. Bríd offers a cup of tea to each arrival, and each says no, they'll wait. I begin.

"What offers the best life for people? Farming? Owning your own business? Working in a good industry, or a shop, or the building trade? Or something else?" I'm testing my questionnaire.

The factory workers are adamant: working in a good industry is the runaway winner, with farming way down the list, although all here live on farms. Next in line is running your own business, but the farmers disagree: farming is harder, but it's a better life – be your own boss, out in the fresh air. Farming isn't a "business."

"Of course you get perks from the government for farming," Tommo says. "And the dole; a lot of farmers are on the dole, too. So you couldn't live just by farming in its purity."

"And you couldn't live by the factory in its purity," The Fear Ruadh says. "It's subsidized."

Bríd scoops batter from a bowl and dollops scones onto a baking sheet. Old Seán McBrearty and his son, Tony Seán, come in, and we move up. Tony is a weaver in the factory, as was his father.

The Fear Ruadh turns to Tommo. "The chairman of Gaeltarra Éireann came out in the *Irish Independent* a week ago and said Gaeltarra lost one-hundred-sixty-thousand-seven-hundred-and-fifty-one pounds last year. Up nearly forty thousand from last year." He taps out every single number. "The whole thing could go down the road tomorrow, and what would you have?"

"My farm," Tommo says.

"You couldn't live on it," The Fear Ruadh says. "You'd need the dole, and a lot of other things. Maybe taking in visitors, but you'd be up against farmers already doing the same thing. You'd have to piece your bits together to make it all work, the way we do."

"Tell me this," Jimmy Condy, the factory worker, asks. "Would you like your daughter to marry into a farm?" Maybe he thought that was a clincher, but surprisingly most of the other men say aye, they wouldn't mind. After university. Or at least a good secondary or technical education. The younger men say you have a better chance of marrying here if you have a job in the factory.

"What changes would you like to see in the village?"

"Another factory," Jimmy Condy says. "Not a government one. More young fellows would stay if they had the security."

"A café," Tommo says. "More shops. Better setups for games and sport."

"Do some people think they're too good to work in the factory?"

"Oh, no, I never heard that," a farmer says. The factory workers say, "Yes," with one voice, and I've heard it often in the factory.

The Fear Ruadh returns to his suspicions. "Them big shots up in the Dáil, they say they want to keep the language alive, but in their own factories you lads don't speak it. Inspectors check on the little wains in school to make sure it's Irish they're speaking, but no one checks on ye in the factory."

Bríd pulls a batch of fairy cakes out of the second oven, ices them, removes the scones and butters them, makes two large pots of tea, cuts some sandwiches, and passes plates to me, Jimmy Condy, The Fear Ruadh, Old Seán, Pádraig the Post, the teacher, the pipe smoker, the factory workers, and her father.

"Bríd, sit down you, don't be so unsociable," Tommo says, and then, "Let you get up and give poor Mary a cup," when a startled lady calls in.

I stay to help Bríd clean up. We talk about the poems she's shown me.

"I've given up writing. I've nothing to write about. And listen you, don't pay any mind to that old talk, that guff about marrying a farmer.

The girls won't do it. And a university girl marrying into a farm? They're all leaving here, even the girls in the factory."

"What would you like to see here? You've heard the men."

"A bus station."

"But are you staying, yourself, or going?"

"What choice have I?"

At home, I find a letter from a young professor in my department interested in the relationship between changes in fashion and the geopolitical situation. He asks for more detail on "that elderly lady's clothing."

## You've Let Your Name Down

I don't know what went wrong. Maybe I made the very mistake Annie warned me about, asking about what people eat. Or maybe I ... but I really don't know.

One day my host, Billy, made boxty, a traditional potato dish, for me. It was delicious and he recited the recipe.

Late night visitors are common here, and a few days later, around 10:00, Billy ushered a young man into the parlor. It was David Wagstaff, the Trinity graduate I last saw in the Spiddal factory, charming the Connemara girls.

"Sorry," he'd said sheepishly, pushing back his wet hair. "I've been here a few days; I'm learning the ropes in different factories. I'm off again at the dawn." I welcomed a fresh eye on the factory. He understood what I was doing and warned me about things he was learning the hard way.

About 11:00 our hosts sent in tea and biscuits, and David left before midnight.

The next day I wrote up his comments in my usual shorthand, locked them in my case, and then remembered: boxty! I wrote Billy's recipe on an index card for my mother's recipe box. Mrs. B. was making my mother's Hungarian kolache, and my mother might like to try boxty.

That evening I went to Coguish townland to interview Hugh O'Neill, an astute and respected member of the Kilcar Parish Council. The council, once defunct, was re-formed recently, with the parish priest and curate as honorary president and vice-president. Among the twenty-eight other members, all men, each representing an area or a business/professional sector, two were factory workers and one an outdoor weaver. A few of them, former and current, were there at Hugh's.

I was curious to know how their council gets things done.

"A couple of lads ease things along. They're behind the scenes, they don't take any credit. In Carrick, it seems everyone is an individualist." True, I think, but that's part of the charm.

They said people wanted better roads, schools, a playground, a clinic. They're angry about the industrial estate going to Gweedore; Kilcar could have been an employment hub for the entire peninsula. But they admit most of the peninsula isn't Irish speaking, whereas Gweedore and its hinterland are.

This morning there's a strange coolness in the house. I ask more about boxty and get a curt answer. A question on folklore is ignored. I go to my study, baffled. A few minutes later Billy comes in. "We want you to leave," he says. "You've let the name of the house down."

"But how?"

He says nothing for a moment. Then, "Well, that young fellow was here all hours that night."

"But he wasn't," I say. "He left at midnight," a respectable hour. But this isn't just about my almost Victorian discussion with David. "And you copied down what we eat," he says. "You'll write a book and make out we're poor in Kilcar, eating food like boxty." He waves my index card. I hadn't noticed it missing. "Anyhow," he says, "who knows what you're up to here."

"But I eat with you every night. I know what you eat, it's the same as what I'd eat at home."

"You were seen taking pictures. You'll make money if you put them on a calendar. You'll make us out to be living in thatched cabins, weaving our own clothes."

Indeed, I had taken *a* picture: that single dark shot of the thatching process. Then I remember my own early decision to be careful about picture-taking; the few published pictures of Kilcar, Carrick, and Glen tend to feature old-fashioned skills, ancients dressed in shawls and petticoats, people in battered work clothes, a half-simple old woman. And I remember Annie's seemingly strange advice: "Don't ask what we eat." But these can't be what it's about, surely? I'm annoyed he'd read my recipe card, and I glance toward my other notes, but they're in shorthand, locked up, and I have the key.

"I wonder, do you believe in God at all?" he asks. "You've let down our name."

Tonight, I move back to Mrs. B.'s.

## Gossip, Pranks, and Nicknames

Anthropologists don't write much about their failures. They talk in seminars about other anthropologists' failures and peccadilloes: roving eyes, breakdowns, over-luxurious field quarters. I learned this firsthand months ago: an academic couple, non-anthropologists, who think of this area as "theirs" invited me to give a talk at Queen's University. I showed them a paper I might use, and then presented it, in a seminar consisting of the two of them and the famous folklorist Edward Estyn Evans. Once they returned to the village, twisted quotes floated around. I think of Raymond Firth's request to his readers as he published *We the Tikopia*: that "nothing which they find herein will be used to the discomfiture of the people ..."

I really don't know how to take my recent eviction from the house. And James doesn't help, implying it's only what he expects of Kilcar. Neither does Mrs. B.

"Now you see how easy it is to blacken a woman's name," she says.

I don't get a chance to fret much. "We haven't seen so many Kilcar people in Carrick since Fair Day," Michael Boyle says. Some of my Kilcar visitors to Mrs. B.'s house are "passing through," they say, to Teelin or Glen. All of them, veterans of my research, try to explain what they think happened in Kilcar, and if they don't, Mrs. B. questions them smartly.

My hosts didn't understand what I was doing, they say, or maybe they thought a married woman shouldn't remain alone with a young man. It says something for my single-mindedness that I thought of David as a factory manager, not the predatory young male of their imaginations. The explanations make sense, sort of. One day "Better" assures me he never, ever told my Kilcar host family I was a communist. Why would he, he asks, and I so good as to get him a telephone?

A telephone? But I didn't. Ó Móráin, I suppose.

I'm invited back to Kilcar to meet more people, borrow records, go to the school. I return to my discussions with Tommo, Jimmy Condy, and The Fear Ruadh who tells me to "pay nobody any mind." Not exactly the mantra for successful fieldwork.

One phrase sticks in my mind: I've let down the name of his house, my Kilcar host said. The importance of one's name and the name of one's house, and how to protect them, seems central to how the community runs itself. This morning, Brian Vocational drops in. I give him a cup in his hand.

"I explained this to you before," he says. "I said the lowest level of local government was quite high, it's up at the county level. We have no village mayors, no official local council. We tend to handle minor problems ourselves. Letting down, for example - letting down your family, your townland, parish, county, country, profession, sex ...

"A person who's rude to a foreigner lets Ireland down. If a shopkeeper here cheats someone from Kilcar he lets Carrick down. If he cheats a local he's let himself down. The local ship's pilot who betrayed the Fenian ship *Erin's Hope* to the authorities in 1867 let Carrick down. He had to leave the country. The Teelin man who reported some of his neighbors to the dole officer because they were doing too well to be eligible ..."

I know this story. The Teelin villagers thought he'd let himself down; the Kilcar people directly across the bay thought he'd let Teelin down. This makes me wonder whether "letting down" works in the same way as my map of where townland members stand on the village street, where the villagers stand in Killybegs, and so on. "Yes," he says, "depending on who you've offended: another family, townland, village, whatever. If you murder someone in your own village, it will probably be family versus family, but if you murder someone in another, it's between the two villages. And of course if the victim is a visiting Ohioan, let's say, it's another story."

Who have I let down? Myself? Carrick? Southwest Donegal? America? Or is it anthropologists? Females? Atheists? The permutations seem endless, but anyone here would know which has more weight, and when. Brian continues: a parish priest let his adopted village, Carrick, down by hiring a native of his home village as a teacher in the school. "The boundaries are invisible and shifting, but they're real, and we all know which will come into play. A bit like your bloody bushes and shrubs."

"So what happens?" I remember how James Mary Agnes handled the case of the stolen butter. But he erected a boundary, a real one.

"Gossip, pranks, nicknames, ridicule. For the more serious cases, ostracism. A shopkeeper of your acquaintance sells, among other things, stale bread. How do you think she got the name 'Madame Blue Mould'?

"Of course," he says, "you can get a nickname just for getting above yourself. 'Jack Ruby' got his name when he came home from America at the time of Kennedy's assassination. He never stopped going on about how much better things were in America. I've told you before: you don't stand up around here except to get shot down. Every small town in the world is the same."

I ask about a poaching case, to see if I've got the hang of the system. Local bailiffs were hired at £4.10 a week by Gael Linn, which owns the bay, to protect it against poachers. "I've heard some bailiffs didn't report them. Is it because that would have been letting Carrick down?"

"Yes," he says, rising as he sees Annie and Mrs. B. coming down the road from Novena. "Also, who was going to turn in their neighbor for four pounds and ten pence a week?"

The ladies salute him as he leaves. I explain our discussion.

Annie reels off nicknames in Teelin. "Sputnik, now, he got his name because he's always going up and down the road. It's from the time you Americans had all that business about the moon."

My nickname used to be The Cailín Ruadh, The Red-Haired Girl. Probably not now.

~

Tonight I review the maps of where people stand on the street; the ideas about "letting down" the house, the area, the country; and the predictions about which area will complain when another gets a factory. All are about invisible boundaries, pulsing and shifting depending on circumstances. They're as old as Ulster mythology, with its alliances, splits, and regroupings, as are some of the legendary protagonists: Fergus, Eoin, Conor, Cormac, Felim, Conall, all names I hear on the street every day.

## Old Accusations

I'm lying. I pretend what happened in Kilcar hasn't taken a feather out of me, as they say. But it's taken most of my plumage.

I do what anyone in my place would do: I write a letter to Conrad Arensberg.

His works on Ireland are famous – *The Irish Countryman*, and with Solon Kimball, *Family and Community in Ireland*. He is still loved in the area he studied. Did anything like that ever happen to him?

I avoid being alone with most men except my old helpers, and of course old Máirtín, who is, presumably, not an Occasion of Sin. Taking photos is out, and I avoid looking communist or atheist. I'm actually not married now; the papers arrived last week.

I'll bet name-place expert John O'Donovan never had this kind of trouble. Then I recall he was held prisoner by his Donegal host for almost two weeks for non-payment of rent.

Today I'm back in Kilcar, waiting for the factory to open and watching the thundering brown river behind it as it breaks over rocky ledges. Noreen McBrearty calls to me from across the road. Noreen "married into" Carrick from Kilcar. She's made it her business to find out what went wrong.

"Some people thought you were working for the government, being down at the factory poking around all the time. Investigating."

"Investigating what?"

"A man died in the factory a few years back. A warehouse manager. It's still fresh in people's minds. They're bitter about it. The men don't like working in the warehouse anymore." She studies me, perhaps to see how much I know.

"It was all politics," she says. "No one wants it raked over again, it was awful enough the first time."

"I didn't know that."

But I should have. Those Dáil debates I looked at months ago, the surprising exchanges between two senior deputies. I copied them because the Kilcar factory was mentioned, one of the few mentions I'd found, and then forgot them. I go back to Mrs. B.'s and search my notes:

MR. MACENTEE: (Tánaiste) [deputy prime minister] The deputy was responsible for the death of one man ...

(INTERRUPTIONS.)

MR. LINDSAY: Did the chair hear that? The Tánaiste has just accused me of having the life of one man on my hands. I object to that remark and I want to say, here and now, that the responsibility for that rests upon the present government and the attorney general of this day.

MR. MORAN: And all Deputy Lindsay succeeded in doing was in getting one man to commit suicide.

MR. LINDSAY: If that is all that is on Deputy Moran's conscience, it is a good thing.

MR. MORAN: I never suggested Deputy Lindsey had a conscience.

(TÁNAISTE): Order. These personalities should cease.

Piecing the few other sessions together, I see that the warehouse manager may have got caught up in the complex shenanigans of a Dublin tweed agent, the central figure in the missing tweed. Dáil inquiries showed a loss of £100,000. Noreen said the factory manager, Mr. Redington's father, was called only on the last day of a three-week inquiry and was able to clear the warehouse manager, but too late to contain the man's grief at the loss of his name. What remains is an anguished community and this schoolboy banter in the Dáil.

"Don't take too much notice," Noreen had said. "Just keep your head up."

But maybe my hosts received "hints" their lodger might be prying into the warehouse tragedy. At best, they'd be labeled as innocent fools if a sensationalized story appeared in print, in "The Book," or in the newspapers. At worst, they'd be ostracized. All this has happened before; a local family might be hospitable to a stranger, only to find themselves and their community described in the British tabloids as "primitive" or "quaint." The name of the house went down.

I don't go back to Kilcar and the factory today. I'm shy of everyone looking at the "spy."

## Lunch, Bushes, and Factories

"I have an ancient plenipotentiary from Kilcar with me." James ushers Peadar Malloy into Mrs. B.'s kitchen. "We were talking about what people here want."

I'm surprised to see them together, they're such different operators. James lives in his head, a gifted dreamer. Peadar prides himself on being out and about, a shrewd operator, the "cute" man. Odd, because Peadar is a historian and James an engineer.

"We want to explain what a factory is," James says. "You explained the difference between tea and dinner to me, and between bushes and shrubs to both of us, so we thought we'd give it a go ourselves. Because when we try to bring in a factory, we get something different."

"What?"

"A workshop or even what we here call a class, but not a factory," James says.

"And when we say 'factory' we see now that we don't mean 'factory,' so it's not entirely their fault," Peadar adds.

"You two shouldn't be allowed out together."

"It's not funny," James says. "We've spent a lot of time on this." He jabs a finger at a stack of closely written index cards. Peadar puts them in four piles. "Industry, factory, workshop, class," he says. "You're such a busy lady, so we'll only show you the one, 'Industry.'"

The card says

✓ regular employment
✓ high % of local breadwinners
✓ mechanized or semi-mechanized
✓ compact physical setting
✓ organized management structure

"Any business that has all these is an industry. If it's missing one, it's a factory, like the vegetable factory. Missing two, it's a workshop, like the

Gael Linn furniture factory. And if it's missing three or more, say only few breadwinners, not mechanized, not in one place, it's a class, like the women knitting."

"A class?"

"In the old days the Congested Districts Board set up training and employment for women, lace making, sometimes in an old school. A 'class' is what we call it."

"So," James says, "you can see our problem."

"Not entirely."

"In our heads, we want an industry. We ask for a factory and what we get is a workshop or a class. All the parties involved, the locals and the government, call it a 'factory.' But the government understands these things one way, and we understand them another. The boundaries are being muddled."

"Is the Kilcar factory a factory?" I ask.

"Yes, the only one around."

"And what about small businessmen? The government doesn't understand them, either," I say. "Poor 'Better' had so much trouble just trying to get a telephone for his shop."

"He told you he has a shop?" James asks. "Where?"

"On the street here." Even as I say it, I realize it can't be right.

"Is that the same lad that thinks he owns the commonage?" Peadar asks James. "The Scourge of Communism?"

"The very same. A *duine le Dia*, but a great memory for old tales."

So. A simple person, a person with God. Even as I studied my maps of the shops on the village street, I didn't catch on because a couple of them are rarely staffed, and a shop's name and the owner's are often different. And I assumed he was waiting for his phone.

Peadar stands, stiffly unfolding himself. "I told you there are some kind of mental problems the community can handle, without the person being sent away. That's one."

I have a reply from Conrad Arensberg. I see why they loved him in County Clare and am shocked to see he was younger than I when he began his fieldwork there. No, he didn't have trouble, but maybe people just didn't mention it to him. He's delighted with my topic; he has a great interest in action programs and factory–community relationships, and he includes a copy of his *Culture and Community*. He asks if I've adapted traditional research methods to my circumstances, and would I send him any ideas. As a footnote, he says he grew up not very far from Youngstown, near Pittsburgh, and asks how it's doing. Fine, I say; I don't mention that the Pittsburgh Mafia has a lethal turf war going on in Youngstown.

A nice man. I bet he never got a nickname.


## Having the Builders In, Round One

I'm ready! Seosamh Ó hÓgartaigh of Gaeltarra, the amiable "Joe," has drilled to exhaustion an army of drivers, managers, bed and breakfast owners, and mimeograph operators with their reams of questionnaires. Irish-speaking sociology graduates are poised, like dogs at a track, to administer the questionnaires at the same moment in thirteen factories. Standby coders and computer technicians await his signal. I'll tour some of the thirteen. Annie has packed her sister's best clothes. But are we going?

No.

We're Having the Builders In. Having *the* Builder In: Conor comes to say he's starting. He asks what's this Mrs. B. wants done, and without a flicker of exasperation, she repeats it: "The water pipe, bathroom, linoleum, jammed front gate, gravel to fill the ruts in the driveway ..."

"That's right," Conor says, waving a dismissive hand. "Tomorrow, first thing." So far, so good; I'm glad I'll be gone and out of the way.

But this afternoon Mrs. B. hurts her wrist badly, tripping in the driveway ruts.

"I'll take you to the hospital. I'll be gone tomorrow and you need an X-ray."

"I can't, maybe they'd keep me in. Conor will be here tomorrow."

"*Aon seans*," as I've learned to say. No chance. We drive to the hospital in Donegal Town.

They keep her in. The X-ray machine shows what could be a torn ligament. Mrs. B. doesn't want to worry her children because "it's only a wee bang."

Next morning, I ring Gaeltarra Éireann and tell Seosamh Ó hÓgartaigh, "Joe," about Mrs. B. "You can't be too careful with a wrist," he says. "I'll postpone our trip – gives me time to knock the 'book Irish' out of some of our Dublin researchers."

The line breaks up. "Eileen? Conor here. I'm in a fierce rush. What? C'mere to me, you're breaking up. Speak into the mouthpiece, there's a girl. I'll be over to you in an hour."

"I won't be here, Mrs. B.'s in hospital. She's hurt her wrist. I'm on my way to see when she's coming out."

"That's shocking. Can I do anything? You can't be too careful ..."

"She'll be over the moon if you just start her work."

"Well, I wouldn't like to enter the premises without yourself or your agent being there to effect ingress."

Conor likes an audience, an awed acolyte or two he can shoo out of the way, muttering as he works. Also, tea.

"Please, just start. She won't be back today. She did some real damage to herself on that driveway."

"The driveway!" He sounds horrified. "She had no business going next or near that driveway."

"But, we can't get out the front gate ..." I stopped, since he's to fix the front gate, too, and I'd probably be told she had no business going next or near that, either.

"Well, I'll tip down to your place to see what's what," he says.

"Will you have the bathtub with you?" I'm pushing my luck.

"I'm working on it. All the baths on the go these days are the wrong size. They don't make ordinary baths anymore. Hollywood has this country ruined." I start to ask what was wrong with the one we had, but he interrupts: "I'll tell you what, why don't I meet you at the builder's suppliers in Killybegs on your way to Donegal Town, it would be nearly handier for me, you can show me the bits and bobs she might like, switches for the electrician and taps for the plumber and the like. Then you can pop over to the hospital, and I'll be about my business."

I'm getting fresh clothes for Mrs. B. when the phone rings. She must be wondering where I am. But it's Mattie the plumber. "Eileen, I just heard from Conor. As long as you'll be in Killybegs will I meet you there so I can show you some bargain taps I got."

"I don't know ... Conor told me ..." There's a loud crack and a "whoooosh" outside.

"They'll do Mrs. B. grand," he says. "Otherwise I'm going to put them in my own place today. The wife's been at me for months, she's on her high horse because she has to turn our kitchen taps on and off with a wrench. Although wasn't it far from taps we were reared?"

"Actually ..."

"And now lookit, nothing only gold taps will do some of the gobshites on the go today."

I want to say it wasn't far from taps I was reared, growing up in Ohio. My family was poor but watered. Funny how these guys flatter me that I'm nearly one of their blood kin when it suits them ("You know yourself builders are the worst in the world for mess"), and how I might as well be from a tree top in Borneo when they don't ("Ah, now, they might do that across the water where you come from, but people in Ireland think concealed wiring is very dodgy. They like to see all their wiring.") I say nothing, just agree to the taps, hang up, and start outside to investigate the whoosh.

Conor rings. "It's well for some to be sitting with their feet up."

"I was just on my way to ..."

"I've got a lead on a bathtub so it will be an hour, anyhow, before I can meet you in Killybegs. Will you give a ring to Damian the electrician, get him over to your place no later than 3:00 sharp? He's a terrible one for getting hold of, the same Damian. Anyhow, it would be better coming from yourself. He'll just give me a load of old guff about how he's run off his feet."

Despite this flattery, I know Conor and his sidekicks would prefer to be dealing with a man, but there's a nice chivalry creeping through. Each of them has warned me against other villains: dodgy concrete purveyors, pampered stonemasons ("Sure haven't they the life, out in the fresh winter air all day?"), and all the greedy gits selling their old rubble as topsoil. "If you don't mind me saying so," Conor has told me, "they can see you coming."

"While you're at it," he says now, "would you ring the quarry and ask them to send the gravel over tomorrow? I put the fear of God into them, told them absolutely not till next week, so you could get the car in and out easy before your trip, but there's a fellow free tomorrow will help me spread it before you leave."

I ring the quarry. Would they mind sending the gravel a week early so Conor can spread it tomorrow? No bother, they say, it was delivered half an hour ago. The whoosh, right behind my car. It's pearly white, the expensive kind people put around graves. The wrong stuff.

James arrives, leaving his shop in the hands of "the girl," a woman older than my mother. "The lads and I will shift the gravel into that hole by the side gate so you can back out." Two of the three lads are his visiting nieces. "But if Conor gets his hands on this fancy stuff he might take a notion to mix you up the dearest cement this side of the Taj Mahal."

"How're ya keeping?" Conor bellows when I run in to answer the phone. "Okay, no joy with the bathtub. And now I can't move without some fecker, sorry, asking me to fix something. They have me crucified, but I said, 'That American one will skin me if I don't get over to her job today.'"

"I'm on my way to see how Mrs. B ..."

"Not to worry, she's fine, sitting up here large as life."

"You're at the hospital?"

"Of course. *Someone* has to be. But she's coming out, just a sprain. I'm dropping her over to Killybegs to stay with her friend Mrs. McNeilis for a while. You can bring her things there. She can't go home with all the uproar we'll be making."

This is the first I've heard of uproar.

"And I ran into Noel from the carpet shop here. He'll hop over to take up the lino in the pantry and put in new stuff."

"This gravel ..."

"If we don't stop blathering, I'll never get there."

I gather some things for Mrs. B. James and the lads move the last of the pricey gravel.

One of them asks me shyly if I like it here. I say och, aye, it reminds me of home.


## Having the Builders In, Round Two

At Mrs. McNeilis's, Mrs. B. is propped on a settee with her sprain in plaster.

Conor, ducking and blushing with delight, is being grilled on his marriage prospects. They list a couple of likely girls, and he dismisses one: "She got married! She already has one in the wheelbarrow and another in the mixer. Oh, sorry ladies," he says, as he sees their faces. "I'm off now; don't be detaining me. I've left this number with the gang at Mrs. B.'s in case they have any questions." Mrs. McNeilis chases after him with a newspaper-wrapped bacon sandwich.

We settle down to our tea and scones. "I was just saying I got my first love letter at sixteen," she says, opening a box. "It was from a teacher ..."

"Show her the rest," Mrs. B. smirks.

"Seventy-five more," she says. "I read them often."

"All from the one man, of course," Mrs. B. says.

"Yes, and no dowry, either. It's further south they have dowries."

"We marry for love up here," Mrs. B. says. "Be sure you say that in 'The Book.'"

The phone rings. Phone calls usually herald bad news, so Mrs. McNeilis sets her face accordingly and rushes out. "No!" I hear her say in a low voice. "That's shocking. With a knife? Wait now till I get her."

"Eileen, how're ya?" Damian, the electrician shouts. "Conor gave me this number. How's Mrs. B.? I'm at her house. Do you know where's the switches Conor bought? He said they were sitting here waiting on me for weeks. I said I'd get them myself, but oh, no, I'm not tasty, he said ... listen, I'm ringing from the public box because Mrs. B.'s landline is banjaxed. The carpet shop fellow, Noel, cut it when he was laying the lino. Yeah. Give some people a knife and you can do nothing only stand back and admire the carnage. Oh, Noel, there you are. You're off now? Sound man. Eileen, there's another fellow beside me here, J.P., he's Mattie Jennings's helper, he wants to speak to you."

"Nye than!" says a young Belfast voice, complete with its music. "J.P. here, part of the work cree? I've just popped in to organize thengs for Mattie? I'm his helper? He said he wanted the water turned off for whan he changes the taps? Yee don't have a volve inside, right? I turn it off eightside at the sayde gate, right? But someone's dumped a load of gravel up against it? I'll shuft it, no worries."

Damian's voice again. "Will I put in these new taps for you as long as I'm here? Mattie left them in before he took off, fishing. No, he'll not be back today, didn't he tell you?" And then, to someone near him, "Well, to what do we owe this gracious appearance, Your Worship?"

"Hello? Is that you, Eileen? Conor here. Damian, stop farting around. Sorry, Eileen. C'mere to me, Eileen, some fecker's dumped a power of gravel into the pit I've dug by the side gate to check the water pipe. Cement? Me? No bloody fear. I have more to be doing than mixing up cement for fun. No, I know you're in Killybegs, didn't I just leave you? I rushed over here with Jackie to check on Damian, haven't I the switches just sitting here waiting on him?"

"Would you believe it?" cries Damian, taking the phone back, breathless. "I disconnected the old taps and went looking for a washer and just now when I got back, what happened me only the place was flooded! That little shite, J.P., Mattie's helper, he turned the water back on when I told him Mattie'd effed off for the day, fishing. What? Hold on. Okay, J.P.'s after telling me where the valve is at the side gate, but someone's left a load of gravel fornenst it. The new taps got an awful clatter with all the high jinks here today, but they're grand."

I put the phone down. "Everything all right?" Mrs. B. asks, and I say yes, fine. "They used the public phone box, so don't worry."

"They would, of course. They'd know my phone is only for emergencies."

The phone rings again and Mrs. McNeilis startles like a meerkat. I say I'll take it.

"Good night, Eileen, good night, Eileen, I'll see you in my dreams!" a lovely tenor carols over the phone. "Good one, huh? Just kidding," Mattie says. "By the way, Damian's got Mrs. B.'s phone rigged up again so we're using it. I'm leaving now, probably won't get back today, the wife's taken a wee turn. Conor was foosthering around making up a big batch of cement here, for what I don't know. I left some taps with J.P. at your place for Mrs. B. to look at, not the ones I got for her earlier. Scratched. These ones are fierce expensive, but I figured you'd fancy gold. I know how Yanks want the best."

"I thought you'd left, Damian said you went off fishing." My head is reeling, I need a chessboard with little builders, plumbers, and electricians to keep track of who's where, doing what.

"Me, is it? Fishing!?" Mattie cries. "I was out in the van ..."

"Fixing the reel on his fly rod," Damian shouts, furious. "He's going poaching salmon, leaving the rest of us gobshites to do his work. Get away from me Mattie, stop acting the maggot. I'm off myself now, Eileen, back when the place dries out to switch the sparks back on for you and Mrs. B. If you're talking to Conor this weather, would you ever ask him is he getting those switches, or what? He won't be getting them for the next fortnight, anyhow."

"Why not?" I ask.

"Builders' and suppliers' holidays. Always two weeks in late summer."

"The builders' holiday was in August," I sound school-marmish.

"It was pouring in August," he says, laughing, and hangs up.

We decide it's best for Mrs. B. to stay with Mrs. McNeilis.

When she returns home, Conor has installed an old velvet chaise by the fire, a pillowed lair with everything she could desire to hand. During the day he brings her tea on a tray with a lightly boiled egg on her good china.

I quiz Conor about when the work might be finished, given the builders' holidays. He seems shocked: "What kind of man do you think I am at all, would I leave Mrs. B. here in an incompleted state without all her requisites, the windows not fitted and all?"

I say this is the first I've heard of windows. "Oh, where's my head, that's Richard Mullen's house. I must be distracted by your beauty."

Mrs. B. scowls and he returns to re-re-wiring the one-bar electric fire.

Magically, one day the whole project comes together, the pipes, the taps, the linoleum, the water pipe, the gate, and various other tasks never asked for, all in chaos in the morning, all in shining order in the evening. Mrs. B. pays Conor, and Conor hands back a tidy sum for the phone calls Mrs. B. found on her bill. She goes to make a cup of tea in his hand, with her good one.

Conor and I stand in the hall Jackie has just painted, inhaling the oddly comforting smell of new plaster. I'm amazed at the project's fine finish. Conor props the heel of his hand against the wall and says nonsense, anyone going the road could do nearly as well. When he straightens up, there's an oily black handprint on the sparkling white paint. "There you are. The Stamp of Authority." He rubs at it with a dirty rag, making it worse.

"Leave it alone, let you," Mrs. B. says, coming back. "Your mother would've had your hide for that."

Conor asks if I've ever watched a man in a pub with a fresh pint. "You know how it is. He's bought the pint, it's his, he turns away from it, keeping an eye on the other fellow, of course, waiting for it to settle, for the conditions to be just right. Only then he turns back to it. The same with the building trade. You get the contract, it's yours ... you get the idea." He kisses the top of Mrs. B.'s head and leaves.

How could any of these builders work in a factory?

"This is the way we do it," Mrs. B. says, well satisfied. We have everything now but the bathtub.

# November/Mí na Samhna 1967

## Journeys and Voyages

"You'll call in and give us the *scéal* about your journeys?" James shouts from the door as the Morris Minor judders around the final corner toward home. Annie and I have finished our tour of factories in Connemara and Donegal, and we have interviewed local folklorists, historians, businesspeople, schoolmasters, and nuns. Annie, as the daughter of a legendary musician, was a big hit with audiences in the evenings, singing almost-lost songs. My dream of seeing the boiler-making/lobster factory in Carna was dashed; the village was closed for a funeral.

I missed a lot in those six weeks: the Ram Fair is over, the cows are back in their byres, the lambs taken from the older sheep, the sheep injected, the ram put in with the sheep, and the spirits of the dead propitiated on All Souls Day. Con Cassidy has placed his potatoes in a hay-lined pit and covered them. Willie John died of emphysema. Sheepishly, James tells me he sent offerings.

"Willie had a grand death," Mrs. B. says, but I heard a brattish lad near the Central Bar say he "died roaring." I write to ask how my father is doing.

~

"You're like Rapunzel," Mrs. B. says about my new notes. "Pity it's only paper you're spinning." But she clears the spare room, and I cover the floor, bed, and chests with layers of papers, bookmarked reports, and the survey results from 347 factory workers (all workers present on the day) and almost 500 vocational school students. I've triangulated every way I know how. My job now is to weave a coherent picture of the people I've talked to and the places I've been throughout the last year.

Tonight, hail sweeps around the brown whins and piles up at James's doorway. Inside, he abandons the bar to the drinkers and wedges himself into a corner of the snug. "The Journey of the Red-Haired Anthropologist" he announces to the other guests: Michael Boyle, Shane Cannon, and three refugees from Kilcar, Peadar Malloy, Dan Gillespie, and The Fear Ruadh, each with a Guinness or a Club Orange. Annie's mother, the triumphantly wild-haired Mary Kate, a hot whiskey in hand, settles in for the night, laughing. "Like the Voyage of Bran!" she shouts.

Journeys, voyages, and pilgrimages crisscross the whole of ancient Irish mythology. They're still so fresh that even the modern traveler who makes a day trip to Letterkenny may feel the need to compare his outing to that of the legendary Bran or Máel Dúin or Brendan. In fact, until 300 years ago, which is living memory around here, The Book of the Dun Cow, a twelfth-century manuscript brimming with adventures, belonged to the O'Donnell clan of Donegal. The Fear Ruadh is an O'Donnell, and I see him squaring his backside on the bench, ready to launch into tales of Máel Dúin's boat or the capers of Conn of a Hundred Battles.

James is an O'Donnell, but a "different O'Donnell," and he heads him off. "When Bran visited the Isle of Joy, all the people stared and laughed. They wouldn't talk to him. Nothing similar happened to you, I suppose?"

Michael Boyle laughs. "I mind the time Máel Dúin was pelted with nuts by a woman."

How can I compete with that? Or with the time Bran finds himself a fairy lover? Or even with the fleas, sour beer, and sprained ankles of John O'Donovan? What wonders can I produce?

"There's about one woman for every three men in the Irish country-side," I offer.

"You were counting?" Mary Kate asks, delighted.

I'd love to say yes, but it was the bards at the Agricultural Institute who sent me yet another report. In rural areas, they say, there are only 375 women for every 1,000 men aged 35–44. "A little more than a third of a woman for every man," I say. Mary Kate asks James to translate "a third of a woman" into Irish.

"I knew the women were a bit thin on the ground, all right," The Fear Ruadh says. "Michael here had a wild siege finding one for himself."

The Fear Ruadh is another person who's convinced I'm writing a tell-all book with unflattering photographs. "In the end," he says, "Bran sailed across the sea and was never heard from again. That's what you'll do when you finish your book."

I don't bite. I'm still searching the knotted thicket of data in my head for the thread that unfurls my tale.

But what interests them most, as always, is a map of what routes I took, how wrong I was, and how there's no place as nice as southwest Donegal. They like to hear about those afternoons Annie and I spent in bitterly cold country schools with no electricity or water, and the hours lost on dark roads where the only entertainment local youths had was turning the signposts around. "I suppose no one asked had you a mouth on you, either," Mary Kate says, rejoicing in the barbarism of people in other counties. "Races," she calls them; the County Kerry people, the Carrick villagers, the Teelin people, each is a race, or a tribe, or in Irish, a *dream*.

My hard-won figures and statistical tests fade for the moment as I recall some of the people behind them. "There was a girl in Galway," I say. She'd worked in the factory for two years. "I'm off to London now. I hand up most of my wages to the mother, but now I've the forty pounds saved." Enough to get her across on the boat and cover the first month's rent with girlfriends who got her a job in their factory.

"'When do you think you'll go?' I asked. 'The day after tomorrow,' she'd said. Her parents didn't know yet."

"She might only tell them the night before," Mary Kate says. "The poor mother."

"I want to see the *world*," the girl had said, her voice trailing off in a wail. Otherwise, she saw no life except to marry a local man with a scrap of land. "And then live my mother's life all over."

She said she'd come home often, and I could imagine her return, dressed in London fashions, bringing gifts for the little brothers and sisters.

"The wee creature," The Fear Ruadh says. "She won't come back. Just a few times at the beginning." My statistics agree: I'd studied primary school roll books covering the last fifty years. The teachers and old people helped me recover the stories: half the students had emigrated, and once gone, few came back, even to visit. Not much has changed over the years.

I thought of the girls in the Mayo factory who could tell me exactly where they intended to work in London and what they'd be doing: Smiths of Cricklewood, making clocks. "We have more relatives in that factory than we have in the whole of Ireland," one girl boasted.

"The mothers." I hear Mary Kate's ragged voice and see the face of legendary women: mythical queens, goddesses, mothers. I realize I haven't asked myself the question until now: will Annie go, too, the spark of a girl who lights Mary Kate's life?

The face of that girl in Galway; she's not just one girl, but many. She's the face of the factories. The majority of the workers are young single females, and two-thirds of them intend to emigrate.

A man sticks his head into the snug and asks for "a lock of fags," a box of cigarettes, and James struggles up from our jammed bench. Soon we all drift out. I collect my maps and charts and notes, hoping tomorrow I'll pull another thread through the tangle.

~

That night, Mrs. B. shouts up the stairs: "He says he *needs* you!" It's Cathal MacGabhann on the phone.

"I studied the thirteen factory results, and I've wrangled money for seven year-long community studies. Through Irish. You direct it."

I picture my grey-haired self writing my own thesis years from now.

"We'd pay for seven researchers, travel, training, expenses ... a salary for your good self, of course."

I think it's a first: how many other accountants think anthropology is a practical tool for planning?

"You won't find seven anthropologists here."

"Bring them in, if need be," he says. "A man in Kerry has invented a humane way of teaching Irish. He's dying to try it. Let me know."

I consult my family and my professors. Yes, they say. Maybe I can use a bit of that year to type up my shorthand field notes. MacGabhann adds the final incentive: The charmer, Seosamh Ó hÓgartaigh, would work with me.

## Criminal Conversation

My divorce papers came through. But before I can tell Mrs. B., she springs a question on me.

"Did you ever hear of such a thing as Criminal Conversation?" Mrs. B. asks.

Indeed I have. I once shared a taxi with Leo the Lips.

"No, Criminal Conversation is an Irish crime. If a married woman has an affair with another man, her husband can sue the man for Criminal Conversation. I knew a man so popular he got sued twice."

A petite young woman with a shiny black wing of hair over her eye comes in. She's Gemma Marshall, staying with Mrs. B. to improve her Irish while I've been away. "Her grandmother was a distant friend of my mother," Mrs. B. says. Gemma shakes the rain off and puts a thick book on the side table. I presume we'll change the subject in the young lady's presence, but no.

"Wives can't sue for Criminal Conversation," Mrs. B. continues. "The husband can play around with a doxy as much as he likes." "Doxy" is new to me, but I can guess its meaning.

"Yes, the husband can sue the other man even if the wife is dead," Gemma adds. "Of course, he won't get as much. But if she's living, the court figures out the wife's value and the husband gets that. A good housewife is worth more."

"Gemma is studying to be a barrister," Mrs. B. says. "She says if a man beats his wife, even if she has to go to hospital, she can do nothing. Or the Gardaí, either. He can't be kept away from the house because it's his, not hers. He could be a layabout, and she the worker paying the bills, but she has no share in the house. If he likes, he can sell it and go live with the doxy."

"And the wife can't divorce him," I commiserated. Ireland doesn't allow divorce.

"No, but he can divorce her," Mrs. B. says.

"Surely not?"

"He can go abroad," Gemma says. She gets the big book and leafs through it until she finds what she wants. "He can establish an official residence there, a domicile, and get a divorce. But a woman's official domicile is wherever her husband's is. If he moves to Spain, say, that's her domicile even if she's never set foot in the place, and even if she doesn't know where he is. Of course, no one can get a divorce in Ireland, but if she goes to Britain to get one, it won't be recognized in Ireland because her legal domicile is wherever her husband is."

"Brian Vocational suggested Gemma give a little talk to the girls' laundry class, on anything, just to give them a break. So she talked about Ireland's laws on women. It woke them up."

Gemma leaves for a dance. Mrs. B. and I talk about women trapped in violent marriages. What we would do in their shoes. "I'd pray to the good Lord," Mrs. B. says. "He'd see me right. But you Americans, I suppose you'd sneak up behind the fellow and hit him with a hammer. Knock him off."

I try to match her Wild West bravado. "Well, if I did, what woman would vote to hang me like a dog?"

"None, women can't serve on juries here."

I've forgotten. Only landowners can serve on juries, and few women own land. Houses and land belong to the husband.

Mrs. B., being a widow, is a landowner.

"But I'd never be called. We're told it's because the courthouses have no women's toilets. A woman must sign up if she wants to serve - men don't have to, they're on call. But who wants to sign up to something where you can't go to the toilet?"

I kneel down for the Rosary, and Mrs. B. calls out "*In ainm an Athair*," in the name of the Father ... But I'm distracted, wondering. I've asked so many women to draw a map of the village. How sad if the "real" domicile of one of them might be somewhere in Spain.

I forget to ask Brian how Gemma's talk went down.


## Windows as a Good Investment

The farm. The field. The stone boundary walls webbed across the landscape like a fisherman's loosely thrown trawl net.

Ideas about the farm, its care, its activities, its rights, get woven into the factory, the weft threaded through the factory's warp. Most of what rural workers bring to the factory can be traced back to farming: "What is work?" "Who does it?" "How should it be done?"

"You won't believe what happens in this place," managers say. But you would, if you looked out the window.

On any small farm around the world, the family is the business unit. Workers aren't recruited, they're born or marry in. Just as a small farm draws on family first before outsiders, the factory draws on people from this village before the next: Kilcar before Carrick; this peninsula before people further inland, Donegal before neighboring counties. Boundaries, again.

The farmer's aim is to make "a living." A man fences, shears sheep, repairs a tractor, treats a sick cow, and drains land, sometimes all in one day. Neighbors help neighbors. The seasons dictate the work schedule. But factory work is based on a different business model. It's divided into tiny operations, with a clear-cut division of labor. People with specific skills produce, on time, what the market demands. In a manager's mind, cooperative multitasking leads to chaos. Johnny Condy had told me about a hand weaver who helped another man adjust a machine loom in the Kilcar factory. Mr. Slippers shooed the weaver away like a scolded child and told him to get back to his own work.

Just as Michael Boyle defers to "the boss," old Máirtín, and Conor to his father, Eugene, a factory worker defers to managers even though he often thinks he'd do a better job. Workers would like more "say," but they won't speak up at a meeting and don't want the job themselves: "You wouldn't want to boss your neighbors." Well, who would? I remember Brian Vocational's comment: "You only stand up around here to get shot down."

I asked Jimmy Condy why Donegal workers are thought to be the best. Managers say they value overtime, piece work, incentive schemes, while southerners just "work for a living." Modestly, Jimmy denies this, but when I say nothing, he admits Donegal people are a world apart.

"It's the windows," he says. In the old days, in Donegal's province, Ulster, a landlord couldn't raise the rent just because the farm had been improved: putting in windows, for example, or draining. If the farmer sold his tenancy to someone else, the improved value stood to him. This and other rights were extended to the rest of Ireland in the Land Acts, 1870 and 1881, but clearly Jimmy thought that was too recent to see an effect on productivity yet.

James had a simpler explanation: "Long before the factory, we *were* a factory, or a clatter of little factories. In the 1830s, twenty-four-hundred weavers in this area worked at home for cash."

I tried another idea. Inexperience – is that the answer? The northern factories are older businesses. And outside Donegal, most of the workers are under twenty-five. Few have ever held another job. Their rawness drives some managers, many of them under thirty themselves, to distraction. "It's like herding cats," one said. Fred Driver, the British manager in Kiltimagh, County Mayo, sits halfway between north and south. "Yes, things happen here that wouldn't happen in Dublin," he told me. "But things happen in Dublin that wouldn't happen in Britain, and things happen in Britain that wouldn't happen in Germany. We must build a new kind of industrial tradition, and it's the manager who has to adjust first."

"Ah, well," Jimmy Condy says, "as soon as the young leave here and go to England, they learn fast enough. They're well able for it."

Maybe they don't want to let Ireland down.


## Colmcille, Patron Saint of Development

Did he go or was he pushed?

That's my question about St. Colmcille, or Columba, yet another lad for whom I have a weakness. Glencolmcille is named after him, as is the cathedral in Youngstown, St. Columba's. Leave it to Youngstown to name our cathedral after a sixth-century cut-throat.

The royal Colmcille, said to be the great-great grandson of Niall of the Nine Hostages, was an impressive figure, large in stature and voice, charismatic, cranky, and hot-tempered. As a monk still in his twenties, he founded a number of churches and monasteries. Then the waters muddy. Some records claim he was discovered copying the illuminated manuscripts of another monk. He argued this was permissible, but a high king and long-time foe, Diarmuid, disagreed. The furious Colmcille took an army into battle against his detractors. Three thousand people were killed: martyrs, perhaps, to copyright? Colmcille left for Iona, off Scotland. Was he self-exiled, suffering from remorse at the loss of so many lives? Or was he driven out by the aggrieved Diarmuid? Or was the whole thing part of local politics, as it often is today? In exile, Colmcille did a lot of community development, although even then, not without troublesome skirmishes.

I discussed this today in a final visit to Father McDyer. Are his community development plans working? Aye, he says, but he could do with less carping about his motives. He assures me he's not a megalomaniac. I ask if, war and copyright violations aside, he sees some parallels between his life and that of the besieged Colmcille? He laughs his booming laugh, stretches his rangy frame, and says, "Maybe."

I go home to my surveys and notes, parsed, dissected, left to marinate, and now in the end, faced up to. For the government's plan to work, someone has to be willing to sell land, someone has to be willing to buy it, someone has to stay and farm it, and someone has to be willing to go into the factory as a result. And those someones must be willing to speak Irish.

The other "facts" I've gleaned so far: over 52 per cent of all the young workers (aged 15 to 30) plan to emigrate. Factories won't keep them here. They say they want to see the world, or have their own business, or be their own boss. The factory is a convenient waiting area until they get everything "ready for off." The figures are lowest for the two factories that employ the most men.

Maybe the next generation offers more hope? Maybe vocational school students? My surveys up and down the coast shows these students have been among the most likely to emigrate. They're not interested in factory work, not even in management. And the Carrick Vocational School? With the Kilcar factory so close by, will they be persuaded to stay? No. Of the 125 students, two-thirds of the girls intend to emigrate, while only 20 per cent of boys do. Their main reason for emigrating is to find a job. "Would you stay at home if you could find a job locally?" I asked. Almost all the boys said yes, and three-quarters of the girls. So far, good.

"Would you work in the factory?" I asked. This is the longest established factory in the Gaeltacht, and nearly half the students have relatives in it. The shocker: all 125 said no.

What about the plan for land consolidation: "Farmers will go into the factory and sell their land." But at least two-thirds of Gaeltacht farmers are over fifty. In a study of southwest Donegal, the Agricultural Institute says more than 90 per cent are over forty. And most of the factories employ young women who don't own land, nor are they likely to be heirs.

Land sales are rare and the pieces that make up the farm are often unconnected, inconvenient scraps. Most of the potential "consolidators" are elderly.

But suppose farmers did sell and bigger farms offered a better living and Irish speakers stayed at home and worked in factories. In about half of today's factories, people aren't speaking Irish, even if most can.

Do people care that much about Irish? It's hard to say.

# December/Mí na Nollaig 1967

## The Breakthrough: A Few Ranches

I'm in the village trying to line up a dark-haired man for Mrs. B. Anyone will do, she says. I've often had to do this for my mother. Michael Boyle catches me eyeing a shy-looking youth leaning against James's wall. "Is that fellow old enough to be considered a man?" I ask.

"That wee bairn? Tell Mrs. B. I'll find her a dark-haired man to call to her house first thing on New Year's Day. But I didn't think she held with that superstitious old codology."

"He must bring a lump of coal with him. Otherwise she'll have a year's bad luck."

"He will," Michael says. "Now, I hear from James you're nearly finished here. So tell me this and tell me no more: *An mbeidh muid ag labhairt Gaeilge an am seo an bhliain seo chugainn?*" As he sees me hesitate, he laughs: "Will we be speaking Irish this time next year?"

"Very funny." I don't need the translation; I'm hesitating over my answer.

"Sure, that's the whole point of your study? You'll let me know, so, when you find out." He lopes off, striding, as always, as if he's heading uphill in a gale.

Next year seems safe enough, but if young people leave, who will pass it on? In 1943, the anthropologist Ralph Linton described Irish as "moribund." This year, the only potential new Irish speakers were the few infants born in the two parishes and the few new factory managers. The managers have no impact. Their Irish isn't strong, isn't local, and they're reluctant to force the language on workers who are speaking English, perhaps to spare the managers any embarrassment.

What does "Irish speaking" mean, anyhow? Almost everyone here is self-reported as "Irish speaking" in the Census. A better measure might be the *deontas*, the grant households get if their schoolchild passes a test for native fluency. All the local primary schools are Irish speaking, but it's hard to achieve native fluency unless the parents speak Irish at home, and they will, at least until the child leaves school.

Some of those parents believe their children are part of a cruel experiment. Irish holds their children back when they emigrate, shuttling them into low-paying construction jobs and cleaning, like my own family when they went to America.

I've learned people in some parts of Galway and Donegal see Irish simply as their "natural" unremarkable language. But in other communities, strongly Irish speaking, people skillfully leverage their position with the government. A bustling, hustling place like Gweedore, in northern Donegal, is a prime example. In the middle are places like Kilcar and Carrick where people know Irish well but don't speak it as much. When they don't get the benefits Gweedore does, they conclude the government isn't serious.

So. The farmers on their plots, the workers in their factories, the children in their schools, their belief, or not, in the language. But I've missed a dimension. I've had a great seat at the theater, seeing and hearing the

actors, but I ignored the stage: The Land. Governments use big, seduc-
tively vague words to capture the minds of its citizens: "freedom," "liberty,"
"justice." The Irish government uses words like "farm," "factory," and
"Irish speaker" in the same loose, dreamy way. I, too, have been seduced.

But I'm saved again by the Agricultural Institute, which takes a less
romantic view of things. We already know the land isn't great. Now their
draft *West Donegal Resource Survey*, a multiexpert symphony of good sense,
says that even with improvement, it's only suitable for poor grazing, and
then only if three-quarters of the *entire* peninsula is combined into a few
ranches. Only a small number of people would have work.

Would the government subsidize employment for the landless rest?
Would private manufacturing investors be attracted to these remote
areas? If not, what happens to the people and their music, dancing,
games, oral and written tradition, their literature? What happens to Irish
without people?

I look again at the urbanite's view. Is it laziness or a lack of "economic
mentality" that keeps these people from looking for factory work? Here's
where living with people, watching and listening, suggests an answer.
There's a long tradition of supplementing farm or fishing income, from
*poitín*-making or smuggling to today's dole, to create a family's "economic
pie." A farming family may earn less than a factory employee, but not
much less when home production of their food and turf is included, and
it's a safer strategy.

And no one I've met is afraid of hard work: the women in the region's
lace factory work extraordinary hours, fourteen or more in high season.
Michael Boyle's "pie" includes his backbreaking work on some of the
worst land in Ireland. As soon as his children are old enough to move
the sheep or dig or sweep, their labor is needed, too. A woman's work,
between keeping house, caring for a garden, looking after small animals
on a farm, and knitting twenty or thirty hours a week for about sixpence
an hour, amounts to more time than she'd spend teaching or working in
the civil service, supposing, as a married woman, the state allowed her to.

Nor are the men standing around on the street loafing, as some urbanites think. And they aren't always gathering market information, as I'd thought. But their daily work follows patterns different from the regimented timetables of office or factory workers. Even their agricultural decisions are misinterpreted. For years, experts criticized locals; they didn't use enough fertilizer, and they wouldn't invest in more modern machinery. According to Michael, every farmer has told them these things won't help. Now the Agricultural Institute supports him: even if local farmers did everything they've been advised to do, it wouldn't make much difference.

The weak link in the government's plan is not lazy workers, a poor "economic mentality," or, as I've learned from the records, mental instability. It's the land.

A factory delays emigration, offers a decent living, and keeps some money in the community. Most of all, it's a source of pride. Kilcar workers know their products are world class, and lace is one of the biggest attractions in Irish airport shops. Hand-woven tweed and sweaters are sold on Fifth Avenue in New York and Knightsbridge in London. A man digging in a field here may be wearing his now-retired "good suit" made of the finest tweed in the world, and his judgment of the cloth is as nuanced as that of a connoisseur of fine wines.

But the biggest impact of factories is that they've shaped the idea of what "development" is. An empty, generic "advance factory," one that will lure an entrepreneur to "beyond the beyond," is near the top of every local development committee's wish list. But it will take a lot more than a factory to save the language.

### Not Worth the Fingernail on Pádraig Pearse's Little Finger

I'm in for a difficult morning. Mrs. B. is at the bottle of whiskey again.

"I must feed my cakes," she says. She disappears and returns with three large parcels wrapped in greaseproof paper and silver foil. She pulls back the tops and with a skewer pokes about ten well-spaced holes into the dark innards. My job is to measure out exact half-teaspoons of whiskey and pour one into each hole. She's been doing this weekly for the past month but it's my job now because her spectacles are no longer up to the job. She made the Christmas cakes while I was away, but a few days before I left I watched Margaret Cannon making hers. This irritated Mrs. B., who prides herself in having her own made before anyone else, in August if necessary.

Margaret, also a non-drinker, stirred whiskey-steeped currants, sultanas, nuts, and candied fruits and peels into a rich dark batter smelling gloriously of cinnamon, vanilla, orange, ginger, and cloves. While she was poking at the fire in the bowels of her stove, I saw Shane empty a half bottle of Guinness into the batter. Margaret said she allows for this when preparing the mix, suspecting he'll do it because that's the way his mother did. The process, from steeping to the cake's "first feed" of whiskey, will take about three days. Right before Christmas, another half cup will go into the marzipan, the hard almond paste icing. But for now, the cake is wrapped, put into a tin, and hidden where only the woman of the house can find it.

Christmas preparations make me homesick. Until now I've been distracted by things like interviewing, mapping, and Conor crashing around the house, painting the bathroom avocado when Mrs. B. wanted aqua, then repainting it "another Spanish color," flamingo. "She'll love it once she gets used to it."

"I didn't think I'd miss my family so much," I say.

"Of course you would," Mrs. B. says, as she cleans out the ashes. "You're old enough to be your sister's mother. I missed *my* children."

"When they were away at school?" I ask, because unless they're attending the local vocational school, visible from Mrs. B.'s kitchen window, they must leave home for secondary school.

"No! When *I* was away at school, teaching in England. Because of the Marriage Bar! It's only in the last while that married women can teach in

Ireland, and only because primary school teachers are scarce. But back then, I had a young family, I needed the income, I had to go. By all that's right, I should have been the headmistress of the school just around the corner here.

"I went to England for four years," she says. "My youngest child was nine. I came home in the holidays, and we got a girl in to look after the children. I'll never forget it. But we were both teachers, so it was unthinkable that our children wouldn't go to secondary school, and we needed the money to pay for it."

She takes the heavy ash bucket out through the pantry door to empty it and comes back through the front door. Something is up, no one, not even herself, is allowed in the front door with an ash bucket, and bucket or no, it's considered bad luck to go out one door and in another. I hear muffled bangs from her bedroom, and she returns waving a copy of a document whose strong font even I recognize: the Proclamation of the Irish Republic. "Pádraig Pearse read this from the General Post Office in Dublin during the Easter Rising in 1916." She stabs at a paragraph. "'Equal rights and equal opportunities to all its citizens ... cherishing all the children of the nation equally ...' He was executed a week later. And James Connolly, a great friend to us women, a few days after. And what kind of a government did we get instead? Even now, half the children in the country leave school at thirteen, or even younger. Their family can't pay to send them to secondary, or they need their wages, or ..."

Her glasses sit crooked and her silver hair springs free in front. "And how can you cherish the children if their mother has to leave the country to earn their school fees? Who did that help but England? England got themselves a good teacher.

"And would you listen to this? Not long ago, Archbishop McQuaid tried to stop girls from sitting the exam for secondary school. And from playing competitive sport. Would you believe the badness?"

"But that's over, now," I say. Last November, Donogh O'Malley, the minister of education, revolutionized the education system by making secondary school free and providing rural transport.

"If we'd had the likes of Donogh in my day, I could have educated my children without leaving. And if Pearse and Connolly lived, I might have had my rights and opportunities. Don't even talk to me about the 1937 Constitution. We were finally free of Britain, all except the women!"

Back to her bedroom, a place I've never visited. She seems to have a miniature Library of Congress in there.

"Article 41.1 of the Constitution! 'The State recognizes that by her life within the home, woman gives to the State a support without which the common good cannot be achieved ... The State shall, therefore, endeavor to ensure that mothers shall not be obliged by economic necessity to engage in labor to the neglect of their duties in the home.' You know, the women that fought in The Rising, like Countess Markievicz, and that Scottish sniper. It wasn't for this."

I must look up that Scottish sniper.

"The Church, the government, not one of them worth the fingernail on Pádraig Pearse's little finger." She marches out to store the bucket. I'm struck once more by her bearing; Queen Méabh had nothing on her.


## The Bus


"I presume you're referring to Dr. Kane," I heard Mrs. B. say on the phone yesterday. She handed it to me, eyebrows raised, and went into the pantry.

"Eileen? Conor. How're ya keepin'?"

"What did you say to Mrs. B.?"

"Nothing. I was just acting the maggot. C'mere to me, I want to ..."

"But what did you say?" I whispered, because she was still looking at me.

"I said, 'Is that darling girleen still with you?' Only joking. Sure, if I meant it, I wouldn't be saying it, would I? And you a freshly unmarried woman?" He laughs. "So. You wouldn't be going anywhere near Donegal Town tomorrow?"

"Yes, I have to interview a manager."

"Could you collect me in Meenacloy and give me a lift to town?"

"The van's not working?"

"You know yourself how it is. It needs repairs, but it will get me as far as Meenacloy. A fellow there will look at it. I'll leave it with him."

"I can give you a lift back after my interview."

"Sound. But no worries, I'll make my own way. About ten tomorrow?"

This morning I set out at 9:30. The trip seems straightforward enough: along the coast into Killybegs, then left into the hills. After that, I ask. People say Meenacloy is miles away, so I drive flat out, careening around the bends to a boggy, scrubby lunar waste where I see a man digging, chest deep in a ditch. He leans companionably on his spade, settling in for a chat. I tell him I'm on my way to Meenacloy. "This is Corker Mór," he says. Big Corker. Meenacloy is about a half mile behind me.

Back I go, and as I re-enter the forbidding misty wilderness that must be Meenacloy, many thoughts run through my head. The first, as a Youngstowner, is that Conor is planning to kill me, but at least the man in Corker Mór will know where to direct the search party. The second is I am going to kill Conor.

I nearly do as he appears, semaphoring wildly, as if I might miss him on this, the last road God made. "I worried you'd gone off wrong entirely and ended up in Corker Beg." Corker Beg is "Little Corker," which I can only imagine.

"How could I have missed you?"

"I was in the bushes," he says demurely. "Bush, I mean," for there's only one in the immediate landscape.

"Just a sec," he calls, and goes behind the bush. He returns hastily and lifts something heavy into the back with a thud. "Let's get out of here. We call it Pago Pago back in my village."

"Has fire been discovered in your village yet?"

"Now, now, be nice. Did you tell anyone you were coming here?"

"No," I say, forgetting Mr. Corker Mór.

"Good." He reaches into the back seat for what? A map? A hatchet? I knew a girl in Youngstown who came home from school and found her mother chopped up in a washtub. We peer into the back, I for anything strange, he for his cigarettes.

We set out. "What's that heavy thing on the floor?" I ask.

"A case. I'm leaving for England."

He might expect a lot of questions, but not, probably, the only one I can think of: "This can't be the best place to start from?"

"I sold the van to a fellow here in Meenacloy this hour."

"And you're on the run from him now?"

"Of course not. Amn't I just trying to catch the bus from Donegal Town to Dublin so I can get on the boat tonight?" He turns to me. "Not a word about this at home."

"But why are you going to England?" What really shocks me is he's sold the van, with all its lovingly fitted tiny drawers and shelves, peg boards for tools, jar lids screwed to the ceiling for the glass jars holding his nails, and the camp stove and old stool for lunch and tea.

"Work. I have to. My brother Ollie's got it in his head to leave. If he does I'll be left with the farm and my father and my own business I'm trying to build. It's not on. The farm makes very little; it's just a home for us and some sheep really, but while my Da is alive, we've got to keep it up, somehow."

"Ollie seemed happy enough the time I saw him?"

"He takes notions. He's always been a divil for the radio, *The Kennedys of Castleross*, *Saturday Spin*, *On the Farm*." He stubs out the cigarette.

"So a cousin from Dublin came here a while back and made a fuss of him and invited him to visit. She has television of course, and he saw *The Riordans* on it. Now he's thinking he's like Benjy on *The Riordans*, just a lonely farm boy and everyone else away having a great life. He wants to live in Dublin or Castleross now."

"Castleross isn't a real place."

"You must have seen yourself – he's not a hundred per cent, but fair dues to him, he can farm. If he goes now ..."

"But you said yourself he's not ... surely he'll be back soon enough?"

"He will, of course, he always is, but 'soon enough' is no good if there's sheep to shear and turf to cut and the cows and potatoes and chickens *and* a building business to run. I'm ahead of him this time, though. Two nights ago I found a box in the shed with his few good bits and pieces, shoes and a coat and a little money, and I knew it would only be days before he'd be gone again. I'm not living this way, me, Muggins, picking up the pieces. And it would kill the old fella to see the place go down. It won't outlast him, maybe, but while he's alive, I owe him that much."

He waves me left at a fork.

"So at the end of all, I've decided to go to England, rather than waiting to see. I'll get work on the Underground tunnels, the Victoria Line or some other yoke, whatever, we have a cousin there, and I'll make enough to buy a decent van and a few things for the farm so I won't have to kill myself when he gets a notion to go the next time. If he comes back then, okay, but I won't be banking on it."

I think of turning the car back toward Owenteskiny and old Eugene, but I know he'd jump out.

"What about Jackie?"

"It's no bother to him. He's a painter. Fully qualified last month."

"He apprenticed to you?"

"Certainly. The guiding hand of an older man. If I do nothing, the place will collapse around me, the business will fail, you've seen yourself what it takes to keep all the balls in the air, the carpenter, the plumber, the this, the that ...

"I have the jump on him now and he'll have to stay. Say nothing until I'm well away on the bus. You won't, anyhow, what's this you have? Not exactly the Seal of Confession, but you can't tell anyone what someone else tells you?"

This is news to me.

"And you shouldn't anyway because everyone will be asking why I picked *you*." He laughs. "That's a good one, I hadn't thought of that." I had.

"Would you ever look at that!" he says, as clouds skim a silver-sliver day-moon. "A teeny tiny moon! And it could look bigger if we traveled a long distance. But it's us that's changed, not the moon. Surprise! Parallax!" He ducks my blow. "And you might look different when I view you from a distant point, England, say, but I doubt it."

In Donegal Town, a small group waits outside the hotel for the bus: young people with suitcases, mothers pressing newspaper-wrapped sandwiches into their hands.

"What will Eugene and Ollie think when you don't come home?" I ask.

"They'll know I'm gone. I've never spent a night away from home in my life. They'll know."

The bus arrives. He squeezes my shoulder. "I'm not testing your hearing now," he says, and goes.

# January/Mí Eanáir 1968

## What's the Alternity?

Two weeks since Conor left.

Our Christmas was the Irish ideal: quiet. Irish people ask each other "How did you get over the Christmas?" not "How did you get *on* over the Christmas?" and the correct answer is "It was quiet." I suspect this can include drunken, uproarious, knock-down, marriage-fracturing yuletides, but one never probes, even if the speaker's arm is in a sling.

"He's sent no letter," Mrs. B. says, referring to one of the reasons for our subdued Christmas, "and Eugene is grieving. We'll go over. Eugene is a friend of my mother's and he'll be delighted to see me. You needn't let on you know anything or mention your own role in this."

"Mine?"

"Of course. Felim Doogan, Charlie's boy, was on the Dublin bus with Conor and saw you through the window. What I don't know is whether he's coming back. Eugene is sick about it."

"He'll come back."

Country men without women often live in houses as bleak and austere as their outbuildings. Their doors are open to the bitter winds, or
fuggy rooms are choked with smoke and cluttered with ugly functional-
ity: a rancid armchair under the bare light bulb, a derelict cooker used
as a cupboard, small bits of machinery to be repaired, a basin and towel
for washing feet by the fire, all for convenience, none for aesthetics,
although the farmer has a very neat eye for the land and its spare buildings. Sometimes the few remnants of the last woman in the house sit
incongruously on a shelf or dresser, the good blue delph pitcher and
a crazed ceramic vase vying with a tin of sheep de-wormer. But here, I
see traces of Conor everywhere: an exquisitely grained table, a carved
chest.

"I can't believe one of mine would do this to me, Nellie," he says,
taking Mrs. B.'s hands. "I know he worried Ollie might slip away, but he
could have told me. The worry I've had."

"I'm sure he's trying to make enough to keep everything going. He'll
come back."

"Will he?"

"He will, of course. Felim Doogan was on the bus with him and I
think he said something like that." I'm astonished at her lie, but Mrs. B.
must be satisfied her Lord will overlook it.

"You know Conor was twice the man ..."

"You're right, he was twice the man of anyone in his class," Mrs. B.
says quickly, as Ollie appears at the door behind Eugene, with the same
absent smile as ever. Conor said he wasn't a hundred per cent, as I'd
guessed, but I wonder what per cent he actually is.

"Conor will return. Just pray to Our Blessed Lady, and she'll never
fail you," Mrs. B. says. Ollie blesses himself quickly at the words "Our
Blessed Lady."

"I will so," Eugene says, slowly rising from his chair. "Anyway, Nellie,
what's the alternity?"

## The Center Cannot Hold

"Big meeting of the committee tomorrow night. People from Carrick and Kilcar, weapons left at the door. Ready?" Shane Cannon calls as he swings in behind me at the petrol pump.

"I'd love to be a fly on the wall."

"No need. You're the star speaker!"

In the pub, James is reading something that looks like the Dead Sea Scrolls. "The Spinning Wheel Census of 1796," he says. "It has a good few names from this area." Beside him on the bar is a fully fledged anchor, flukes akimbo.

With a sharp snap, he closes it, cutting his finger. This is the real thing; how often I've seen my father cut his finger like this. But it differs from my father's anchor.

"Yes, it's like a third cousin once removed," James says. "A distant friend, you might say."

"It's beautiful," I say, having seen a dozen trial versions in my childhood.

He beams. "I've gone for a patent."

"The committee meeting?" I don't ask whether he's a member now; the membership has become quite fluid, what with horse-trading over county, official, political, and factional representation.

"People have me demented asking what's going into that book of yours."

"Who's coming?"

"The Development Committee, some from the Kilcar Parish Council, and the odd few others." The Carrick Parish Council has never materialized, despite all the drama.

"I haven't got my work sorted out in my own head yet."

"I think you do. Anyhow, we all want to learn from you. In the words of St. Colmcille in 575, 'A man without guidance is weak/Blind are all the ignorant.'"

So I search for a string, a line, a strand that might help me to explain what I've found. Sometimes I've imagined it as a thread fishing in and out through the warp of my interviews, maps, and records, emerging in a richly textured web. But what I have, instead, is the end of a granny knot, a shoe-lace tie. When I pull, the tie falls apart. As Yeats said, the center cannot hold.

"Ach, your old knots," Mrs. B. says. "Just tell them the story. Everyone loves a story."

Here's one, a story about borders, edges, boundaries, and the places and people who fall outside them, who don't fit in. "We're 'beyond the beyond,'" James had said.

They live in a liminal place where they don't get special Gaeltacht attention because they can speak Irish, but don't always, and they don't get help from other departments because they're in the Gaeltacht. Where civil government is so remote that local sanctions, such as nicknames and gossip, are used to keep order, and "letting your name down" is ruin-ous. Where shadow systems flourish, even for getting a telephone. Where people can't work in their own country.

Where the maps men and women draw are so different that it's hard to know if they're of the same village. Where the unspoken boundaries of alliances and divisions radiate outwards and draw in again, depending on one's perceived affiliation at any particular moment. Where even the cat-egories of mental illness vary from "official" ones, and the mental hospital is reserved for cases the community can't handle, including the homeless poor, geriatrics, and mothers of the illegitimate. Where a "factory" means one thing to the government, another to local people. A lonely place, liv-ing on the edge of Irish and English, home to centuries of survivors.

But I won't tell this story.

To clear my head, I drive out to the cliffs in Glencolmcille and stand on the edge of Europe. To the west, nothing between me and Newfound-land; to the south, Lisbon, Porto, and Conakry. Behind me, the great figures of Europe and beyond, contemporaries of Niall of the Nine Hos-tages: Attila the Hun, Augustine, Constantine.

How many stories I've heard here, ancient Ulster tragedies about Niall kissing the hag "properly"; Cú Chulainn being cooled in a barrel after seeing the bared breasts of the enemy women; Deirdre of the Sorrows ending up with the wrong man; Méabh getting her period at exactly the wrong moment, something that speaks to every woman? Some of these minor points stick in my memory, perhaps because they all involve women, but in fact each is a major tragedy.

The story of the Kilcar factory, the story I must tell them, has all the markings of a mythical tragedy, like Cú Chulainn's or Niall's: a mighty hero, flawed; a spectacular fall, partly his own fault. The punishment exceeds the crime. An insight emerges, but at great cost. The factory, the source of work and pride for many, has a flaw: it's English speaking, so it fails to become an industrial estate.

The story won't be as gripping as that of Cú Chulainn. No one wants to hear a tragedy about manufacturing as a pillar of government policy, especially those people doing the manufacturing. But it's the only story I can tell; people must cast it as they see fit. I've had a good education and grant money that allowed me to study. But people here have a scholarly tradition, personal experience of what I studied, and they'll have to live with the outcomes, whatever they'll be. We each have a stake, but the stakes are worlds apart.

But maybe a story won't do it. This wild, wind-scoured place, these scattered lives, the golden myths, the fraught history, the wrong-sided boundaries, also demand a role. Perhaps a symphony might do them justice, or a heroic poem, or even, God forbid, an interpretive dance. But a PhD thesis?

## The Government Does Nothing for Us

That's most of the Carrick Development Committee over there, and behind them The Perpetual Smile, "Better," Madame Blue Mould, and Jack Ruby. A few men huddle in the back as if they were in church. Jimmy

Condy and The Fear Ruadh from Kilcar study the school's big map of Ireland, where earlier I placed stickers showing the factories I studied. A few sullen-looking youths lounge in the corner.

Mrs. B., lips set tight to forewarn anyone who might dream of giving me trouble, is well placed at the side; James, with his bundle of yellowed documents, sits between Liz and a serene Michael Boyle; Tommo, Bríd, Peadar Malloy, and some of the Kilcar Parish Council are here, as well as Father Stevens and two of the teachers. Art Sweeney and Mrs. Campbell arrive from Glencolmcille. Brian Vocational and Chairman Leo chat amiably with James, which surprises no one, it seems, but me. And who is that dapper fellow sitting alone at the back? He gives me a nod and taps some rolled-up sheets of paper. Is he from the government? Here to challenge my findings? And I'm worried people who helped me may regret it if their neighbors blame them after they hear some of my ideas. But one thing no longer worries me: my professor claims women's voices aren't suited to public speaking. I've heard Margaret Mead on television, and she sounds fine.

What about those women behind the long table, with cakes and a kettle already on the boil? And the Cannon twins, helping Margaret set out scones? In fact, Mrs. B., at the side, is part of that group; she's still "leaving politics to the men."

The new parish priest, Father Shiels, waves to me to the front of the room. "Tonight we're saying goodbye to Miss Kane, Eileen, who's been with us now for quite a while."

So this is a goodbye party. Or not: some of the members of the Carrick Development Committee and the Kilcar Parish Council open notepads. "Know your audience" is the first rule of public speaking, but what is this audience? I'm not sure what they expect: from what I heard as I came through the door, a few think I'm from the government, some Teelin people think I'm collecting folklore, and "Better" now suspects I've come halfway around the world to have an affair with James. I'm told he's been calling me "The Borrowed Bride," the title of yet another ancient tragedy.

Each group has people who think I'm writing The Book that will make my fortune.

"Will I say something about what I've been doing?" I ask Father Shiels.

"Well ... I suppose ... well, surely, if you like."

What?

"*Cad é do scéal?*" The Fear Ruadh calls. What's your story?

Okay, a story, one I only learned from a letter last evening.

"I have a secret story, about a respectable family gone bad. About power and greed, and the death of an Ulster man." A few look around, smirking; others sit to attention.

"*Fadó Fadó*, a long time ago, a Norman knight, Adam Stanton, built Castle Carra down in County Mayo. He was a proud, religious man.

"The Red Earl of Ulster, proud and religious, too, assumed that his title would be passed down in a dignified way. One day his son, Edmond Burke, went missing.

"Edmond's cousin was one of the culprits. He wanted Edmond's title, so he got Adam Stanton's grandsons, or maybe his great-grandsons, to kidnap Edmond. But when His Eminence, the Archbishop of Tuam, ordered them to free Edmond, they panicked. They tied a stone to his neck, put him in a sack and drowned him in Lough Corrib."

"Better" gasps.

"They were punished. The Stanton family went into exile for many years. Some changed their name. We still have Adams in my family today; I'm told the first Adam Stanton was my ancestor." I look at James, as if to ask "Have I got it right?" and he nods, laughing. I must send a note to thank the little historian in the Valuation Office.

"So everyone has secrets. I came here to learn only one. Is the government's plan for the Gaeltacht working?"

"No," someone says. "We told you that the first day."

"*What* plan?" "Better" shouts. I glance at the dapper man at the back. Maybe he'd like to explain it? He just smiles, so I recite my litany: farm consolidation, factory, emigration reduced, the language survives. I know the thorn: consolidation.

"Selling our land?" The Fear Ruadh calls out. "No other farmer in his right mind would buy it. Who needs more rocks?"

A man with an upright bush of silver hair stands much faster than I thought a man of his age could. "The young men coming into the factory have no land to sell. Their fathers are still living. Or they may not be the heirs at all. Or their people didn't come from farms."

Michael says, "Government big shots take no notice of us. The Doctor here knows all about that. She told me people in Dublin said we have no economic sense."

People look at me accusingly.

I say a lot of outsiders, "sensible in every other way," think any country person living on more than an acre is a full-time farmer. And I don't mention the entire government plan for Carrick seems to depend on one man, Finbarr Doherty, the only full-time farmer who isn't signing on for the dole, a real "farmer." And he lives in another area. The Agricultural Institute's draft *West Donegal Resource Survey* refers quite often to "the farmer" this, "the farmer" that. Well, that's him, by the tea table. I wonder if he understands the full extent of his burden.

"And some Dublin people think farmers don't understand what's good for them. They think farmers would have a better living in a factory," I say.

"If they think we have no economic sense, why did they think we'd go into the factory?" The Fear Ruadh calls out.

Farmers and factory workers argue about which life is safer. My confidential draft of the *West Donegal Resource Survey* seems to have escaped James's custody and traveled around the parishes. The two local agricultural advisors look surprised. Factory workers say it shows the land is suitable only for ranches. The farmers say they've been using the land for centuries for the only thing it's good for – part of a living. And they add that the factory could disappear any moment.

"It won't, not in our lifetime," an older factory worker says.

"The cake has fallen through, Margaret," a dour woman announces on the side.

"Well, it has ice cream in it. I never expected we'd be kept waiting so long." Margaret shoos the standing women toward vacant chairs.

An old farmer stands. "They want us to sell up and go into the factory. At my age? Most of us are well over fifty. Look at my hands," he shouts, holding them up. I think he means they're arthritic, but it's the size we notice: they're like shovels, hard to imagine in a precision factory. "And if I don't go in, them people, they'll say I'm lazy ..."

The bush-haired man shoots up again. "They always say that. For fifty years, did anyone ever see old Máirtín Boyle sitting down?" he shouts. "Or the ladies here, knitting every spare hour God sends?" He looks around the room. "Or the Teelin fishermen? It might look like sport to holidaymakers, but those Dublin lads should try making their living at it."

"Strangers see local men standing here on the street and think they're dossers," I say. This seems to surprise some of the seers who stand outside the Central Bar.

"Those strangers' families couldn't be long out of the countryside," James says. "How easy they lose the common sense their people before them had."

For a second I hear Conor laughing. I remember the note I took: "The apparent displacement of objects caused by actual change of point of observation." Parallax. One minute Dublin planners see the Gaeltacht and its people as romantic, their language at the center of national identity, and the next as lazy, backward, and unable to grasp economics. Gaeltacht people look east, hoping educated planners can help them, but then look at the local outcomes and conclude the planners are blindfolded, out of touch, promoting one desperate scheme after another. All within a distance of less than 200 miles. "We compress time and expand distance," as James told me.

The cake on the tea table is more like a pancake now.

One of the youths lounging at the back shouts, "Ye're all going on, saying the farm will do you, the factory will do you, it will see you out. No room for us lads, though, it's only the boat to England has room for us." It's Jackie. "Sorry, but it's always the same feckin' old blather. Fertilizer, no fertilizer, always in the right. The government, locals, everybody's right. Not us, though."

"Ah, now," James says. But we're electrified. Young people don't speak out in adult company, and certainly not this way. I recognize the youths now: the cherubic boys who made maps for me, who were horrified when the discussion of courting places got out of hand. Their voices have deepened a bit since then, and their lips curled.

"I've heard you say yourself the factory here in Kilcar is the biggest, with the best workers. What the government wants. And now them two big industrial estates are going to other places, not to us," Jackie says to me.

Peadar slumps in his chair. "The language," he says.

"All of us speak Irish," Jimmy Condy roars. "But most of our children *have* to emigrate. So they need English. Will the government pay for translators to go with them so they can work? Won't that cost more than helping them to live here?"

A Teelin man stands. "The government doesn't care about Irish. I'll tell you how I know."

He has the stance of a man who farms in a gale. "In the summer, my wife and I keep city children attending the Irish college in Teelin. Their people send them so they can get enough Irish to go to university and into government jobs. My own children serve them food, make their beds. But we have no money to send ours to secondary school, let alone university. So the well-off city children with poor Irish go to university and get good jobs, and our children with perfect Irish don't."

"They have family who can pay big money," The Fear Ruadh sneers.

"Our children have family who speak great Irish," the bent man says.

"The city wains, they'll get the few words of Irish but they'll know nothing about Mael Dun, or Bran, or Conall Cernach swallowing a giant boar." Nods all around when James lists these. He pushes his luck: "Or MacConglinne's oozy lard." Blank faces.

"We have the vocational school, but I don't know will many of them want to go into the factory," Michael Boyle says. "My boy didn't."

None want to, according to my survey.

"We don't want to go to London, diggin' the Victoria Line, either," Jackie mutters.

"But don't we want to see the world?" the smallest boy protests.

"I don't need to see it from the back of a spade. I'd be as able to see it with a good education; the same way the city lads do."

"And you," Jackie jutting his chin at me. "Here we thought you were bringin' jobs."

Their courage fades and they stumble out the door. One turns back and slams it.

The women have said little. Sometimes a hand darts up and is withdrawn as fast when a man stands. One has retreated several times. But now she stands, a woman I always thought of as the local version of a haughty socialite. "You mentioned laziness. I just want to say one thing. And I wish she was still with us to hear me. My mother went blind making lace."

People murmur, shocked. James and Peadar nudge each other to stand. The cake, in its pool of ice cream, smells delicious.

James pulls the pack of index cards out of his jacket pocket. I hear a groan. "We need to have clear heads about what we want. We say we want a factory, but what most of us really have in mind is an industry and all that goes with it. Maybe we won't get that, but shouldn't we know what we *don't* want?"

"You," I hear a wag muttering.

Peadar rises. "Until now we've been grateful for anything. That furniture factory was a good example: a few youngsters, learning a trade alone in their own homes, just a stopgap till they leave. It wasn't a factory; not even a workshop."

"Or the vegetable co-op, seasonal," the bush-haired man says. "Or all girl workers. They quit when they marry, or else emigrate. We should be able to explain ourselves to investors. We're not lazy or stupid. We survived on bad land; we have the official stamp of the government that it's bad." He holds up the *West Donegal Resource Survey*.

Leo, Carrick's chair, rises. "We're talking about more than the Kilcar factory tonight. Whatever we need in Carrick and Kilcar, that's what the whole west needs, too, Irish speaking or not. Or is the government willing to let the west just wither away?"

James nods. "Exactly. We need to take more control. We need to have a real role when a business comes in. Straight talk on both sides. Look at that trout farm. We told them ..."

"We know, James," Peadar says.

"So," James says, waving his cards, "Know what we want, find out how to get it. And who are we? Before Miss Kane came here, they told her in Dublin, talk first to the priest, the headmasters, the sergeant of the Gardaí, and the doctor. Now tell me, which of those is on Carrick's Development Committee?"

"Only a few teachers," Shane says. "And I ask you, what do teachers know about development?"

"The Kilcar Parish Council is quite representative," a man says. "We have panels from each townland or area, and representatives of the fishermen, the forestry men, the factory workers ..."

A strong public speaker interrupts from the side. "Yerrah, your old panels, your committee of teachers. Ye have no woman on either committee. Who represents *me* and my hands crippled from knitting? Or the women who have nowhere to go but the church or the shop? What's here for them? Or the young people, like those lads who spoke up?"

So Mrs. B. is not leaving politics to the men.

James reads something from notes written on his hand. "I had a bit of a brainwave," he announces. "What is our strength?"

People avoid his eye, as they did in school when they didn't know the answer to a teacher's catechism question.

"We're in the middle of nowhere!" he shouts triumphantly. The roads are bad, and the electricity and transport are dodgy. We need to attract ..." He extends his palms, like a director encouraging a choir.

"No? Then I'll tell you. We need to attract environment-free businesses. Businesses that need nothing but brains. Keeping records! And the European Union is coming in. and they'll need people to handle their documents. And Irish is our official language, so all kinds of things, edicts, orders, what have you, will have to be translated into Irish. *Good* Irish."

"We need a factory, James," someone calls.

He deflates. "Well, before anything, we should go round to all the people in the villages. Including the ladies," he says, bowing to Mrs. B. "Businesspeople, tradesmen, fishermen, people interested in tourism, teachers, shopkeepers. Most of all, young people. What do they need? Why? How much of it can we do for ourselves? How do we get help with the rest? Then we meet again. Some of the ideas will be the same; better transport, probably. So we start, maybe with the easiest, maybe with something everyone agrees on. We figure out how much we can do, ourselves. Who else could help? *Then* we go to Dublin with a strong case. Active, involved people, not just moaners."

Mr. Bush-Hair laughs. "You left out us old lads standing on the street. We want to be consulted." I hadn't recognized him without the cap.

"And let some of ye make the tea next time," Mrs. B. says, moving toward the table.

"Thank you," I say to the group, who are already gathering their things. Many of the people here helped to produce my information, although maybe not the interpretation I've put on it. No one has attacked me,

though, but that's not people's way here. Someone flays you alive, someone else tells you later.

"We'll have to be our own anthropologist now," James laughs.

At the back, men stand aside shyly and women pour tea and force cake
on people. "Stay your hand, Margaret," the arthritic old man protests as
she cuts a tombstone of a piece. His huge hand dwarfs it.

"How did you find out about the Stantons?" James asks, laughing, as
we walk out into an unseasonal sleet. "Better" is on our heels.

I say the historian took an interest in my story and sent me some
details yesterday. "He was a bit worried I might be upset about the way the
Stantons killed their prisoner." Me, from the Murder Capital of the U.S.

"I was saving the Red Earl story as a parting gift," James said. "As a boy
I had a great interest in him. And the Stantons supported the other lad,
the cousin, because he was their local overlord, one of their own. Maybe
they weren't a hundred per cent bad."

"I wouldn't bother that woman," I overheard "Better" saying to Shane.
"A wee bird told me she has Mafia connections. If you crossed them lads,
they'd go through you for a shortcut."

The dapper, silent man touches my sleeve and hands me his rolled-up
sheets. He gives a farewell salute and disappears in the crowd.

The sheets are a puzzle. "Do you know what these are?" I ask James,
sheltering in a doorway.

"It's the races his best dogs are running in," James says. "That's John
Joe Mulhern, the car mechanic from Donegal Town. Didn't he replace
your exhaust pipe the day before you descended upon us?" It was true,
what I was told. John Joe washes up well.

Across the street I see Jackie and the lads in a doorway, passing a bottle
around. Jackie comes over. The lads jeer and whistle.

"Sorry I spoke out at your meeting. I didn't mean to."

"You were right."

"It's just I was thinking of Conor. My uncle was back from London
last week. He took me to the pub and said it's a dog's life. Worse."

"Stop messin'!" he roars at the young fellows. He's coming into his own.

"Conor could have been anything, an engineer, anything at all," he says.

~

Later, James takes my notebook. At the end of the list of Irish words and phrases he's written so often, he adds a new one: *Anois, cad é?* Now what?

I know what. "I'm taking Cathal MacGabhann's offer. You're the first person here that I've told." I don't need to tell Mrs. B. She already knows it in her "waters."

# February/Mí Feabhra 1968

## Things I Didn't Know

I'm nervous about leaving. Am I missing that nugget, the keystone, that would give me better insights? Do I need more time? Bur I really need some sleep ...

Deliver me, Lord, from the wicked,

Preserve me from the violent,
Protect me from enchantment
From sudden death
From evil conduct
From cursing or being cursed
From secret intrigues
And from quarrels over land boundaries,
Preserve me from the furious warrior
Who likes to spread terror

Whose hair is always bristling ...

Bristling hair!? The dream fades. I claw at my nightgown, twisted up around my neck, throttling me. Psalm 140? They say you can leave the Church but it never leaves you.

I remember now, it's not the Bible, it's "The Evening Prayer of the Society Islands in French Polynesia." I read it for an anthropology class. It's probably the only prayer that mentions quarrels over land boundaries.

Now that I'm close to leaving, almost everyone in the two parishes has come to put me straight, to air grievances and slights, or to tell me what I should put in "The Book."

A man: "The guards were called on this fellow, he had changed some ragwort into a pig and sold it at the market. Well, he put the guard up on a table and set him to laying eggs. I was going to sell that to the Folklore Commission, but I said to myself you'd pay better."

A shopkeeper: "My brother got a job as a bus driver, but when the tinsel wore off, he went to Canada in 1953. Did you ever run into him there? He's the only person who really knows what's what here."

A man in his fifties: "Forget all this stuff people are telling you. I'll tell you this: many people here think nothing of 'heavy petting' as long as the formalities are observed by both parties. I'll bet no one let you in on that one."

"There was this ninety-year-old man, he worked for ten pence a day at Cladnagearah pier. One time he took thirty-four and three-quarter yards of homespun from his valley and sold it at a shilling three farthings a yard and came home with the correct amount. How did he do that when he never went to school? Could you do that, with all your education?"

A teacher: "People used to say that February first was the first day of spring, but now they realize that it's too cold at that time. So in your book, shift it to late April, May even."

Several people who avoided talking to me: "Why did you listen to (James, Mrs. B., Brian Vocational, Peadar, Michael Boyle, the factory manager, etc.)? Useless. Anything you needed to know, you could have come to me."

The doctor: "The house next to Mrs. B's, the Red House, is the place everyone meets. It's a 'gossip house,' like in the old days. You could have lived there and finished up your work in six weeks."

Mr. Slippers: "You've talked to all the wrong people. You should ask a person, 'Who's your worst enemy?' and then you should go talk to that one. It's more scientific that way."

The curate: "There's a heap of women here you should have talked to. If a fly farts, they know about it."

A "returned Yank": "Did he tell you he owns that land? Let me see your ordnance survey map. Well! All I can say is God bless your innocence. You'd better start over."

~

Start over?

    ... And let me and my spirit live
    And rest in peace, O my God!

# March/Mí an Mhárta 1968

## The Eye of a Friend

I'm leaving tomorrow. I've spent weeks saying goodbye. People here shep-
herded me until I became an adult they could talk to. They "put manners
on me" when I failed. And they contributed hundreds of hours answering my questions and steering me right when I asked the wrong ones.

They're used to saying goodbye to young people, but I'm not used to
emigrating. I've extracted the dry, people-free facts required for a PhD
thesis, and now I can give Michael Boyle and Tommo and Shane the
ordnance survey maps they've worked on for so many nights, chasing the
nineteenth-century Condys and Charlies down through the generations
to the Felims and Dannys of today. I won't forget Michael's face as his
finger followed the lines that encompass his life and those of his ancestors. Soon I'll forget the stories of why Charlie Doogan's farm is called
Mary Condy Harley's, or how Máirtín "married in" to his farm. But I
won't forget Margaret or Eugene or The Fear Ruadh or Bríd or Chairman Leo ... Con Cassidy will go back to his music. Peadar will have more
time for football.

James and Liz are cocooned in the warmth of their old kitchen sofa.

"Eileen of the Ruddy Hair," he says. "Like our great goddess, the red-haired Macha, she made Ulstermen weak. And like them, we'll be weak for nine generations now."

"Isn't she the one who turned herself into a leper?"

"Only in passing. She's the one who gave birth to twins while racing on horseback."

We turn to community development. He's already asked local women if they're willing to offer bed and breakfast to tourists. He himself can't accommodate any of the hoped-for influx; he has no spare room, only "your own," although it's over a year since I slept in it.

"And," he says, "the environment-free idea is taking off." He shows me a business card: "Translation Services" and "James O'Donnell, Stiúrthóir." "Put that in your notebook: *stiúrthóir*, 'director.' I'm counting on Leo to be my right-hand man."

I notice a thick roll of blueprints squashed between the cushions.

"Starting all over," he says. "It's half the fun." If Mrs. B. hadn't told me he's just won the patent on his anchor, I'd have believed him.

"I've enjoyed my time talking to you," he says, "but your father's the only person I know who has a perfect understanding of the difference between a funicular railway and an incline elevator." He taps the prints. "I'm hoping to get him over."

He hands me Worsley's *The Trumpet Shall Sound* and I present him with Levi-Strauss.

It's hard to reconcile a future without James.

And then there's Mrs. B.

I try to bring in enough turf, dust enough rooms, fill the holy water font high enough, shake out the kitchen table oilcloth hard enough to last her for the next ... what? Weeks? Year? Five years? Is this what emigrating daughters do for their mothers the night before they go?

"I'm still very excited about the community meeting we had," I chirp. "What do you think will happen?"

"I don't think he'll come back. I know it in my waters."

We're quiet for a while. "Of course he will. The bathtub ..." and I realize how ridiculous that sounds. It's like something out of an ancient Irish legend; I'm holding Conor hostage over a bathtub. Or holding the bathtub hostage to lure him back.

What do the people who are left behind think about? When my grandmother, a young girl then, left Ireland, her own grandmother said, "I'll never see you again." My grandmother remembers waving from the horse and cart taking them away, until each was out of the other's sight. I remember the bus leaving Donegal Town, and I don't want to think about it anymore. Tomorrow, leaving this house, will be worse.

I picture driving away, the Morris trailing a bejeweled woolly web glinting with bits of parallax, the black breast, Padraig Pearse's fingernail, *Fanny Hill*, cow injections, and Maggie Ruadh's undergarments. All the bits that mean something to me.

"So, what will come from the community meeting?" I ask Mrs. B.

"It's early days. There's an old saying, 'A good beginning is half the work.'"

A bit optimistic, I think.

"But probably not much will happen in my time." She may have twenty years in front of her, so I sink a little more.

As I pack to leave for the lads in Dublin and a night at the Trocadero, the professors in Pittsburgh and my family in Youngstown, I decide to speak up, at last.

"Some people think you're a bit strait-laced. Strict."

She laughs.

"But I see a very different person." I have to think how best to describe her to herself. "Red-blooded, open, ready for anything. Were you always this way?"

"*Is maith an scáthán súil charad,*" she says. "The eye of a friend is a good mirror."

And that's all I get.

Tonight we race through the Rosary in English and Irish, I kneeling before the warmth of the Stanley, Mrs. B. facing the other way, on her knees with her elbows on the seat of her rocker. The television is on, sound off, but toward the end I turn and see she's watching the racing results. "*In ainm an Athair agus an Mhic ...*" she intones, "In the name of the Father ..." and winks at me when she kisses her beads and puts them away. We bank up the fire for the night.

# Epilogue

## What Happened to the People?

Conor never came back: when Eugene died, he stopped writing. A returned emigrant from Straleel said he'd talked to Conor while they were shoveling rubble on the Victoria Line extension to Pimlico. Later, another saw him eating in a "transport cafe," and "he wasn't looking the best." He noticed he'd lost some fingers, the man said, but he didn't like to ask about it.

The young priest left the priesthood when his mother died.

Terry Stewart, stand-in manager of the Spiddal doll factory, became a director in the European Commission, and later, director general of the Institute of European Affairs. Dónall Ó Móráin added the chair of the Irish national broadcasting system to his role in Gael Linn. Cathal Mac-Gabhann became chair of the new Údarás na Gaeltachta, the Gaeltacht Authority. Seán MacRéamoinn became a national treasure. Seosamh Ó hÓgartaigh became an important civic leader in Galway, and his distinguished son, Ciarán, is currently the president of NUIG, the National

University of Ireland, Galway. Fred Driver lived out his life as an honored citizen of Kiltimagh. Father McDyer became the parish priest of Carrick – how I wish I'd been there.

Mrs. B. died in 1984 at age ninety. Margaret died when the twins were teenagers and Shane, their father, followed soon after, but their children and grandchildren have exceeded the dreams their parents had for them. Many of my friends in both villages lived to see the millennium, and in 2021, the couturier Mary O'Donnell still thrives. Fans of traditional music can buy Con Cassidy's music on the internet. The Trocadero Restaurant, where the "lads" helped me to graduate from the cultural knowledge of a four year old to their own byzantine cynicism, still flourishes.

## What Happened to My Study?

As you've read, Gaeltarra Eireann offered to fund a larger study. I designed it and trained seven anthropology students who had relevant research credentials. The American members were taught Irish in a six-week experimental language course, pioneered by a charismatic teacher, the "humane" Diarmuid Ó Donnchadha. Each learned the dialect of the community in which their year-long study would be done. The course was so successful that one researcher, a Japanese American, was invited to converse in Connemara Irish on television. A common Irish response was, "That girl speaks lovely Irish, and our own can't be bothered to learn it!"

As an experiment, the results of three of the community studies were sent back to the relevant community and displayed for comment in an accessible place. We made corrections, and the other comments were incorporated into an appendix. The final report contained the analysis and conclusions, plus edited versions of the community studies. The study has been used to help policymakers, planners, and managers understand Gaeltacht life and the rural economy. It helped them to see that "farmer" is a social-entrepreneurial concept, and that the concept of "factory" is itself a cultural production. People can see a clip of the young me being interviewed about this study on television in the RTE Archives (see the bibliography).

I kept all the field notes, and the unedited versions of the studies. Not the greatest way to advance ethnography, or build a reputation, but at the time, we didn't have much guidance on the ethics of handling materials about small, identifiable, literate communities, and still don't.

What happened to the ordnance survey maps? In 2020, a Placename Committee of experts was set up to determine the "correct" names. Most of the work will be done online. Online! I mourn poor John O'Donovan, with his quill pen and grubby lodgings.

~

Some recommendations I presented to the sponsoring body, Gaeltarra Eireann, after my community studies:

1. There should be a new Gaeltacht commission or authority, with elected members representing all the Gaeltacht communities and their interests, to replace Gaeltarra Éireann, which focused mainly on factories. In 1980, as a result of input from many bodies, Údarás na Gaeltachta, the Gaeltacht Authority, was established with Cathal MacGabhann as its first chief executive. It continues to this day.

2. Strangely, for a government committed to the Irish language, it was almost impossible for non-Irish-speaking adults to get help if they wanted to learn it. Diarmuid Ó Donnchadha's well-published success with my American researchers showed how adult learners could succeed. I approached Gael Linn and they hired him to provide a range of courses. These courses continue to this day, fifty years on.[1]

---

1 You can read Diarmuid's story in *The Irish Times*.

Other language/cultural immersion/holiday courses are available
around the country now: *Oideas Gael*'s courses in Glencolmcille
include archeology folklore, music, and hiking as part of their
courses.

3. Ireland was on the cusp of being able to consider what James Mary
Agnes called "environment-free" economic activities. For example,
when the government was in the process of applying for European
Union admission, bilingual, highly literate rural areas such as
Carrick and Kilcar could become processors and repositories
for certain kinds of Irish–English and English–Irish documents.
Telephone fax machines had just become available, but rural phone
service would have had to be improved.

Sixteen years ago, a scholar, Una Byrne, who had connections
to Carrick, arranged for a never-used advance factory to become a
center in which the full text of books in Irish are being translated
for inclusion in a Royal Irish Academy database.

4. The study results had an effect on the direction that Gaeltarra
Éireann took at that time. My assistant, Ellen Hanrahan Clancy,
was hired as their sociologist/anthropologist under the direction of
the estimable Seosamh Ó hÓgartaigh, who also developed a serious
interest in anthropology. New managers were given familiarization
courses in the area before being posted to a factory, and established
managers were given access to our study of their particular area.

What else happened to my study?

Well, the Wenner-Gren Foundation, which waited patiently for 56
years to see the results of its funding, will see it now. Thank you.

## What Happened to Me?

Despite my worries, I got my PhD in 1970, joined the faculty of the
University of Pittsburgh, and while there, directed the National Science

Foundation's Field Training Program in Europe for three years. I later set up the first and still only department of anthropology at Maynooth University in Ireland. I had great students, support from senior faculty, and excellent "external examiners" (required in Irish universities) to attend and supervise the exam results. They included Ulf Hannerz, John Blacking, and Ward Goodenough. I also chaired the Irish government's advisory board on aid to developing countries.

I always wished I'd known the Kilcar people better, and I'd always wondered about what went wrong there. Did people fear I was writing The Book? Unlike the people whom anthropologists tend to study, many of these people were more literate than I was, immersed in a tradition of great writers, histories, ancient manuscripts, and scrolls. They knew the power of the written word, and in my case, possibly feared it, perhaps because of factory suicide.

Or was it "Better" and his communist fantasies? Or the young David Wagstaff, innocent of any romantic notions?

I didn't know. Would another researcher have been more self-aware, cautious, respectful?

A few years later I got an unexpected insight when I met the priest-headmaster of a secondary school in northern Donegal. The man, later the Bishop of Raphoe, came from Kilcar and had a keen interest in the factory.

"I understand from Fitzgerald that young Wagstaff was a communist," he said. "Very worrying to us."

Fitzgerald? Oh, Mr. Slippers.

"He was no more a communist than I was," I protested.

"Ah," he said, making a steeple of his fingers and standing up. The interview was over.

I didn't write The Book until now, and it's a different kind of book, the "backstage." My original research shaped the additional studies that Gaeltarra had asked for, and my PhD drew on the results. Even then, I restricted its circulation until anthropology and I could figure out how to respect the rights of identifiable people in tiny villages, rather than thinking of them as mere "subjects." We're still not entirely successful.

## What Happened to Youngstown?

On September 19, 1977, "Black Monday," Youngstown's twenty miles of steel mills and factories began closing without warning. As my father predicted, they saw him out; he'd died five months earlier of lung cancer, hastened by emphysema. By then all the Gaeltarra Éireann factories I'd studied were gone too, although not on my recommendation.

Youngstown was recently described as the "Fastest Shrinking City in the United States," having lost 60 per cent of its population since the 1960s. We're no longer "Bomb City," and the Mafia is weakened, although a retired FBI man assured me recently that it wasn't gone. But we've dropped to ninth in the country for violent crime.

## What Happened to Carrick and Kilcar?

Both villages have survived; in the last Census, 2016, Carrick gained about a hundred people and Kilcar twenty. Most people are self-reported Irish speakers, speaking Irish daily (although in practice, not exclusively). From the outside, the Kilcar factory building looks the same; inside it's a community center with a library, computer facilities, a crèche, art spaces, meeting rooms, and an impressive state-of-the-art historical society. Studio Donegal, a private weaving company, sits at one end, and upstairs you'll see the original looms, some handweavers at work, and yarn being spun. Downstairs, international visitors buy tweed designer clothing. As of 2022, the European Commission has given the name "Donegal Tweed" the same protection as products such as "Champaigne." This protects against cheap imitations; no one can use the name unless the product is locally produced. The village also has a new retail estate. Recently, the Kilcar Parish Council had its fiftieth anniversary. In Carrick, a successful fish-processing cooperative has replaced the vegetable co-op factory.

In 1983, the British Open University filmed the villages' struggles with industry, posted in 2016 on YouTube: "South West Donegal Tradition and Change." In it, you'll see some of the people I've written about: the redoubtable Father McDyer, still wrestling with local opposition, and the affable Tom Redington, philosophical about perennial government–local misunderstandings. Just as in the 1960s, urban pundits comment on the workers' lack of an "industrial tradition," remoteness, poor road and telephone systems, and "laziness."

Today people communicate through the internet, and distance is irrelevant in most businesses. Pádraig Twin and Séamus Twin run their joint high-tech business from two different countries. Environment-free, as James Mary Agnes predicted.

But old ways die hard. The villagers still rush to extend condolences to someone who isn't dead, just out of town for the day.

## What Happened in Mental Illness Research?

I never found out why the 1960 Letterkenny records contained blanks where the diagnosis should be, and then an unbroken string of "schizophrenia" entries, followed by a string of "ditto" entries. But I followed the mental health research for a few years after that, befriending Dermot Walsh, Aileen O'Hare, and Ivor Browne, each of whom were producing groundbreaking research or psychiatric practice in their own ways. What emerged was that in mental hospital records, no clear distinction was made between the number of cases at a particular time, say a year (*prevalence*), and the number of new cases that year (*incidence*). Most mental hospitals counted prevalence. The result was that a person who went into the hospital three times during a particular period was counted as three people. Incidence rates were much lower, although were not, even then, as low as they should have been in relation to mental illness: they still included people, such as elderly bachelors or homeless day laborers, who were not mentally ill.

... But why go on when someone has covered all this and much more, and much better. Brendan Kelly is professor of psychiatry at Trinity College, Dublin. His monumental work, *Hearing Voices: The History of Psychiatry in Ireland*, is certainly the most comprehensive to date, and in places, adroitly diplomatic.

He covers all the heartbreaking social reasons why people found themselves in the hospital, as well as the "political, legal, economic, demographic reasons and clinical practice reasons."

He concludes that "the epidemiological evidence is now clear: despite a high rate of psychiatric hospitalization, there is insufficient evidence to conclude that Ireland ever had a higher rate of mental disorder than elsewhere." In relation to schizophrenia, sometimes described as high, and "spiraling," there is "convincing evidence that the overall rate of schizophrenia in Ireland in recent times is no higher than the world-wide average."

If you are serious about looking at mental health in Ireland, *Hearing Voices* is the definitive work.

For an excellent museum-curated exhibition of the Letterkenny hospital's history, see the Donegal County Museum's "A World Apart: The Donegal District Lunatic Asylum."

For modern photographs of the grounds, see the *Donegal Daily*'s "150 Years of St. Conal's Hospital."

## What Happened to Irish?

According to the 2016 Irish Census, the Gaeltacht had 96,000 people, of whom 66 per cent spoke Irish; 21,000 spoke it daily. Looking at daily

Map 5. Gaeltacht areas of Ireland in 2007. This map shows the extent of the areas' decline, when compared with the maps on page 12.

speakers in small towns, four of the top five are in Donegal. But ahead of all are the villages of Carraroe and Gweedore, the areas Gaeltarra chose for its industrial estates, now gone.

The Census reports that fewer than one in four families with school-going children in the Gaeltacht raise their children through Irish. The exceptions: the figure rises to 50 per cent among families in Carraroe and three small islands connected to the area.

In Ireland overall, the 2016 Census shows that of the total population of 4.76 million, 1.76 million people said they could speak Irish. A catch here is the number who speak it *outside* of school: 586,535. Within that group, 74,000 people speak it on a daily basis and 111,500 on a weekly basis. The overall language figures represent a drop from the 2011 Census: there are 13,000 fewer Irish speakers. While Irish is taught in all schools, *Gaelscoileanna* schools, now numbering almost 260, are becoming more popular and provide a good primary and secondary education through Irish.

For more about Irish, including the political and cultural associations, see the *Sightlines* website (Sightlines.ie).

## What Happened in Anthropology?

I began this book with applied anthropology, and that's where I'll finish.

But first: It's true that anthropology has seen many major theoretical and philosophical trends since the 1960s, moving from modernism and its emphasis on the natural sciences to more humanistic paradigms. These trends include postmodernism, feminist anthropology, critical realism, ontological reflections, and a concerted focus on globalization. We raised concerns about anthropological "privilege," the impossibility of objectivity, and for some a rejection of "culture" as the lodestone of anthropology. Reputations were built and challenged. A few disavowed their previous brainstorms. On the *Sightlines* website (Sightlines.ie), I will present a brief discussion of some of those major movements in academia. If you are a student, the "Questions" section of the website will help you to move from the *Sightlines* era to today's anthropology.

But Stanley Barrett has pointed out that most of the people in the field are "no-name" anthropologists who don't commit themselves to any of the more recent trends. "Keep Calm and Carry On" is their motto, doing fieldwork and communicating the essentials of anthropology in their classrooms. In my case, I'm doing applied anthropology.

*Applied Anthropology/Public Anthropology*

Applied anthropology has a long history: British social anthropologists began to organize professionally in the 1860s, when slavery was an issue. At that time and later, British colonial administrators drew on anthropologists for perspectives on the nations they had colonized, as did the United States Bureau of Indian Affairs, in its often repressive dealings with Indigenous groups. In World War II, about half of all American anthropologists were working directly for the government. David H. Price's *Anthropological Intelligence* provides a comprehensive account.

Today, it's critically important for students considering a career in anthropology to assess the job market. What are your prospects? In 1971, when I returned to the University of Pittsburgh and a job, the career prospects for doctoral graduates were good.

Now, a recent study by Speakman and colleagues shows, in painful detail, the academic career prospects for today's graduates. It looks at hiring trends in U.S. universities offering bachelor's, master's, or doctoral degrees in anthropology and found that in the period 1985–2014, only a little over 20 per cent of doctoral graduates obtained tenure-track positions, which comprise only about 30 per cent of all positions. (The remaining academic jobs are now lower-paid, non-tenure-track positions, part time or full time, with many on short-term contracts.) Another finding is that between 1994 and 2004, eleven universities accounted for about 40 per cent of all graduate job placements, and while females now outnumber male graduates, in the period 2009–14 the number of male hires are disproportionately represented in the subfield of sociocultural anthropology, which represents more than half of all hiring.

Despite this bad news, the field of applied anthropology is not a residual category for people who can't get academic jobs (indeed, some academics also do it); it's for those interested in the application of anthropological insights and methods to investigate and solve practical problems. The Society for Applied Anthropology webpage provides a list of institutions that offer specialized degrees, and if you look at the American Anthropological Association's webpage on "Careers," you'll see that the extensive range of full-time jobs, as well as consultancies, is impressive.

"Public anthropology" as a recognized field is more recent and focuses on using various media to influence public opinion by arguing for social change in relation to the big issues of the day. It's not unheard of for an anthropologist to do both, as I have done in relation to girls' education in countries where participation is low, Hedican provides an explanation of the many subfields of anthropology that fall under the umbrella of "practicing anthropology," of which "applied" and "public" are just two; and an excellent sampling of some of the major areas in which public anthropology can make a contribution.

Some areas in which applied anthropologists are sought, either as employees or consultants, include human rights, business, community development, government, international development, education, environment, agriculture, health, disaster, gender issues, and more recently, terrorism and war. Within any one of these, each has subtopics: in business, they might range from large tech companies and media companies to department stores and architectural practices; in government and civil affairs, from the military to law enforcement agencies to civic and special interest groups.

Some of the most frequent users of anthropological advice are international development agencies, including governmental, non-governmental, and multilateral agencies such as lending banks. On the *Sightlines* website (Sightlines.ie), I will provide an up-to-date listing of the major employers of anthropologists. Some applied anthropologists operate as independent practitioners rather than as employees, and there's a particularly arcane in-the-know process for seeking work, which I outline on the website. Even private groups seek our advice: I was asked to help reorient an order of nuns whose elderly white members were now outnumbered by young African sisters. Together, they decided to meet a changing world and "Africanize." I facilitated their discussions as they reflected and redesigned.

Applied anthropologists take on a variety of roles. Within a sector such as education or health, for example, anthropologists apply their skills to policy analysis, needs assessment, program design and implementation, impact assessment, and as evaluators at all stages. They may act as consultants, managers, researchers, negotiators, advocates, brokers, and trainers. In addition to having an anthropological background, you need to have expertise in the area of the world, the sector, and your role. In my work in sub-Saharan Africa, I had to understand the education sector in a particular country, with specific reference to girls' education, and I assumed various roles.

Whatever your role, your topic, or your employer, the ethical and professional considerations are foremost: your obligations to the commissioning group; the rights and concerns of the stakeholders whom your research may affect; your own integrity; and your self-identification as an anthropologist.

*Participatory Research*

Almost everything I learned from my time in Donegal in the 1960s has helped me in my later research. I realized that people are active partners in producing findings. I hadn't liked the concept of people as "subjects," doing research "on" them, claiming "objectivity." Later, my embryonic mapping with various groups paved my way to using participatory research and its graphic analytical tools. But what I didn't know in the 1960s, nor did many, was that at the time of my research, an agronomist, Robert Chambers, was already developing participatory approaches in agricultural research. His 1997 book, *Whose Reality Counts: Putting the Last First*, is one of his many publications that offers valuable insights for social scientists.

The umbrella term for participatory research is participatory learning and action (PLA), which can be used in a wide range of disciplines and settings. In PLA, the researcher is just *one* partner in the research; the aim is to include everyone involved, especially the disadvantaged and those most likely to be overlooked. Once a group learns to use

PLA, it can apply it to new problems and can pass the approach on to others.

On the *Sightlines* website (Sightlines.ie), I will be adding more information on participatory research and a short tutorial on one way of doing it.


## Now You've Reached the End ... Come to Ireland!

If you take the night flight from New York to Dublin, at dawn you'll fly over the west coast of Ireland. Although you'll be groggy, from this height you'll see things you'll never see on the ground: high kings, wars over land or a brown cow or women; a warrior-queen, bards, monks scribing in their towers, Patrick wrestling a snake, a lady pirate, the arrival of Norsemen and Anglo-Normans, earls fleeing, patriots being executed here and there, priests hiding in cupboards, mappers making the most complete map in the world, a few men struggling to find place names for the maps, the 2 million bodies of the starved, the 2 million people fleeing on big ships, the flash of guns as sixteen patriots are executed; the resulting fury, and a ragtag army taking on the British; countrymen killing their fellow countrymen, treaties being signed; women being left out, a divided and warring world in the northern parts, factories coming in, churches losing their faithful; every second person writing a book, making a film, dancing, or acting. Down through history, a lot of this was done by Irish speakers. Some spoke it as their birthright; others had it beaten into them.

You have only twenty minutes to take this in, because it disappears as you fly into Dublin, over Google's headquarters and the Facebook offices.

You've come to the end of the book, but not the end of *Sightlines*, which continues on the *Sightlines* website (Sightlines.ie). There you will find questions for most chapters and help in answering them. Over time, you'll also find a discussion of all the items listed at the end of the Preface. I can only say *Go n-éirí leat!* May you succeed.

# Bibliography

ACYLS Newsletter. "Out of Context." *American Council of Learned Societies* 3 (Summer, 1952): 11–16.

American Anthropological Association. "Anthropology Careers & Employment (ACE)." https://careercenter.americananthro.org/jobs.

Arensberg, Conrad M. *The Irish Countryman*. New York: The Natural History Press, 1968. First published 1937 by Macmillan.

Arensberg, Conrad M., and Solon T. Kimball. *Culture and Community*. San Diego: Harcourt Brace, 1965.

———. *Family and Community in Ireland*. Harvard, MA: Harvard University Press, 1940.

Arensberg, Conrad M., and Arthur H. Niehoff. *Introducing Social Change*. New York: Aldine, 1964.

Barrett, Stanley R. *Anthropology: A Student's Guide to Theory and Method*. Toronto: University of Toronto Press, 1999.

Beck, Lewis White. "The 'Natural Science Ideal' in the Social Sciences." In *Theory in Anthropology*, edited by Robert A. Manners and David Kaplan. Chicago: Aldine Publishing, 1968.

British Open University. *South West Donegal Tradition and Change*. YouTube Video, May 18, 2016. https://youtu.be/WhaJbwkL1RU.

Byrne, Anne, Ricca Edmondson, and Tony Varley. "Arensberg and Kimball and Anthropological Research in Ireland." *Irish Journal of Sociology* 23, no. 1 (2015). https://journals.sagepub.com/doi/10.7227/IJS.23.1.3.

Chambers, Robert. *Revolutions in Development Inquiry*. London: Routledge, 2008.

——. *Whose Reality Counts? Putting the Last First*. London: Intermediate Technology Development, 1997.

Davies, James, and Dimitrina Spencer. *Emotions in the Field: The Psychology and Anthropology of Fieldwork Experience*. Stanford: Stanford University Press, 2021.

Dineen, Patrick, Foclóir Gaedhilge agus Béarla. *An Irish-English dictionary, Being a Thesaurus of the Words, Phrases and Idioms of the Modern Irish Language*. Irish Texts Society by the Educational Co. of Ireland, 1927.

Director, Ordnance Survey of Ireland. *The Irish Grid: A Description of the Co-ordinate Reference System used in Ireland*. Dublin: Government of Ireland, 1996.

Donegal County Museum. "A World Apart: The Donegal District Lunatic Asylum." https://www.donegalcoco.ie/media/donegalcountyc/museum/DDLA 2020.pdf.

*Donegal Daily*. "DD History: 150 Years of St. Conal's Hospital." https://www .donegaldaily.com/2016/05/26/dd-history-150-years-of-st-conals-hospital.

Firth, Raymond. *We the Tikopia*. Stanford: Stanford University Press, 1963.

Foster, George. *Traditional Cultures and the Impact of Technological Change*. New York: Harper, 1962.

Fox, J.R. "Kinship and Land Tenure on Tory Island." *Ulster Folklife* 12 (1966): 1–17.

Geertz, Clifford. "Under the Mosquito Net." *New York Review of Books* (September 14, 1967): 12–13.

Goodenough, Ward Hunt. *Cooperation in Change*. New York: Russell Sage Foundation, 1963.

Health Research Board. "Census of Irish Psychiatric Units and Hospitals 2013." Dublin: Health Research Board, 2013.

Hedican, Edward J. *Public Anthropology: Engaging Social Issues in the Modern World*. Toronto: University of Toronto Press, 2016.

*Irish Times*. "Innovative Teacher Had Lifelong Goal to Advance Use of Irish Countrywide." June 2, 2012. https://www.irishtimes.com/life-and-style/people /innovative-teacher-had-lifelong-goal-to-advance-use-of-irish-countrywide -1.1063695.

Jacobs, Steven. "The Use of Participatory Action Research within Education: Benefits to Stakeholders." *World Journal of Education* 6, no. 3 (2016): 48–55.

Jennings, C. "Psychiatric Care in Eight Register Areas: Statistics from Eight Psychiatric Case Registers in Great Britain, 1976–1981." Southampton, UK: University of Southampton, n.d.

Kane, E. *Girls' Education in Africa: What Do We Know about Strategies That Work?* Africa Region Human Development Working Paper Series. Washington, D.C.: World Bank, 2004.

——. "It Turns Out That Economists Are Now a Girl's Best Friend," *Irish Times*. March 8, 2005. https://www.irishtimes.com/opinion/it-turns-out-that-economists -are-now-a-girl-s-best-friend-1.421293.

———. *The Last Place God Made*. HRAFlex Books ER6-001. New Haven, CT: Human Relations Area Files, 1977.

Kelly, Brendan. *Hearing Voices: The History of Psychiatry in Ireland*. Newbridge, Kildare: Academic Press, 2015.

Kemmis, Stephen. "Participatory Action Research and the Public Sphere." *Educational Action Research* 14, no. 4 (2006): 459–476.

Lessa, William, and Evon Z. Vogt. "Navajo Prayer ..." In *Reader in Comparative Religion*, 6–7. Evanston, IL: Row, Peterson and Co., 1958.

Linton, Ralph. "Nativistic Movements." *American Anthropologist* 45 (1943): 230–340.

Meyer, Kuno, trans. *The Project Gutenberg eBook of Ancient Irish Poetry*. Various authors. April 17, 2010. https://www.gutenberg.org/files/32030/32030-h/32030-h.htm.

Malinowski, Bronislaw. "Methods of Study of Culture Contact." International African Institute, Memorandum 15. London: Oxford University Press, 1938.

Malinowski, Bronislaw, Norbert Guterman, Valetta Malinowska, Raymond Firth, and Mario Bick. *A Diary in the Strict Sense of the Term*. New York: Harcourt, Brace and World, 1967.

Medico-Social Research Board (MSRB). *Census of Irish Psychiatric Hospitals 1982*. Dublin: Medico-Social Research Board, 1982.

———. *The Three-County and St Loman's Psychiatric Case Registers, 1974 and 1982*. Dublin: Medico Social Research Board, 1987.

Minkler, Meredith. "Using Participatory Action Research to Build Healthy Communities." *Public Health Reports* 115, no. 2-3 (March/April & May/June 2000): 191–97.

Ni Nuallain, Mairin, Aileen O'Hare, and Dermot Walsh. "The Prevalence of Schizophrenia in Three Counties in Ireland." *Acta Psychiatrica Scandinavica* 82, no. 2 (1990): 136–40.

O'Hare, Aileen. "Irish Psychiatric Case Registers: Their Contribution to Health Care." *Medical Informatics Europe* 82 (1982): 16.

O'Hare, Aileen, and Dermot Walsh. *Irish Psychiatric Hospitals and Units Census 1981*. Dublin: Medico-Social Research Board, 1983.

Price, David H. *Anthropological Intelligence*. Durham, NC: Duke University Press, 2008.

———. *Lessons from Second World War Anthropology*. 2002. http://web.mnstate.edu/robertsb/445/lessons_from_second_world_war_anthropology.pdf.

Reeves, William, ed. *Life of Saint Columba, Founder of Hy. Written by Adamnan, Ninth Abbot of That Monastery*. Dublin: Dublin University Press, 1874.

Robins, Joseph. *Fools and Mad: A History of the Insane in Ireland*. Dublin: Institute of Public Administration, 1986.

Rosskam, E. "Using Participatory Action Research Methodology to Improve Worker Health." In *Critical Approaches in the Health Social Sciences Series. Unhealthy Work: Causes, Consequences, Cures*, edited by P.L. Schnall, M. Dobson, and E. Rosskam, 211–28. Amityville, NY: Baywood Publishing Co., 2009.

RTE Archives: "Donegal Gaeltacht Challenges." 1972. https://www.rte.ie
/archives/2017/0109/843669-donegal-gaeltacht.

Society for Applied Anthropology. Resources. https://www.appliedanthro.org
/about/resources.

Speakman, Robert J., Carla S. Hadden, Matthew H. Colvin, Justin Cramb,
K. C. Jones, Travis W. Jones, Isabelle Lulewicz et al. "Market Share and Recent
Hiring Trends in Anthropology Faculty Positions." *PLoS One* 13, no. 9: e0202528.
https://pubmed.ncbi.nlm.nih.gov/30208048.

Spicer, Edward H. *Human Problems in Technological Change*. New York: Russell Sage,
1952.

Symmons-Symonolewicz, Konstantin. "Bronislaw Malinowski in the Light of His
Diary." *The Polish Review* 12, no. 3 (Summer 1967): 67–72. https://www.jstor.org
/stable/25776725.

Taylor, Lawrence. *Occasions of Faith: An Anthropology of Irish Catholics*. Philadelphia:
University of Pennsylvania Press, 1995.

Walsh, Dermot. "Psychiatric Deinstitutionalisation in Ireland 1960–2013." *Irish Journal
of Psychological Medicine* 32, no. 4 (July 7, 2015): 347–52.

——. "The Ups and Downs of Schizophrenia in Ireland." *Irish Journal of Psychiatry* 13,
no. 2 (1992): 12–16.

Printed and bound by CPI Group (UK) Ltd, Croydon, CR0 4YY

13/04/2025

14656519-0004